Beyond the C++ Standard Library

Beyond the C++ Standard Library

An Introduction to Boost

Björn Karlsson

✦✦Addison-Wesley

Upper Saddle River, NJ • Boston• Indianapolis • San Francisco
New York • Toronto • Montreal • London • Munich • Paris • Madrid
Capetown • Sydney • Tokyo • Singapore • Mexico City

The publisher offers excellent discounts on this book when ordered in quantity for bulk purchases or special sales, which may include electronic versions and/or custom covers and content particular to your business, training goals, marketing focus, and branding interests. For more information, please contact:

U. S. Corporate and Government Sales
(800) 382-3419
corpsales@pearsontechgroup.com

For sales outside the U. S., please contact:

International Sales
international@pearsoned.com

Visit us on the Web: www.awprofessional.com

Library of Congress Catalog Number: 2005927496

ISBN-10: 0-321-13354-4
ISBN-13: 978-0-321-13354-0
Text printed in the United States on recycled paper at R.R. Donnelley in Crawfordsville, Indiana.
Fifth printing, April 2009

In memory of the dead, in honor of the living.

Contents

Foreword

Good things are happening in the C++ community. Although C++ remains the most widely used programming language in the world, it is becoming even more powerful and yet easier to use. Skeptical? Bear with me.

The current version of standard C++, which was finalized in 1998, offers robust support for traditional procedural programming as well as object-oriented and generic programming. Just as old (pre-1998) C++ was single-handedly responsible for putting object-oriented within the reach of the workaday software developer, C++98 has done the same for generic programming. The integration of the Standard Template Library (STL) into standard C++ in the mid-1990s represented as much a paradigm shift as did Bjarne Stroustrup's adding classes to C in the early 1980s. Now that the majority of C++ practitioners are proficient with concepts of STL, it's once again time to raise the bar.

Applications of the power of C++ are still being discovered. Many of today's C++ libraries, and mathematical libraries in particular, take routine advantage of template metaprogramming, a fortuitous but unforeseen result of the brilliant design of C++ templates. As higher-level tools and techniques come to light in the C++ community, developing increasingly complex applications is becoming more straightforward and enjoyable.

It is difficult to overstate the importance of Boost to the world of C++. Since the ratification of C++98, no entity outside of the ISO Committee for Standard C++ (called WG21) has done more to influence the direction of C++ than has Boost (and many Boost subscribers are prominent members of WG21, including its founder, my friend Beman Dawes). The thousands of experienced Boost volunteers have, in unselfish, peer-reviewed fashion, developed many useful library solutions not provided by C++98. Ten of its offerings have already been accepted to be integrated into the upcoming C++0x library, and more are under consideration. Where a library approach has been shown to be wanting, the wisdom gained from the cross-pollination of Boost and WG21 has suggested a few modest language enhancements, which are now being entertained.

In the rare case that you haven't heard of Boost, let me ask...do you need to convert between text and numbers or (better yet) between any streamable types? No problem—use Boost.lexical_cast. Oh, you have more sophisticated text processing requirements? Then Boost.Tokenizer or Boost.Regex might be for you, or Boost.Spirit, if you need full-blown parsing. Boost.Bind will amaze you with its function projection and composition capabilities. For functional programming there is Boost.Lambda. Static assertions? Got 'em. If you're mathematically inclined, get your pencil out: You have Boost.Math, Graph, Quaternion, Octonion, MultiArray, Random, and Rational. If you are fortunate enough to have discovered the joy of Python, you can use it and C++ together with the help of Boost.Python. And you can practically pick your platform for all of the above.

Björn Karlsson is a Boost enthusiast and a heartfelt supporter of the C++ community. He has published useful and well-written articles in the *C/C++ Users Journal* and, more recently, for The *C++ Source*, a new online voice for the C++ community (see www.artima.com/cppsource). In this volume, he motivates and illustrates key Boost components, and shows how they work with and extend the C++ Standard Library. Consider this not only an in-depth tutorial on Boost, but also a foretaste of the future version of Standard C++. Enjoy!

—*Chuck Allison, Editor, The C++ Source*

Preface

Dear Reader,

Welcome to *Beyond the C++ Standard Library: An Introduction to Boost*.

If you are interested in generic programming, library design, and the C++ Standard Library, this book is for you. Because the intended audience for the book is intermediate to advanced C++ programmers, there is little coverage of basic C++ concepts. As the title suggests, the focus of this book is on the Boost libraries—general usage, best practices, implementation techniques, and design rationale.

Almost from the day I discovered Boost, the people behind it, and the extraordinary libraries in it, I've wanted to write this book. It is amazing that a language as mature as C++ still offers room for exploration into higher-level abstractions as well as technical detail, all without requiring changes to the language. Of course, this is what sets C++ apart from many other programming languages: It is specifically and intentionally designed for extension, and the language's facilities for generic constructs are extremely powerful. This exploration is at the core of the Boost libraries and the Boost community itself. Boost is about making programming in C++ more elegant, more robust, and more productive. As discoveries are made and best practices are shaped, a great challenge faces the C++ community; to share this knowledge with others. In isolation, there is limited value to these remarkable findings, but when exposed to a larger audience, a whole industry will evolve.

This book shows how to use a selection of the wonderfully useful Boost libraries, teaches best practices for their use, and even goes behind the scenes to see how they actually work. The Boost libraries' license grants permission to copy, use, and modify the software for any use (commercial and non-commercial), so all you need to do is visit www.boost.org and download the latest version.

For all the C++ Standard Library aficionados out there, it is well known that a new revision of the Standard Library is in progress. From a standardization point of view, there are three primary areas where the C++ Standard Library is likely to change:

- Fixing broken libraries

- Augmenting missing features to existing libraries

- Adding libraries that provide functionality that is missing in the Standard Library

The Boost libraries address all of these areas in one way or another. Of the 12 libraries covered in this book, six have already been accepted for inclusion in the upcoming Library Technical Report, which means that they will most likely be part of the next version of the Standard Library. Thus, learning about these libraries has excellent long-term value. I hope that you will find this book to be a valuable tool for *using*, *understanding*, and *extending* the Boost libraries. From that vantage, you'll want to incorporate those libraries and the knowledge enshrined within them into your own designs and implementations. That's what I call reuse.

Thank you for reading.

Björn Karlsson

Acknowledgments

A number of people have made all the difference for this book, and for my ability to write it. First of all, I wish to thank the Boost community for these astonishing libraries. They—the libraries and the Boosters—make a very real difference for the C++ community and the whole software industry. Then, there are people who have very actively supported this effort of mine, and I wish to thank them personally. It's inevitable that I will fail to mention some: To all of you, please accept my sincere apologies. Beman Dawes, thank you for creating Boost in the first place, and for hooking me up with Addison-Wesley. Bjarne Stroustrup, thank you for providing guidance and pointing out important omissions from the nearly finished manuscript. Robert Stewart, thank you for the careful technical and general editing of this book. Rob has made this book much more consistent, more readable, and more accurate—and all of this on his free time! The technical errors that remain are mine, not his. Rob has also been instrumental in finding ways to help the reader stay on track even when the author strays. Chuck Allison, thank you for your continuous encouragement and support for my authoring goals. David Abrahams, thank you for supporting this effort and for helping out with reviewing. Matthew Wilson, thank you for reviewing parts of this book and for being a good friend. Gary Powell, thank you for the excellent reviews and for your outstanding enthusiasm for this endeavor. All of the authors of Boost libraries have created online documentation for them: Without this great source of information, it nearly would have been impossible to write this book. Thanks to all of you. Many Boosters have helped out in different ways, and special thanks go to those who have reviewed various chapters of this book. Without their help, important points would not have been made and errors would have prevailed. Aleksey Gurtovoy, David Brownell, Douglas Gregor, Duane Murphy, Eric Friedman, Eric Niebler,

Fernando Cacciola, Frank Griswold, Jaakko Järvi, James Curran, Jeremy Siek, John Maddock, Kevlin Henney, Michiel Salters, Paul Grenyer, Peter Dimov, Ronald Garcia, Phil Boyd, Thorsten Ottosen, Tommy Svensson, and Vladimir Prus—thank you all so much!

Special thanks go to Microsoft Corporation and Comeau Computing for providing me with their excellent compilers.

I have also had the pleasure of working with two excellent editors from Addison-Wesley. Deborah Lafferty helped me with all of the initial work, such as creating the proposal for the book, and basically made sure that I came to grips with many of the authoring details that I was previously oblivious to. Peter Gordon, skillfully assisted by Kim Boedigheimer, took over the editing of the book and led it through to publishing. Further assistance was given by Lori Lyons, project editor, and Kelli Brooks, copy editor. I wish to thank them all—for making the book possible and for seeing it through to completion.

Friends and family have supported my obsession with C++ for *many* years now; thank you so much for being there, always.

And finally, many thanks to my wife Jeanette and our son Simon—I am forever grateful for your love and support. I will always do my best to deserve it.

About the Author

Björn Karlsson works as a Senior Software Engineer at ReadSoft, where he spends most of his time designing and programming in C++. He has written a number of articles about C++ and the Boost libraries for publications such as *C/C++ Users Journal*, *Overload*, and the online journal *The C++ Source*.

Karlsson is a member of the advisory board for *The C++ Source* and has been a member of the editorial board of *C/C++ Users Journal*, where he is also one of the columnists in the Experts Forum. He participates in the Boost newsgroups and is one of the Boost-Users moderators.

Organization of This Book

This book is divided into three main parts, each containing libraries pertaining to a certain domain, but there is definitely overlap. These divisions exist to make it easier to find relevant information for your task at hand or to read the book and find related topics grouped together. Most of the chapters cover a single library, but a few consist of small collections.

The typesetting and coding style is intentionally kept simple. There are a number of popular best practices in this area, and I've just picked one I feel that most people are accustomed to, and that will convey information easily. Furthermore, the coding style in this book purposely tries to save some vertical space by avoiding curly braces on separate lines.

Although the examples in most books make heavy use of using declarations and using directives, this is not the case here. I have done my best to qualify names in the interest of clarity. There is an additional benefit to doing so in this book, and that is to show where the types and functions come from. If something is from the Standard Library, it will be prefixed with `std::`. If it's from Boost, it will be prefixed with `boost::`.

Some of the libraries covered by this book are very extensive, which makes it impossible to include detailed explanations of all aspects of the library. When this is the case, there's typically a note stating that there is more to know, with references to the online documentation, related literature, or both. Also, I have tried to focus on the things that are of the most immediate use, and that have a strong relation with the C++ Standard Library.

The first part of this book covers *general libraries*, which are libraries that are eminently useful, but have no other obvious affinity. The second discusses important *data structures and containers*. The third is about *higher-order programming*. There's no requirement to read about the libraries in a specific order, but it certainly doesn't hurt to follow tradition and start from the beginning.

Before getting to the in-depth look at the covered Boost libraries, a survey of each of the currently available Boost libraries will introduce you to the Boost libraries and give context for those that I'll address in the rest of the book. It gives an interesting overview of the versatility of this world-class collection of C++ libraries.

Introduction to Boost

Because you are reading this book, I expect that you are somewhat familiar with the Boost libraries, or that you at least have heard of Boost. There are a great number of libraries in Boost, and there are few, if any, that will not be of at least some interest to you. As a result, you will most definitely find libraries you can put to immediate use. The Boost libraries range over a wide variety of domains—from numeric libraries to smart pointers, from a library for template metaprogramming to a preprocessor library, from threading to lambda expressions, and so on. All of the Boost libraries are compatible with a very generous license, which ensures that the libraries can be freely used in commercial applications. Support is available through newsgroups, where much of the activity of the Boost community takes place, and there is at least one company that specializes in consulting related to the Boost libraries. For an online introduction to the Boost community, I strongly suggest that you visit Boost on the Web at www.boost.org.

As of the time of this writing, the current Boost release is 1.32.0. In it, there are 58 separate libraries. The following pages introduce all 58 of those libraries sorted by category and give a short description of what the libraries have to offer. For the libraries not covered in detail in this book, have a look at the documentation provided at www.boost.org, which is also where you go to download the Boost libraries.

String and Text Processing

Boost.Regex

Regular expressions are essential for solving a great number of pattern-matching problems. They are often used to process large strings, find inexact substrings, tokenize a string depending on some format, or modify a string based on certain criteria. The lack of regular expressions support in C++ has sometimes forced users to look at other languages known for their powerful regular expression support, such as Perl, awk, and sed. Regex provides efficient and powerful regular expression support, designed on the same premises as the Standard Template Library (STL), which makes it intuitive to use. Regex has been accepted for the upcoming Library Technical Report. For more information, see "Library 5: Regex."

The author of Regex is Dr. John Maddock.

Boost.Spirit

The Spirit library is a functional, recursive-decent parser generator framework. With it, you can create command-line parsers, even a language preprocessor.[1] It allows the programmer to specify the grammar rules directly in C++ code, using (an approximation of) EBNF syntax. Parsers are typically hard to write properly, and when targeted at a specific problem, they quickly become hard to maintain and understand. Spirit avoids these problems, while giving the same or nearly the same performance as a hand-tuned parser.

The author of Spirit is Joel de Guzman, together with a team of skilled programmers.

Boost.String_algo

This is a collection of string-related algorithms. There are a number of useful algorithms for converting case, trimming strings, splitting strings, finding/ replacing, and so forth. This collection of algorithms is an extension to those in the C++ Standard Library.

The author of String_algo is Pavol Droba.

---

1. The Wave library illustrates this point by using Spirit to implement a highly conformant C++ preprocessor.

Boost.Tokenizer

This library offers ways of separating character sequences into tokens. Common parsing tasks include finding the data in delimited text streams. It is beneficial to be able to treat such a sequence as a container of elements, where the elements are delimited according to user-defined criteria. Parsing is a separate task from operating on the elements, and it is exactly this abstraction that is offered by Tokenizer. The user determines how the character sequence is delimited, and the library finds the tokens as the user requests new elements.

The author of Tokenizer is John Bandela.

Data Structures, Containers, Iterators, and Algorithms

Boost.Any

The Any library supports typesafe storage and retrieval of values of any type. When the need for a variant type arises, there are three possible solutions:

- Indiscriminate types, such as `void*`. This solution can almost never be made typesafe; avoid it like the plague.

- Variant types—that is, types that support the storage and retrieval of a set of types.

- Types that support conversions, such as between string types and integral types.

Any implements the second solution—a value-based variant type, with an unbounded set of possible types. The library is often used for storing heterogeneous types in Standard Library containers. Read more in "Library 6: Any."

The author of Any is Kevlin Henney.

Boost.Array

This library is a wrapper around ordinary C-style arrays, augmenting them with the functions and `typedefs` from the Standard Library containers. In effect, this makes it possible to treat ordinary arrays as Standard Library containers. This is useful because it adds safety without impeding efficiency and it enables uniform syntax for Standard Library containers and ordinary arrays. The latter means that it enables the use of ordinary arrays with most functions that require a container type to operate on. Array is typically used when performance issues mandate that ordinary arrays be used rather than `std::vector`.

The author of Array is Nicolai Josuttis, who built the library upon ideas brought forth by Matt Austern and Bjarne Stroustrup.

Boost.Compressed_pair

This library consists of a single parameterized type, `compressed_pair`, which is very similar to the Standard Library's `std::pair`. The difference from `std::pair` is that `boost::compressed_pair` evaluates the template arguments to see if one of them is empty and, if so, uses the empty base optimization to compress the size of the pair.

Boost.Compressed_pair is used for storing a pair, where one or both of the types is possibly empty.

The authors of Compressed_pair are Steve Cleary, Beman Dawes, Howard Hinnant, and John Maddock.

Boost.Dynamic_bitset

The Dynamic_bitset library very closely resembles `std::bitset`, except that whereas `std::bitset` is parameterized on the number of bits (that is, the size of the container), `boost::dynamic_bitset` supports runtime size configuration. Although `dynamic_bitset` supports the same interface as `std::bitset`, it adds functions that support runtime-specific functionality and some that aren't available in `std::bitset`. The library is typically used instead of `std::bitset`, in scenarios where the size of the bitset isn't necessarily known at compile time, or may change during program execution.

The authors of Dynamic_bitset are Jeremy Siek and Chuck Allison.

Boost.Graph

Graph is a library for processing graph structures, using a design heavily influenced by the STL. It is generic and highly configurable, and includes different data structures: adjacency lists, adjacency matrices, and edge lists. Graph also provides a large number of graph algorithms, such as Dijsktra's shortest path, Kruskal's minimum spanning tree, topological sort, and many more.

The authors of Graph are Jeremy Siek, Lie-Quan Lee, and Andrew Lumsdaine.

Boost.Iterator

This library provides a framework for creating new iterator types, and it also offers a number of useful iterator adaptors beyond those defined by the C++ Standard. Creating new iterator types that conform to the standard is a difficult and tedious task. Iterator simplifies that task by automating most of the details, such as providing the required `typedefs`. Iterator also makes it possible to adapt an existing iterator type to give it new behavior. For example, the indirect iterator adaptor applies an extra dereferencing operation, making it possible to treat a container of pointers (or smart pointers) to a type as if it contained objects of that type.

The authors of Iterator are Jeremy Siek, David Abrahams, and Thomas Witt.

Boost.MultiArray

MultiArray provides a multidimensional container that closely resembles the Standard Library containers and is more effective, efficient, and straightforward than vectors of vectors. The dimensions of the container are set at declaration time, but there is support for slicing and projecting different views, and also run-time resizing of the dimensions.

The author of MultiArray is Ronald Garcia.

Boost.Multi-index

Multi-index offers multiple indices into an underlying container. This means that it is possible to have different sorting orders and different access semantics for one underlying container. Boost.Multi-index is used when `std::set` and `std::map` isn't enough, often due to the need of maintaining multiple indices for efficient element retrieval.

The author of Multi-index is Joaquín M López Muñoz.

Boost.Range

This library is a collection of concepts and utilities for ranges. Rather than having algorithms be specified in terms of pairs of iterators for denoting ranges, using ranges greatly simplifies the use of algorithms and raises the abstraction level of user code.

The author of Range is Thorsten Ottosen.

Boost.Tuple

Pairs are available in Standard C++ (from the class template `std::pair`), but there is currently no support for n-tuples. Enter Tuple. Unlike when using `structs` or `classes` for defining n-tuples, the class template `tuple` supports direct declaration and use as function return type or argument, and provides a generic way of accessing the tuple's elements. See "Library 8: Tuple" for the details of this great library. Tuple has been accepted for the upcoming Library Technical Report.

The author of Tuple is Jaakko Järvi.

Boost.Variant

The Variant library contains a generic discriminated union class for storing and manipulating an object from a set of heterogeneous types. A unique feature of the library is the support for type-safe visitation, which alleviates the common problem of type-switching code for variant data types.

The authors of Variant are Eric Friedman and Itay Maman.

Function Objects and Higher-Order Programming

Boost.Bind

Bind is a generalization of the Standard Library binders, `bind1st` and `bind2nd`. The library supports binding arguments to *anything that behaves like a function*—function pointers, function objects, and member function pointers—

with a uniform syntax. It also enables functional composition by means of nested binders. This library does not have all of the requirements that are imposed by the Standard Library binders, most notably that there is often no need to provide the typedefs `result_type`, `first_argument_type`, and `second_argument_type` for your classes. This library also makes it unnecessary to use the adaptors `ptr_fun`, `mem_fun`, and `mem_fun_ref`. The Bind library is thoroughly covered in "Library 9: Bind." It's an important and very useful addition to the C++ Standard Library. Bind is typically used with the Standard Library algorithms, and is often used together with Boost.Function, yielding a powerful tool for storing arbitrary functions and function objects for subsequent invocation. Bind has been accepted for the upcoming Library Technical Report.

The author of Bind is Peter Dimov.

Boost.Function

The Function library implements a generalized callback mechanism. It provides for the storage and subsequent invocation of function pointers, function objects, and member function pointers. Of course, it works with binder libraries such as Boost.Bind and Boost.Lambda, which greatly increases the number of use cases for callbacks (including stateful callback functions). The library is covered in detail in "Library 11: Function." Function is typically used where a function pointer would otherwise be employed to provide callbacks. Examples of usage are in signal/slot implementations, separation of GUIs from business logic, and storage of heterogeneous function-like types in Standard Library containers. Function has been accepted for the upcoming Library Technical Report.

The author of Function is Douglas Gregor.

Boost.Functional

The Functional library provides enhanced versions of the adapters in the C++ Standard Library. The major advantage is that it helps solve the problem with references to references (which are illegal) that arise when using the Standard Library binders with functions taking one or more arguments by reference. Functional also obviates the use of `ptr_fun` for using function pointers with the Standard Library algorithms.

The author of Functional is Mark Rodgers.

Boost.Lambda

Lambda provides lambda expressions—unnamed functions—for C++. Especially useful when using the Standard Library algorithms, Lambda allows functions to be created at the call site, which avoids the creation of many small function objects. Using lambdas means writing less code, and writing it in the location where it's to be used, which is much clearer and maintainable than scattering function objects around the code base. "Library 10: Lambda" covers this library in detail.

The authors of Lambda are Jaakko Järvi and Gary Powell.

Boost.Ref

Many function templates, including a large number from the Standard C++ Library, take their arguments by value, which is sometimes problematic. It may be expensive or impossible to copy an object, or the state may be tied to a particular instance, so copying is unwanted. In these situations, one needs a way to pass by reference rather than by value. Ref wraps a reference to an object and turns it into an object that may be copied. This permits calling functions taking their arguments by value with a reference. Ref has been accepted for the upcoming Library Technical Report.

The authors of Ref are Jaakko Järvi, Peter Dimov, Douglas Gregor, and David Abrahams.

Boost.Signals

Signals and slots systems, based on a pattern also known as *publisher-subscriber* and *observer*, are important tools for managing events in a system with a minimum of dependencies. Few large applications get by without some variation of this powerful design pattern, though typically they use proprietary implementations. Signals provides a proven and efficient means to decouple the emission of signals (events/subjects) from the slots (subscribers/observers) that need notification of those signals.

The author of Signals is Douglas Gregor.

Generic Programming and Template Metaprogramming

Boost.Call_traits

This library provides automatic deduction of the best way of passing arguments to functions, based upon on the argument type. For example, when passing built-in types such as `int` and `double`, it is most efficient to pass them by value. For user-defined types, passing them by reference to `const` is generally preferable. Call_traits automatically selects the right argument type for you. The library also helps in declaring arguments as references, without imposing restrictions or risking references to references (which are illegal in C++). Call_traits is typically used with generic functions that require the most efficient way of passing arguments without knowing much about the argument types beforehand, and to avoid the reference-to-reference problem.

The authors of Call_traits are Steve Cleary, Beman Dawes, Howard Hinnant, and John Maddock.

Boost.Concept_check

Concept_check supplies class templates that are used to test certain concepts (set of requirements). Generic (as in parameterized) code typically requires that the types with which it is instantiated model some abstraction, such as *LessThanComparable*. This library provides the means to explicitly state the requirements of the parameterizing types for templates. Clients of the code benefit because the requirements are documented and because the compiler can produce an error message that explicitly states how a type failed to meet them. Boost.Concept_check provides more than 30 concepts that can be used for generic code, and several archetypes that may be used to verify that component implementations include all relevant concepts. It is used to assert and document the requirements for concepts in generic code.

The author of Concept_check is Jeremy Siek, who was inspired by previous work by Alexander Stepanov and Matt Austern.

Boost.Enable_if

Enable_if allows function templates or class template specializations to include or exclude themselves from a set of matching functions or specializations. The main use cases are to include or exclude based on some property of the parameterizing type—for example, enabling a function template only when instantiated with an integral type. The library also offers a very useful studying opportunity of SFINAE (substitution failure is not an error).

The authors of Enable_if are Jaakko Järvi, Jeremiah Willcock, and Andrew Lumsdaine.

Boost.In_place_factory

The In_place_factory library is a framework for direct construction of contained objects, including variadic argument lists for initialization. This can reduce the typical requirement that contained types be *CopyConstructible*, and alleviates the need to create unnecessary temporaries used only for the purpose of providing a source object to be copied from. The library helps minimize the work needed to forward the arguments used for initialization of the contained object.

The author of In_place_factory is Fernando Cacciola.

Boost.Mpl

Mpl is a library for template metaprogramming. It includes data structures and algorithms that closely resemble those from the C++ Standard Library, but here they are used at compile time. There is even support for compile-time lambda expressions! Performing compile-time operations, such as generating types or manipulating sequences of types, is increasingly common in modern C++, and a library that offers such functionality is an extremely important tool. To the best of my knowledge, there is nothing quite like the Mpl library in existence. It fills an important void in the world of C++ metaprogramming. I should tell you that there's a book for Boost.Mpl in the works—by the time you read this, it will be available. *C++ Template Metaprogramming* is written by Aleksey Gurtovoy and David Abrahams. You'll want to get your hands on that one as soon as possible!

The author of Mpl is Aleksey Gurtovoy, with important contributions from many others.

Boost.Property_map

Property_map is a conceptual library rather than a concrete implementation. It introduces the `property_map` concept and a set of requirements for `property_map` types, thereby giving the syntactic and semantic requirements that are needed to map from a key to a value. This is useful when generic code needs to state that types must support such a mapping. C++ arrays are examples of `property_maps`. This library contains the *definition* of a concept that may be tested using Boost.Concept_check.

The author of Property_map is Jeremy Siek.

Boost.Static_assert

A common need when doing compile-time programming is to perform static assertions—that is, compile-time assertions. Furthermore, it's nontrivial to get consistent errors, which is what static assertions must produce to signal a failed assertion, across different compilers. Static_assert provides support for static assertions at namespace, class, and function scope. Detailed information is available in "Library 3: Utility."

The author of Static_assert is Dr. John Maddock.

Boost.Type_traits

Successful generic programming often requires making decisions based upon the properties of parameterizing types or adjusting properties (for example, the cv-qualification[2]) of those types. Type_traits offers compile-time information about types, such as whether a type is a pointer or a reference, and transformations that add or remove fundamental properties of types. Type_traits has been accepted for the upcoming Library Technical Report.

The authors of Type_traits are Steve Cleary, Beman Dawes, Aleksey Gurtovoy, Howard Hinnant, Jesse Jones, Mat Marcus, John Maddock, and Jeremy Siek, with contributions from many others.

---

2. A type can be *cv-unqualified* (not `const` or `volatile`), *const-qualified* (`const`), *volatile-qualified* (declared `volatile`), or *volatile-const-qualified* (both `const` and `volatile`); all of these versions of a type are distinct.

Math and Numerics

Boost.Integer

This library provides useful functionality for integer types, such as compile-time constants for the minimum and maximum values,[3] suitably sized types based on the number of required bits, static binary logarithm calculations, and more. Also included are typedefs from the 1999 C Standard header <stdint.h>.

The authors of Integer are Beman Dawes and Daryle Walker.

Boost.Interval

The Interval library helps when working with mathematical intervals. It provides arithmetic operators for the class template interval. A common use case for working with intervals (besides the obvious case of computations including intervals) is when computations provide inexact results; intervals make it possible to quantify the propagation of rounding errors.

The authors of Interval are Guillaume Melquiond, Sylvain Pion, and Hervé Brönniman, and the library is inspired by previous work from Jens Maurer.

Boost.Math

Math is a collection of mathematics templates: quaternions and octonions (generalizations of complex numbers); numerical functions such as acosh, asinh, and sinhc; functionality for calculating the greatest common divisor (GCD) and least common multiple (LCM); and more.

The authors of Math are Hubert Holin, Daryle Walker, and Eric Ford.

Boost.Minmax

Minmax simultaneously computes the minimum and maximum values, rather than requiring two comparisons when using std::min and std::max. For a range of n elements, only 3n/2+1 comparisons are performed, rather than the 2n required when using std::min_element and std::max_element.

The author of Minmax is Hervé Brönniman.

---

3. std::numeric_limits only provide these as functions.

Boost.Numeric Conversion

The Numeric Conversion library is a collection of tools used to perform safe and predictable conversions between values of different numeric types. For example, there is a tool called `numeric_cast` (originally from Boost.Conversion), which performs range-checked conversions and ensures that the value can be represented in the destination type; otherwise, it throws an exception.

The author of Numeric Conversion is Fernando Cacciola.

Boost.Operators

The Operators library provides implementations of related operators and concepts (*LessThanComparable*, *Arithmetic*, and so on). When defining operators for a type, it is both tedious and error prone to add all of the operators that should be defined. For example, when providing `operator<` (*LessThanComparable*), `operator<=`, `operator>`, and `operator>=` should also be defined in most cases. Operators automatically declare and define all relevant operators in terms of a minimum set of user-defined operators for a given type. There is detailed coverage of the library in "Library 4: Operators."

The authors of Operators are David Abrahams, Jeremy Siek, Aleksey Gurtovoy, Beman Dawes, and Daryle Walker.

Boost.Random

This is a library for professional use of random numbers, including a number of generators and distributions that are commonly used in a wide variety of domains such as simulation and security. Random has been accepted for the upcoming Library Technical Report.

The author of Random is Jens Maurer.

Boost.Rational

Integer types and floating-point types are built into the C++ language, and complex numbers are part of the C++ Standard Library, but what about rational numbers? Rational numbers avoid the problems with loss of precision in floating-point types, so their use in tracking money, for example, is popular. Rational provides rational numbers built atop any integral type, including user-defined types (where a type with unlimited precision is obviously the most useful).

The author of Rational is Paul Moore.

Boost.uBLAS

The uBLAS library provides basic linear algebra operations on vectors and matrices using mathematical notation, via operator overloading, with efficient code generation (using expression templates).

The authors of uBLAS are Joerg Walter and Mathias Koch.

Input/Output

Boost.Assign

Assign assists in assigning series of values into containers. It gives the user an easy way of assigning data, by means of overloaded `operator,` (the comma operator) and `operator()()` (function call operator). Although being especially useful for a prototyping-style of code, the functionality of the library is useful at other times too, due to the readable code that results from using the library. It is also possible to use this library to create anonymous arrays on-the-fly using `list_of`.

The author of Assign is Thorsten Ottosen.

Boost.Filesystem

The Filesystem library offers portable manipulation of paths, directories, and files. The high-level abstractions enable C++ programmers to write code similar to script-like operations that are often available in other programming languages. For iterating thorough directories and files, convenient algorithms are provided. The difficult task of writing code that is portable between platforms with different filesystems becomes feasible with the help of this library.

The author of Filesystem is Beman Dawes.

Boost.Format

This library adds functionality for formatting arguments according to format strings, similar to `printf`, but with the addition of type safety. One of the primary arguments against using `printf` and similar formatting facilities is that they are inherently dangerous; there is no assurance that the types that are specified in the format string are matched by the actual arguments. Besides eliminating the opportunity for such mismatches, Format also enables custom formatting of user-defined types.[4]

The author of Format is Samuel Krempp.

Boost.Io_state_savers

The Io_state_savers library allows the state of IOStream objects to be saved, and later restored, to undo any intervening state changes that may occur. Many manipulators permanently change the state of the stream on which they operate, and it can be cumbersome at best and error prone at worst to manually reset the state. There are state savers for control flags, precision, width, exception masks, locale for the stream, and more.

The author of Io_state_savers is Daryle Walker.

Boost.Serialization

This library allows arbitrary C++ data structures to be saved to, and restored from, archives. An archive could be, for example, a text file or XML file. Boost.Serialization is highly portable and offers a very mature set of features, such as class versioning, serialization of common classes from the C++ Standard Library, serialization of shared data, and more.

The author of Serialization is Robert Ramey.

---

4. This is not possible with formatting functions using a variable number of arguments through use of ellipsis.

Miscellaneous

Boost.Conversion

The Conversion library contains functions that augment the existing cast operators (`static_cast`, `const_cast`, and `dynamic_cast`). Conversion adds `polymorphic_cast` and `polymorphic_downcast` for safe polymorphic casts, `numeric_cast` for safe conversions among numeric types, and `lexical_cast` for lexical conversions (for example, between `string` and `double`). You can customize these casts to work optimally with your own types—something that isn't possible with the casts provided by the language. The library is covered in detail in "Library 2: Conversion."

The authors of Conversion are Dave Abrahams and Kevlin Henney.

Boost.Crc

The Crc library provides calculations of cyclic redundancy codes (CRC), a commonly used checksum type. A CRC is attached to a stream of data (from which it is computed), so the checksum can be used later to validate the data. The library includes four sample CRC types: `crc_16_type`, `crc_ccitt_type`, `crc_xmodem_type`, and `crc_32_type`[5].

The author of Crc is Daryle Walker.

Boost.Date_time

The Date_time library provides extensive support for date and time types and operations upon them. Without library support for dates and time, temporal programming tasks are complicated and error prone. Using Date_time, the natural abstractions that one would expect are supported: days, weeks, months, durations (and intervals thereof), addition and subtraction, and so on. The library addresses issues commonly omitted from other date/time libraries, such as handling leap seconds and supporting high-resolution time sources. The library's design is extensible, allowing for customized behavior or added functionality.

The author of Date_time is Jeff Garland.

---

5. CRC32 is used in PKZip, for example.

Boost.Optional

It is common for functions to indicate that the returned value is invalid, but often the returned type does not have a state to indicate that it's not valid. Optional offers the class template `optional`, which is a type that semantically has an additional state, one that is in effect when instances of `optional` are not containing instances of the wrapped object.

The author of Optional is Fernando Cacciola.

Boost.Pool

The Pool library provides a pool memory allocator—that is, a tool for managing dynamic memory in a single, large allocation. Using memory pools is a good solution when allocating and deallocating many small objects, or when memory control needs to be made more efficient.

The author of Pool is Steve Cleary.

Boost.Preprocessor

Using the preprocessor is hard when you need to express common constructs such as recursion, it doesn't have containers, doesn't provide means for iteration, and so forth. Nevertheless, the preprocessor is a powerful and portable tool. The Preprocessor library provides abstractions on top of the preprocessor. These include lists, tuples, and arrays, as well as algorithms that operate on the elements of those types. The library helps eliminate repetitive code, thus reducing your effort, while making code more readable, expressive, and maintainable.

The authors of Preprocessor are Vesa Karvonen and Paul Mensonides.

Boost.Program_options

The Program_options library retrieves program configuration options (name/value pairs), typically provided through command-line arguments or configuration files. The library relieves the programmer from the task of parsing the data by hand.

The author of Program_options is Vladimir Prus.

Boost.Python

The Python library provides interoperability between C++ and Python.[6] It is used to expose C++ classes and functions to Python and Python objects to C++. It is non-intrusive, which means that existing code typically requires no changes to be exposed in Python.

The author of Python is David Abrahams, with important contributions from Joel de Guzman and Ralf W. Grosse-Kunstleve.

Boost.Smart_ptr

Smart pointers are vital parts of any programmer's toolbox. They are used everywhere to avoid resource leaks, share resources, and manage object lifetimes correctly. There are a great number of good smart pointer libraries available, some for free, others part of commercial packages. Smart_ptr is among the best, as proven by thousands of users and the recommendations from leading experts in the field. Smart_ptr includes non-intrusive smart pointers for limiting scope (`scoped_ptr` and `scoped_array`) and sharing resources (`shared_ptr` and `shared_array`), an observing smart pointer to use with `shared_ptr` (`weak_ptr`), and an intrusive smart pointer class (`intrusive_ptr`). Smart_ptr's `shared_ptr` (including the helper `enable_shared_from_this`) and `weak_ptr` have been accepted for the upcoming Library Technical Report. For more about these really smart pointers, see "Library 1: Smart_ptr."

The authors of Smart_ptr are Greg Colvin, Beman Dawes, Peter Dimov, and Darin Adler.

Boost.Test

The Test library provides a matched set of components for writing test programs, organizing tests into simple test cases and test suites, and controlling their runtime execution. The Program Execution Monitor, a component in the library, is also useful in some production (nontest) environments.

The author of Test is Gennadiy Rozental (based upon earlier work by Beman Dawes).

---

6. A popular programming language that you should get acquainted with.

Boost.Thread

Portable threading is tricky business, and there's no help to be had from C++ itself, as the language includes no threading support, nor acknowledges it in any way. Of course, there's POSIX, available on many platforms, but POSIX defines a C API. Thread is a library that offers portable threading through a number of threading primitives and higher-level abstractions.

The author of Thread is William Kempf.

Boost.Timer

The Timer library contains features for measuring time, and aims to be as consistent as possible across different platforms. Although there are typically platform-specific APIs that allow programmers to measure time, there is no portable way of attaining high-resolution timers. Boost.Timer addresses this problem by offering the best possible resolution whilst remaining portable, in return for a certain degree of freedom of guaranteed accuracy and precision.

The author of Timer is Beman Dawes.

Boost.Tribool

This library contains a `tribool` class, which implements three-state Boolean logic. A three-state Boolean type has an additional state besides *true* and *false: indeterminate* (this state could also be named *maybe*; the name is configurable).

The author of Tribool is Douglas Gregor.

Boost.Utility

Some useful stuff just doesn't find its way into a separate library, typically because it is not complicated or extensive enough to warrant a separate library. That doesn't make it less useful; in fact, small utilities often have the most wide-spread use. In Boost, such utilities are contained in the aptly named Utility library. Here, one finds `checked_delete`, a function that ensures that a type is complete upon the point of deletion, the class `noncopyable` to ensure that a class cannot be copied, and `enable_if` for total control of function overloading. There's a lot more to Utility. See "Library 3: Utility" for the whole story.

The authors of Utility are David Abrahams, Daryle Walker, Douglas Gregor, and others.

Boost.Value_initialized

The Value_initialized library helps construct and initialize objects in a generic way. In C++, a newly constructed object can be either zero-initialized, default-constructed, or indeterminate, all depending upon the type of the object. With Boost.Value_initialized, this inconsistency problem goes away.

The author of Value_initialized is Fernando Cacciola.

Part I
General Libraries

It is not obvious what a suitable name for this part of the book should be. With a structure of the book that encompasses distinct domains (such as containers and higher-order programming), names are often palpable; except for what's covered in this part—those little things that we use all of the time: smart pointers, conversion utilities, and so on.

You can't really begin with a division called *Miscellaneous*, or *Ubiquitous*, or *Frequently Used Libraries*. It's true—they are all of these things, but it just doesn't convey their importance properly. Ergo, *General Libraries*, which I'm also hoping will focus on their omnipresence.

One thing that strikes me as odd is the way that we often regard these "simple" components—utilities, if you like—that are of so much use to us. They get a lot of attention in books and articles, but it is surprisingly common to underestimate their value when it comes to selecting them (or creating them) for production code. Is it because we consider small components uncomplicated? Do we willingly sacrifice flexibility on the basis that it's easy to create another small component just like it, but manually adapted to the exact problem at hand? If these are indeed the arguments, we are thoroughly deceiving ourselves. Two million instances of smart pointers in a program make the smart pointers critical, both in terms of efficiency and reliability. Twenty different implementations of common conversions in a program affects the time it takes to code them, but more importantly it also impedes maintainability. Systems are built on layers of abstraction, and the lower levels are often referred to as being comprised of data structures, algorithms, and utilities. If you agree with that, consider the impact of a change, or a bug, or unwarranted inflexibility in any of these small, insignificant, their-importance-forgotten utilities. Shiver. Utilities are vessels that traffic the veins of our programs. They are the oil in our engines of logic and the glue between our barriers of insulation. Enough of crummy analogies; let's just give them the credit they deserve, shall we? We will cover a wide variety of general libraries here, including smart pointers, conversions (both type conversions and lexical conversions), regular expressions, operators, static assertions, and more.

Library 1
Smart_ptr

How Does the Smart_ptr Library Improve Your Programs?

- Automatic lifetime management of objects with `shared_ptr` makes shared ownership of resources effective and safe.

- Safe observation of shared resources through `weak_ptr` avoids dangling pointers.

- Scoped resources using `scoped_ptr` and `scoped_array` make the code easier to write and maintain, and helps in writing exception-safe code.

Smart pointers solve the problem of managing the lifetime of resources (typically dynamically allocated objects[1]). Smart pointers come in different flavors. Most share one key feature—automatic resource management. This feature is manifested in different ways, such as lifetime control over dynamically allocated objects, and acquisition and release of resources (files, network connections). The Boost smart pointers primarily cover the first case—they store pointers to dynamically allocated objects, and delete those objects at the right time. You might wonder why these smart pointers don't do more. Couldn't they just as easily cover all types of resource management? Well, they could (and to some extent they do), but not without a price. General solutions often imply increased complexity, and with the Boost smart pointers, usability is of even higher priority than flexibility. However, through the support for custom deleters, Boost's arguably smartest smart pointer (`boost::shared_ptr`) supports resources that need other destruction code than `delete`. The five smart pointer types in `Boost.Smart_ptr` are tailor-made to fit the most common needs that arise in everyday programming.

---

1. Just about any type of resource can be handled by a generic smart pointer type.

When Do We Need Smart Pointers?

There are three typical scenarios when smart pointers are appropriate:

- Shared ownership of resources

- When writing exception-safe code

- Avoiding common errors, such as resource leaks

Shared ownership is the case when two or more objects must use a third object. How (or rather when) should that third object be deallocated? To be sure that the timing of deallocation is right, every object referring to the shared resource would have to know about each other to be able to correctly time the release of that resource. That coupling is not viable from a design or a maintenance point of view. The better approach is for the owners to delegate responsibility for lifetime management to a smart pointer. When no more shared owners exist, the smart pointer can safely free the resource.

Exception safety at its simplest means not leaking resources and preserving program invariants when an exception is thrown. When an object is dynamically allocated, it won't be deleted when an exception is thrown. As the stack unwinds and the pointer goes out of scope, the resource is possibly lost until the program is terminated (and even resource reclamation upon termination isn't guaranteed by the language). Not only can the program run out of resources due to memory leaks, but the program state can easily become corrupt. Smart pointers can automatically release those resources for you, even in the face of exceptions.

Avoiding common errors. Forgetting to call `delete` is the oldest mistake in the book (at least in this book). A smart pointer doesn't care about the control paths in a program; it only cares about deleting a pointed-to object at the end of its lifetime. Using a smart pointer eliminates your need to keep track of when to delete objects. Also, smart pointers can hide the deallocation details, so that clients don't need to know whether to call `delete`, some special cleanup function, or not delete the resource at all.

Safe and efficient smart pointers are vital weapons in the programmer's arsenal. Although the C++ Standard Library offers `std::auto_ptr`, that's not nearly enough to fulfill our smart pointer needs. For example, `auto_ptrs` cannot be used as elements of STL containers. The Boost smart pointer classes fill a gap currently left open by the Standard.

The main focus of this chapter is on `scoped_ptr`, `shared_ptr`, `intrusive_ptr`, and `weak_ptr`. Although the complementary `scoped_array` and shared_array are sometimes useful, they are not used nearly as frequently, and they are so similar to those covered that it would be too repetitive to cover them at the same level of detail.

How Does Smart_ptr Fit with the Standard Library?

The Smart_ptr library has been proposed for inclusion in the Standard Library, and there are primarily three reasons for this:

- The Standard Library currently offers only auto_ptr, which is but one type of smart pointer, covering only one part of the smart pointer spectrum. shared_ptr offers different, arguably even more important, functionality.

- The Boost smart pointers are specifically designed to work well with, and be a natural extension to, the Standard Library. For example, before shared_ptr, there were no standard smart pointers that could be used as elements in containers.

- Real-world programmers have proven these smart pointer classes through heavy use in their own programs for a long time.

The preceding reasons make the Smart_ptr library a very useful addition to the C++ Standard Library. Boost.Smart_ptr's shared_ptr (and the accompanying helper enable_shared_from_this) and weak_ptr have been accepted for the upcoming Library Technical Report.

scoped_ptr

Header: "boost/scoped_ptr.hpp"

boost::scoped_ptr is used to ensure the proper deletion of a dynamically allocated object. scoped_ptr has similar characteristics to std::auto_ptr, with the important difference that it doesn't transfer ownership the way an auto_ptr does. In fact, a scoped_ptr cannot be copied or assigned at all! A scoped_ptr assumes ownership of the resource to which it points, and never accidentally surrenders that ownership. This property of scoped_ptr improves expressiveness in our code, as we can select the smart pointer (scoped_ptr or auto_ptr) that best fits our needs.

When deciding whether to use `std::auto_ptr` or `boost::scoped_ptr`, consider whether transfer of ownership is a desirable property of the smart pointer. If it isn't, use `scoped_ptr`. It is a lightweight smart pointer; using it doesn't make your program larger or run slower. It only makes your code safer and more maintainable.

Next is the synopsis for `scoped_ptr`, followed by a short description of the class members:

```
namespace boost {

  template<typename T> class scoped_ptr : noncopyable {
  public:
    explicit scoped_ptr(T* p = 0);
    ~scoped_ptr();

    void reset(T* p = 0);

    T& operator*() const;
    T* operator->() const;
    T* get() const;

    void swap(scoped_ptr& b);
  };

  template<typename T>
    void swap(scoped_ptr<T> & a, scoped_ptr<T> & b);
}
```

Members

```
explicit scoped_ptr(T* p=0)
```

The constructor stores a copy of `p`. Note that `p` must be allocated using `operator new`, or be null. There is no requirement on `T` to be a complete type at the time of construction. This is useful when the pointer `p` is the result of calling some allocation function rather than calling `new` directly: Because the type needn't be complete, a forward declaration of the type `T` is enough. This constructor never throws.

```
~scoped_ptr()
```

Deletes the pointee. The type `T` must be a complete type when it is destroyed. If the `scoped_ptr` holds no resource at the time of its destruction, this does nothing. The destructor never throws.

```
void reset(T* p=0);
```

Resetting a `scoped_ptr` deletes the stored pointer it already owns, if any, and then saves `p`. Often, the lifetime management of a resource is completely left to be handled by the `scoped_ptr`, but on rare occasions the resource needs to be freed prior to the `scoped_ptr`'s destruction, or another resource needs to be handled by the `scoped_ptr` instead of the original. In those cases, `reset` is useful, but use it sparingly. (Excessive use probably indicates a design problem.) This function never throws.

```
T& operator*() const;
```

Returns a reference to the object pointed to by the stored pointer. As there are no null references, dereferencing a `scoped_ptr` that holds a null pointer results in undefined behavior. If in doubt as to whether the contained pointer is valid, use the function `get` instead of dereferencing. This operator never throws.

```
T* operator->() const;
```

Returns the stored pointer. It is undefined behavior to invoke this operator if the stored pointer is null. Use the member function `get` if there's uncertainty as to whether the pointer is null. This operator never throws.

```
T* get() const;
```

Returns the stored pointer. `get` should be used with caution, because of the issues of dealing with raw pointers. However, `get` makes it possible to explicitly test whether the stored pointer is null. The function never throws. `get` is typically used when calling functions that require a raw pointer.

```
operator unspecified_bool_type() const
```

Returns whether the `scoped_ptr` is non-null. The type of the returned value is unspecified, but it can be used in Boolean contexts. Rather than using `get` to test the validity of the `scoped_ptr`, prefer using this conversion function to test it in an if-statement.

```
void swap(scoped_ptr& b)
```

Exchanges the contents of two `scoped_ptr`s. This function never throws.

Free Functions

```
template<typename T> void swap(scoped_ptr<T>& a, scoped_ptr<T>& b)
```

This function offers the preferred means by which to exchange the contents of two scoped pointers. It is preferable because `swap(scoped1,scoped2)` can be applied generically (in templated code) to many pointer types, including raw pointers and third-party smart pointers.[2] `scoped1.swap(scoped2)` only works on smart pointers, not on raw pointers, and only on those that define the operation.

Usage

A `scoped_ptr` is used like an ordinary pointer with a few important differences; the most important are that you don't have to remember to invoke `delete` on the pointer and that copying is disallowed. The typical operators for pointer operations (`operator*` and `operator->`) are overloaded to provide the same syntactic access as that for a raw pointer. Using `scoped_ptr`s are just as fast as using raw pointers, and there's no size overhead, so use them extensively. To use `boost::scoped_ptr`, include the header `"boost/scoped_ptr.hpp"`. When declaring a `scoped_ptr`, the type of the pointee is the parameter to the class template. For example, here's a `scoped_ptr` that wraps a pointer to `std::string`:

```
boost::scoped_ptr<std::string> p(new std::string("Hello"));
```

When a `scoped_ptr` is destroyed, it calls `delete` on the pointer that it owns.

No Need to Manually Delete

Let's take a look at a program that uses a `scoped_ptr` to manage a pointer to `std::string`. Note how there's no call to `delete`, as the `scoped_ptr` is an automatic variable and is therefore destroyed as it goes out of scope.

---

2. You can create your own free swap function for third-party smart pointers that weren't smart enough to provide their own.

```
#include "boost/scoped_ptr.hpp"
#include <string>
#include <iostream>

int main() {
  {
  boost::scoped_ptr<std::string>
  p(new std::string("Use scoped_ptr often."));

  // Print the value of the string
  if (p)
    std::cout << *p << '\n';

  // Get the size of the string
  size_t i=p->size();

  // Assign a new value to the string
  *p="Acts just like a pointer";

  } // p is destroyed here, and deletes the std::string
}
```

A couple of things are worth noting in the preceding code. First, a scoped_ptr can be tested for validity, just like an ordinary pointer, because it provides an implicit conversion to a type that can be used in Boolean expressions. Second, calling member functions on the pointee works like for raw pointers, because of the overloaded operator->. Third, dereferencing scoped_ptr also works exactly like for raw pointers, thanks to the overloaded operator*. These properties are what makes usage of scoped_ptr—and other smart pointers—so intuitive, because the differences from raw pointers are mostly related to the lifetime management semantics, not syntax.

Almost Like *auto_ptr*

The major difference between scoped_ptr and auto_ptr is in the treatment of ownership. auto_ptr willingly transfers ownership—away from the source auto_ptr—when copied, whereas a scoped_ptr cannot be copied. Take a look at the following program, which shows scoped_ptr and auto_ptr side by side to clearly show how they differ.

```
void scoped_vs_auto() {

  using boost::scoped_ptr;
  using std::auto_ptr;

  scoped_ptr<std::string> p_scoped(new std::string("Hello"));
  auto_ptr<std::string> p_auto(new std::string("Hello"));

  p_scoped->size();
  p_auto->size();

  scoped_ptr<std::string> p_another_scoped=p_scoped;
  auto_ptr<std::string> p_another_auto=p_auto;

  p_another_auto->size();
  (*p_auto).size();
}
```

This example doesn't compile because a scoped_ptr cannot be copy constructed or assigned to. The auto_ptr can be both copy constructed and copy assigned, but that also means that it transfers ownership from p_auto to p_another_auto, leaving p_auto with a null pointer after the assignment. This can lead to unpleasant surprises, such as when trying to store auto_ptrs in a container.[3] If we remove the assignment to p_another_scoped, the program compiles cleanly, but it results in undefined behavior at runtime, because of dereferencing the null pointer in p_auto (*p_auto).

Because scoped_ptr::get returns a raw pointer, it is possible to do evil things to a scoped_ptr, and there are two things that you'll especially want to avoid. First, do not delete the stored pointer. It is deleted once again when the scoped_ptr is destroyed. Second, do not store the raw pointer in another scoped_ptr (or any smart pointer for that matter). Bad things happen when the pointer is deleted twice, once by each scoped_ptr. Simply put, minimize the use of get, unless you are dealing with legacy code that requires you to pass the raw pointer!

---

3. Never, ever, store auto_ptrs in Standard Library containers. Typically, you'll get a compiler error if you try; if you don't, you're in trouble.

scoped_ptr and the Pimpl Idiom

scoped_ptr is ideal to use in many situations where one has previously used raw pointers or auto_ptrs, such as when implementing the *pimpl idiom*.[4] The idea behind the pimpl idiom is to insulate clients from all knowledge about the private parts of a class. Because clients depend on the header file of a class, any changes to the header will affect clients, even if they are made to the private or protected sections. The pimpl idiom hides those details by putting private data and functions in a separate type defined in the implementation file and then forward declaring the type in the header file and storing a pointer to it. The constructor of the class allocates the pimpl type, and the destructor deallocates it. This removes the implementation dependencies from the header file. Let's construct a class that implements the pimpl idiom and then apply smart pointers to make it safer.

```
// pimpl_sample.hpp

#if !defined (PIMPL_SAMPLE)
#define PIMPL_SAMPLE

struct impl;

class pimpl_sample {
   impl* pimpl_;
public:
   pimpl_sample();
   ~pimpl_sample();
   void do_something();
};

#endif
```

That's the interface for the class pimpl_sample. The struct impl is forward declared, and it holds all private members and functions in the implementation file. The effect is that clients are fully insulated from the internal details of the pimpl_sample class.

---

4. This is also known as the Cheshire Cat idiom. See www.gotw.ca/gotw/024.htm and Exceptional C++ for more on the pimpl idiom.

```
// pimpl_sample.cpp

#include "pimpl_sample.hpp"
#include <string>
#include <iostream>

struct pimpl_sample::impl {
  void do_something_() {
    std::cout << s_ << "\n";
  }

  std::string s_;
};

pimpl_sample::pimpl_sample()
  : pimpl_(new impl) {
  pimpl_->s_ = "This is the pimpl idiom";
}

pimpl_sample::~pimpl_sample() {
  delete pimpl_;
}

void pimpl_sample::do_something() {
  pimpl_->do_something_();
}
```

At first glance, this may look perfectly fine, but it's not. The implementation is not exception safe! The reason is that the `pimpl_sample` constructor may throw an exception *after* the `pimpl` has been constructed. Throwing an exception in the constructor implies that the object being constructed never fully existed, so its destructor isn't invoked when the stack is unwound. This state of affairs means that the memory allocated and referenced by the `impl_` pointer will leak. However, there's an easy cure for this; `scoped_ptr` to the rescue!

```
class pimpl_sample {
  struct impl;
  boost::scoped_ptr<impl> pimpl_;
  ...
};
```

By letting a `scoped_ptr` handle the lifetime management of the hidden `impl` class, and after removing the deletion of the `impl` from the destructor (it's no longer needed, thanks to `scoped_ptr`), we're done. However, you must still remember to define the destructor manually; the reason is that at the time the compiler generates an implicit destructor, the type `impl` is incomplete, so its destructor isn't called. If you were to use `auto_ptr` to store the `impl`, you could still compile code containing such errors, but using `scoped_ptr`, you'll receive an error.

Note that when using `scoped_ptr` as a class member, you need to manually define the copy constructor and copy assignment operator. The reason for this is that a `scoped_ptr` cannot be copied, and therefore the class that aggregates it also becomes noncopyable.

Finally, it's worth noting that if the pimpl instance can be safely shared between instances of the enclosing class (here, `pimpl_sample`), then `boost::shared_ptr` is the right choice for handling the pimpl's lifetime. The advantages of using `shared_ptr` rather than `scoped_ptr` includes being relieved from manually defining the copy constructor and copy assignment operator, and to define an empty destructor—`shared_ptr` is designed to work correctly even with incomplete types.

scoped_ptr Is Not the Same As *const auto_ptr*

The observant reader has probably already noted that an `auto_ptr` can indeed be made to work almost like a `scoped_ptr`, by declaring the `auto_ptr const`:

```
const auto_ptr<A> no_transfer_of_ownership(new A);
```

It's close, but not quite the same. The big difference is that a `scoped_ptr` can be `reset`, effectively deleting and replacing the pointee when needed. That's not possible with a `const auto_ptr`. Another difference, albeit smaller, is the difference in names: Although `const auto_ptr` essentially makes the same statement as `scoped_ptr`, it does so more verbosely and less obviously. After you have `scoped_ptr` in your vocabulary, you should use it because it clearly declares your intentions. If you want to say that a resource is scoped, and that there's no way you'll relinquish ownership of it, spell it `boost::scoped_ptr`.

Summary

Raw pointers complicate writing exception-safe and error-free code. Automatically limiting the lifetime of dynamically allocated objects to a certain scope via smart pointers is a powerful way to address those issues and also increase the readability, maintainability, and quality of your code. `scoped_ptr` unambiguously states that its pointee cannot be shared or transferred. As you've seen, `std::auto_ptr` can "steal" the pointee from another `auto_ptr`, even inadvertently, which is considered to be `auto_ptr`'s biggest liability. That liability is what makes `scoped_ptr` such an excellent complement to `auto_ptr`. When a dynamically allocated object is passed to a `scoped_ptr`, it assumes sole ownership of that object. Because a `scoped_ptr` is almost always allocated as an automatic variable or data member, it is properly destroyed when it leaves scope, and thus frees its managed memory, when execution flow leaves a scope due to a return statement or a thrown exception.

Use `scoped_ptr` when

- A pointer is used in a scope where an exception may be thrown

- There are several control paths in a function

- The lifetime of a dynamically allocated object can be limited to a specific scope

- Exception safety is important (always!)

scoped_array

Header: `"boost/scoped_array.hpp"`

The need for dynamically allocated arrays is usually best handled by `std::vector`, but there are two cases when it makes good sense to use arrays: for optimization, as there is some overhead in size and speed for `vector`; and for expression of intent, making it clear that bounds are fixed.[5] Dynamically allocated arrays are exposed to the same dangers as ordinary pointers, with the added (and all too common) mistake of invoking the `delete` operator instead of the `delete[]` operator. I've seen that mistake in places one could hardly imagine, such as in widely used, proprietary container classes! `scoped_array` does for arrays what `scoped_ptr` does for pointers to single objects: It deletes the memory. The difference is that `scoped_array` does it using the `delete[]` operator.

---

5. These are not clear-cut advantages. Indeed, it is usually best to use `std::vector` until performance measurements suggest the benefits of `scoped_array` are warranted.

The reason that `scoped_array` is a separate class rather than being a specialization of `scoped_ptr` is because it is not possible to distinguish between pointers to single objects and pointers to arrays using metaprogramming techniques. Despite efforts to make that distinction, no one has found a reliable way to do that because arrays decay so easily into pointers that carry no type information indicating that they point to arrays. As a result, the onus is on you to use `scoped_array` rather than `scoped_ptr`, just as you must otherwise choose to use the `delete[]` operator rather than the `delete` operator. The benefits are that `scoped_array` handles deletion for you, and that `scoped_array` conveys that we are dealing with an array, whereas a raw pointer doesn't.

`scoped_array` is very similar to `scoped_ptr`, with the differences that it provides `operator[]` to mimic a raw array.

`scoped_array` is a superior alternative to ordinary, dynamically allocated arrays. It handles lifetime management of dynamically allocated arrays, similar to how `scoped_ptr` manages lifetime for pointers to objects. Remember though, in most cases, `std::vector` is preferable as it is more flexible and powerful. When you need to clearly state that the size of the array is constant, use `scoped_array` rather than `std::vector`.

shared_ptr

Header: `"boost/shared_ptr.hpp"`

Almost all non-trivial programs need some form of reference-counted smart pointers. These smart pointers eliminate the need to write complicated logic to control the lifetime of objects shared among two or more other objects. When the reference count drops to zero, no more objects are interested in the shared object, and so it is deleted automatically. Reference-counted smart pointers can be categorized as *intrusive* or *non-intrusive*. The former expects the classes that it manages to provide certain functionality or data members with which to manage the reference count. That means designing classes with the foresight to work with an intrusive, reference-counted smart pointer class, or retrofitting. Non-intrusive, reference-counted smart pointers don't require anything of the types they manage. Reference-counted smart pointers assume ownership of the memory associated with their stored pointers. The problem with sharing objects without the help of smart pointers is that someone must, eventually, delete the shared memory. Who, and when? Without reference-counted smart pointers, one must impose lifetime management externally to the memory being managed, which typically means stronger dependencies among the collective owners. That, in turn, impedes reusability and adds complexity.

The class to be managed may have properties that make it a good candidate for use with a reference-counted smart pointer. For example, the fact that it is expensive to copy, or that part of its representation needs to be shared between instances, make shared ownership desirable. There are also situations in which there is no explicit owner of a shared resource. Using reference-counted smart pointers makes possible sharing ownership among the objects that need access to the shared resource. Reference-counted smart pointers also make it possible to store pointers to objects in Standard Library containers without risk of leaks, especially in the face of exceptions or when removing elements from the containers. When you store pointers in containers, you can take advantage of polymorphism, improved efficiency (if copying is expensive), and the ability to store the same objects in multiple, associated containers for specialized lookups.

After you've determined that the use of a reference-counted smart pointer is warranted, how do you choose whether to use an intrusive or non-intrusive design? Non-intrusive smart pointers are almost always the better choice on account of their general applicability, lack of impact on existing code, and flexibility. You can use non-intrusive, reference-counted smart pointers with classes that you cannot or don't wish to change. The usual way to adapt a class to work with an intrusive, reference-counted smart pointer is to derive from a reference-counted base class. That change may be more expensive than appears at first glance. At the very least, it adds dependencies and decreases reusability.[6] It also typically increases object size, which may limit usability in some contexts.[7]

A `shared_ptr` can be constructed from a raw pointer, another `shared_ptr`, a `std::auto_ptr`, or a `boost::weak_ptr`. It is also possible to pass a second argument to the constructor of `shared_ptr`, known as a *deleter*. The deleter is later called upon to handle deletion of the shared resource. This is useful for resource management where the resource is not allocated with `new` and destroyed with

---

6. Consider the need to use more than one reference-counted smart pointer class with the same type. If both are intrusive designs, the different base classes may not be compatible and will certainly be wasteful. If only one is an intrusive design, the overhead of the base class is for naught when using the non-intrusive smart pointer.

7. On the other hand, non-intrusive smart pointers require additional storage for the actual smart pointer.

delete (we shall see examples of creating custom deleters later). After the shared_ptr has been constructed, it is used just like an ordinary pointer, with the obvious exception that it must not be explicitly deleted.

This is a partial synopsis for shared_ptr; the most important members and accompanying free functions are shown and subsequently briefly discussed.

```
namespace boost {

  template<typename T> class shared_ptr {
  public:
    template <class Y> explicit shared_ptr(Y* p);
    template <class Y,class D> shared_ptr(Y* p,D d);

    ~shared_ptr();

    shared_ptr(const shared_ptr & r);
    template <class Y> explicit
      shared_ptr(const weak_ptr<Y>& r);
    template <class Y> explicit shared_ptr(std::auto_ptr<Y>& r);

    shared_ptr& operator=(const shared_ptr& r);

    void reset();

    T& operator*() const;
    T* operator->() const;
    T* get() const;

    bool unique() const;
    long use_count() const;

    operator unspecified-bool-type() const;

    void swap(shared_ptr<T>& b);
  };

  template <class T,class U>
    shared_ptr<T> static_pointer_cast(const shared_ptr<U>& r);
}
```

Members

```
template <class Y> explicit shared_ptr(Y* p);
```

> This constructor takes ownership of the supplied pointer p. The argument p must be a valid pointer to Y. The reference count is set to 1 after construction. The only exception that may be thrown from the constructor is std::bad_alloc (which can only happen in the unlikely event that the reference counter cannot be allocated from the free store).

```
template <class Y,class D> shared_ptr(Y* p,D d);
```

> This constructor takes two arguments. The first is the resource that the shared_ptr should take ownership of, and the second is an object that is responsible for releasing that resource when the shared_ptr is destroyed. The stored resource is passed to the object as d(p). Thus, valid values of p depend upon d. If the reference counter cannot be allocated, shared_ptr throws an exception of type std::bad_alloc.

```
shared_ptr(const shared_ptr& r);
```

> The stored resource in r is shared by the constructed shared_ptr, and the reference count is increased by one. This copy constructor never throws.

```
template <class Y> explicit shared_ptr(const weak_ptr<Y>& r);
```

> Constructs a shared_ptr from a weak_ptr (covered later in this chapter). This enables thread-safe usage of weak_ptr, because the reference count of the shared resource pointed to by the weak_ptr argument will be incremented (weak_ptrs do not affect the reference count of shared resources). If the weak_ptr is empty (r.use_count()==0), shared_ptr throws an exception of type bad_weak_ptr.

```
template <typename Y> shared_ptr(std::auto_ptr<Y>& r);
```

> The construction from an auto_ptr takes ownership of the pointer stored in r by storing a copy of the pointer and calling release on the auto_ptr. The reference count after construction is 1. r is, of course, emptied. Throws std::bad_alloc if the reference counter cannot be allocated.

```
~shared_ptr();
```

> The `shared_ptr` destructor decreases the reference count by one. If the count is then zero, the stored pointer is deleted. Deleting the pointer is done through a call to `operator delete` or, if a custom deleter object was supplied to handle destruction, that object will be called with the stored pointer as its sole argument. The destructor never throws.

```
shared_ptr& operator=(const shared_ptr& r);
```

> The copy assignment operator shares the resource in `r` and stops sharing the resource currently being shared. The copy assignment operator never throws.

```
void reset();
```

> The `reset` function is used to stop sharing ownership of the stored pointer. The reference count for the shared resource is decremented.

```
T& operator*() const;
```

> This operator returns a reference to the object pointed to by the stored pointer. If the pointer is null, invoking `operator*` results in undefined behavior. This operator never throws.

```
T* operator->() const;
```

> The operator returns the stored pointer. This, together with `operator*` is what makes the smart pointer look like an ordinary pointer. This operator never throws.

```
T* get() const;
```

> The `get` function is the preferred way of retrieving the stored pointer when it might be null (in which case `operator*` and `operator->` leads to undefined behavior). Note that it is also possible to test whether a `shared_ptr` contains a valid pointer by using the implicit Boolean conversion. This function never throws.

```
bool unique() const;
```

> This function returns `true` if the `shared_ptr` is the sole owner of the stored pointer; otherwise, it returns `false`. `unique` never throws.

```
long use_count() const;
```

The `use_count` function returns the reference count for the pointer. It is especially useful for debugging purposes, because it can be used to get snapshots of the reference count at critical points of program execution. Use it sparingly. For some possible implementations of the `shared_ptr` interface, calculating the reference count may be expensive or even impossible. The function never throws.

```
operator unspecified-bool-type() const;
```

This implicit conversion to a type, `unspecified-bool-type`, makes it possible to test a smart pointer in Boolean contexts. The value is `true` if the `shared_ptr` is currently storing a valid pointer; otherwise, it is `false`. Note that the type that this conversion function returns is not specified. Using `bool` as the return type allows for some nonsensical operations, so typically, an implementation uses the *safe bool idiom*,[8] which is a nifty way of ensuring that only applicable Boolean tests can be used. The function never throws.

```
void swap(shared_ptr<T>& b);
```

It is sometimes convenient to swap the contents of two `shared_ptr`s. The `swap` function exchanges the stored pointers (and their reference counts). This function never throws.

Free Functions

```
template <typename T,typename U>
  shared_ptr<T> static_pointer_cast(const shared_ptr<U>& r);
```

To perform a `static_cast` on a pointer stored in a `shared_ptr`, we could retrieve the pointer and then cast it, but we couldn't store it in another `shared_ptr`; the new `shared_ptr` would think it was the first to manage the resource the pointer refers to. This is remedied by `static_pointer_cast`. Using this function ensures that the reference count for the pointee remains correct. `static_pointer_cast` never throws exceptions.

---

8. Invented by Peter Dimov.

Usage

The primary problem solved by `shared_ptr` is knowing the correct time to delete a resource that is shared by more than one client. Here's a straightforward example, where two classes, A and B, are sharing an instance of `int`. To start using `boost::shared_ptr`, you need to include `"boost/shared_ptr.hpp"`.

```cpp
#include "boost/shared_ptr.hpp"
#include <cassert>

class A {
  boost::shared_ptr<int> no_;
public:
  A(boost::shared_ptr<int> no) : no_(no) {}
  void value(int i) {
    *no_=i;
  }
};

class B {
  boost::shared_ptr<int> no_;
public:
  B(boost::shared_ptr<int> no) : no_(no) {}
  int value() const {
    return *no_;
  }
};

int main() {
    boost::shared_ptr<int> temp(new int(14));
    A a(temp);
    B b(temp);
    a.value(28);
    assert(b.value()==28);
}
```

The classes A and B both store a `shared_ptr<int>`. When creating the instances of A and B, the `shared_ptr` temp is passed to their constructors. This means that all three `shared_ptr`s—a, b, and `temp`—are now referring to the same instance of an `int`. Had we used pointers to achieve such sharing of an `int`, A and B would have had a hard time figuring out when (and if!) it should be deleted. In the example, the reference count is 3 until the end of `main`, where all of the `shared_ptrs` go out of scope, decreasing the count until it reaches 0, allowing the last of the smart pointers to delete the shared `int`.

The Pimpl Idiom Revisited

The pimpl idiom was previously presented in conjunction with `scoped_ptr`, which works well as a means of storing the dynamically allocated instance of the pimpl, if copying is not permitted for the class using the idiom. That is not appropriate for all classes that would benefit from using the pimpl idiom (note that `scoped_ptr` can still be used, but copy construction and assignment need to be implemented by hand). For those classes that can handle shared implementation details, `shared_ptr` comes into play. When ownership of the pimpl is passed to a `shared_ptr`, the copying and assignment operators come for free. You'll recall that when using `scoped_ptr` to handle the lifetime of the pimpl class, copying of the outer class is not allowed, because `scoped_ptrs` are not copyable. This means that to support copying and assignment in such classes, a copy constructor and assignment operator must be defined manually. When using `shared_ptr` to handle the lifetime of the pimpl, a user-defined copy constructor may not even be needed. Note that the pimpl instance will be *shared* among the objects of the class, so if there is state that only applies to one instance of the class, a handcrafted copy constructor is still required. The solution is very similar to what we saw for `scoped_ptr`; just make it a `shared_ptr`, instead.

shared_ptr and Standard Library Containers

Storing objects directly in a container is sometimes troublesome. Storing objects by value means clients get copies of the container elements, which may be a performance problem for types where copying is an expensive operation. Furthermore, some containers, notably `std::vector`, copy elements when resizing as you add more elements, further adding to the performance problems. Finally, value semantics means no polymorphic behavior. If you need to store polymorphic objects in a container and you don't want to slice them, you must use pointers. If you use raw pointers, the complexity of maintaining the integrity of the elements skyrockets. That is, you must know whether clients of the container still refer to elements of the container when erasing them from the container, never mind coordinating multiple clients using the same element. Such problems are solved handily by shared_ptr.

The following example shows how to store shared pointers in a Standard Library container.

```cpp
#include "boost/shared_ptr.hpp"
#include <vector>
#include <iostream>

class A {
public:
  virtual void sing()=0;
protected:
  virtual ~A() {};
};

class B : public A {
public:
  virtual void sing() {
    std::cout << "Do re mi fa so la";
  }
};

boost::shared_ptr<A> createA() {
  boost::shared_ptr<A> p(new B());
  return p;
}

int main() {
  typedef std::vector<boost::shared_ptr<A> > container_type;
  typedef container_type::iterator iterator;

  container_type container;
  for (int i=0;i<10;++i) {
    container.push_back(createA());
  }

  std::cout << "The choir is gathered: \n";
  iterator end=container.end();
  for (iterator it=container.begin();it!=end;++it) {
    (*it)->sing();
  }
}
```

The two classes, A and B, contain a single virtual member function sing. B derives publicly from A, and as you can see, the factory function createA returns a dynamically allocated instance of B wrapped in a shared_ptr<A>. In main, a std::vector containing shared_ptr<A> is filled with 10 elements, and finally sing is invoked on each element. Had we been using raw pointers as elements, the objects would need to be manually deleted. In the example, this deletion is automatic, because the reference count of each shared_ptr in the container is 1 as long as the vector is kept alive; when the vector is destroyed, the reference counters all go down to zero, and the objects are deleted. It is interesting to note that even if the destructor of A had not been declared virtual, shared_ptr would have correctly invoked the destructor of B!

A powerful technique is demonstrated in the example, and it involves the protected destructor in A. Because the function createA returns a shared_ptr<A>, it won't be possible to invoke delete on the pointer returned by shared_ptr:: get. This means that if the pointer in the shared_ptr is retrieved—perhaps in order to pass it to a function expecting a raw pointer—it won't be possible to accidentally delete it, which would wreak havoc. So, how is it that the shared_ptr is allowed to delete the object? It's because of the actual type of the pointer, which is B; B's destructor is not protected. This is a very useful way of adding extra safety to objects kept in shared_ptrs.

shared_ptr and **Other Resources**

Sometimes, you'll find yourself in need for using shared_ptr with a type that requires other cleanup than a simple delete. There is support for such cases in shared_ptr through what is called *custom deleters*. Resource handles, such as FILE*, or operating system–specific handles, are typically released through an operation such as fclose. To use a FILE* in a shared_ptr, we define a class that is responsible for deallocating the resource.

```cpp
class FileCloser {
public:
   void operator()(FILE* file) {
     std::cout << "The FileCloser has been called with a FILE*, "
       "which will now be closed.\n";
     if (file!=0)
       fclose(file);
   }
};
```

This is the function object that we'll use to make sure that `fclose` is called when the resource should be released. Here's an example program that utilizes our `FileCloser` class.

```
int main() {
  std::cout <<
    "shared_ptr example with a custom deallocator.\n";
  {
    FILE* f=fopen("test.txt","r");
    if (f==0) {
      std::cout << "Unable to open file\n";
      throw "Unable to open file";
    }

    boost::shared_ptr<FILE>
      my_shared_file(f, FileCloser());

    // Position the file pointer
    fseek(my_shared_file.get(),42,SEEK_SET);
  }
  std::cout << "By now, the FILE has been closed!\n";
}
```

Note that to get the resource, we need to use the unpronounceable `&*` idiom, `get`, or `get_pointer` on the `shared_ptr`. (I clearly caution against using `&*`. The choice between the other two is less clear.) The example could be made even simpler—if we don't need to do more than call a single argument function when deallocating, there's really no need to create a custom deleter class at all. The example could be rewritten as follows:

```
{
  FILE* f=fopen("test.txt","r");
  if (f==0) {
    std::cout << "Unable to open file\n";
    throw file_exception();
  }

  boost::shared_ptr<FILE> my_shared_file(f,&fclose);

  // Position the file pointer
  fseek(&*my_shared_file,42,SEEK_SET);
}
std::cout << "By now, the FILE* has been closed!\n";
```

Custom deleters are extremely useful for handling resources that need a special release procedure. Because the deleter is not part of the shared_ptr type, clients need not know anything about the resource that the smart pointer owns (besides how to use it, of course!). For example, a pool of objects can be used, and the custom deleter would simply return the object to the pool. Or, a singleton object could have a deleter that does nothing.

Security Through Custom Deleters

We've already seen how using a protected destructor in a base class helps add safety to classes used with shared_ptr. Another way of achieving the same level of safety is to declare the destructor protected (or private) and use a custom deleter to take care of destroying the object. This custom deleter must be made a friend of the class that it is to delete for this to work. A nice way to encapsulate this deleter is to implement it as a private nested class, like the following example demonstrates:

```cpp
#include "boost/shared_ptr.hpp"
#include <iostream>

class A {
  class deleter {
    public:
      void operator()(A* p) {
        delete p;
      }
  };
  friend class deleter;
public:

  virtual void sing() {
    std::cout << "Lalalalalalalalalalala";
  }

  static boost::shared_ptr<A> createA() {
    boost::shared_ptr<A> p(new A(),A::deleter());
    return p;
  }

protected:
  virtual ~A() {};
};
```

```
int main() {
  boost::shared_ptr<A> p=A::createA();
}
```

Note that we cannot use a free function as a factory for shared_ptr<A> here, because the nested deleter class is private to A. Using this scheme, it isn't possible for users to create As on the stack, and it isn't possible to call delete using a pointer to A.

Creating a *shared_ptr* from this

Sometimes, it is necessary to obtain a shared_ptr from this—that is, you are making the assumption that your class is being managed by a shared_ptr, and you need a way to convert "yourself" into that shared_ptr. Sounds like a mission impossible? Well, the solution comes from a smart pointer component that we've yet to discuss—boost::weak_ptr. A weak_ptr is an observer of shared_ptrs; it just silently sits and watches them, but does not affect the reference count. By storing a weak_ptr to this as a member of the class, it's possible to retrieve a shared_ptr to this on demand. To relieve you from the tedium of having to write the code for storing a weak_ptr to this and subsequently obtain a shared_ptr from that weak_ptr, Boost.Smart_ptr provides a helper class for this task, called enable_shared_from_this. Simply have your class derive publicly from enable_shared_from_this, and then use the function shared_from_this whenever you need to access the shared_ptr that is managing this. Here's an example that demonstrates how enable_shared_from_this is used:

```
#include "boost/shared_ptr.hpp"
#include "boost/enable_shared_from_this.hpp"

class A;

void do_stuff(boost::shared_ptr<A> p) {
  ...
}

class A : public boost::enable_shared_from_this<A> {
public:
  void call_do_stuff() {
    do_stuff(shared_from_this());
  }
```

```
};

int main() {
  boost::shared_ptr<A> p(new A());
  p->call_do_stuff();
}
```

The example also demonstrates a case where you need the shared_ptr that is managing this. Class A has a member function call_do_stuff that needs to call the free function do_stuff, which expects an argument of type boost::shared_ptr<A>. Now, in A::call_do_stuff, this is simply a pointer to A, but because A derives from enable_shared_from_this, calling shared_from_this returns the shared_ptr that we're seeking. In shared_from_this, which is a member of enable_shared_from_this, the internally stored weak_ptr is converted to a shared_ptr, thereby increasing the reference count to make sure that the object is not deleted.

Summary

Reference-counted smart pointers are extremely important tools. Boost's shared_ptr provides a solid and flexible solution that is proven through extensive use in many environments and circumstances. It is common to need to share objects among clients, and that often means that there is no way of telling if, and when, the object can be deleted safely. shared_ptr insulates clients from knowing about what other objects are using a shared object, and relieves them of the task of releasing the resource when no objects refer to it. This is arguably the most important of the smart pointer classes in Boost. You should get acquainted with the other classes in Boost.Smart_ptr, too, but this one should definitely be kept close to heart. By using custom deleters, almost any type of resource can be stored in shared_ptrs. This makes shared_ptr a general class for handling resource management, rather than "just" handling dynamically allocated objects. There is a small overhead in size for shared_ptr compared to a raw pointer. I have yet to see a case where this overhead actually matters so much that another solution must be sought. Don't roll your own reference-counted smart pointer class. Instead, use shared_ptr—smart pointers don't get much better than this.

Use shared_ptr in the following scenarios:

- When there are multiple clients of an object, but no explicit owner

- When storing pointers in Standard Library containers

- When passing objects to and from libraries without (other) expressed ownership

- When managing resources that need special cleanup[9]

shared_array

Header: `"boost/shared_array.hpp"`

shared_array is a smart pointer that enables shared ownership of arrays. It is to shared_ptr what scoped_array is to scoped_ptr. shared_array differs from shared_ptr mainly in that it is used with arrays rather than a single object. When we discussed scoped_array, I mentioned that std::vector was often a better choice. But shared_array adds some value over vector, because it offers shared *ownership* of arrays. The shared_array interface is similar to that of shared_ptr, but with the addition of a subscript operator and without support for custom deleters.

Because a shared_ptr to std::vector offers much more flexibility than shared_array, there's no usage section on shared_array in this chapter. If you find that you need boost::shared_array, refer to the online documentation.

intrusive_ptr

Header: `"boost/intrusive_ptr.hpp"`

intrusive_ptr is the intrusive analogue to shared_ptr. Sometimes, there's no other choice than using an intrusive, reference-counted smart pointer. The typical scenario is for code that has already been written with an internal reference counter, and where there's no time to rewrite it (or where the code's not available). Another case is when the size of a smart pointer must be exactly the size of a raw pointer, or when performance is hurt by the allocation of the reference count for shared_ptr (a rare case, I'm sure!). The only case where it would seem that an intrusive smart pointer is *required*, from a functional perspective, is when a member function of a pointed-to class needs to return this,

---

9. With the help of custom deleters.

such that it can be used in another smart pointer. (Actually, there are ways to solve that problem with non-intrusive smart pointers too, as we saw earlier in this chapter.) `intrusive_ptr` is different from the other smart pointers because it requires *you* to provide the reference counter that it manipulates.

When `intrusive_ptr` increments or decrements a reference count on a non-null pointer, it does so by making unqualified calls to the functions `intrusive_ptr_add_ref` and `intrusive_ptr_release`, respectively. These functions are responsible for making sure that the reference count is always correct and, if the reference counter drops to zero, to delete the pointer. Therefore, you must overload those functions for your type, as we shall see later.

This is a partial synopsis for `intrusive_ptr`, showing the most important functions.

```
namespace boost {

  template<class T> class intrusive_ptr {
  public:
    intrusive_ptr(T* p,bool add_ref=true);

    intrusive_ptr(const intrusive_ptr& r);

    ~intrusive_ptr();

    T& operator*() const;
    T* operator->() const;
    T* get() const;

    operator unspecified-bool-type() const;
  };

  template <class T> T* get_pointer(const intrusive_ptr<T>& p);

  template <class T,class U> intrusive_ptr<T>
    static_pointer_cast(const intrusive_ptr<U>& r);
}
```

Members

```
intrusive_ptr(T* p,bool add_ref=true);
```

> This constructor stores the pointer p in *this. If p isn't null, and if add_ref is true, the constructor makes an unqualified call to intrusive_ptr_add_ref(p). If add_ref is false, the constructor makes no call to intrusive_ptr_add_ref. This constructor can throw an exception if intrusive_ptr_add_ref can throw.

```
intrusive_ptr(const intrusive_ptr& r);
```

> The copy constructor saves a copy of r.get() and, if that pointer is not null, calls intrusive_ptr_add_ref with it. This constructor never throws.

```
~intrusive_ptr();
```

> If the stored pointer is not null, the intrusive_ptr destructor makes an unqualified call to the function intrusive_ptr_release, with the stored pointer as argument. intrusive_ptr_release is responsible for decrementing the reference count and deleting the pointer if it becomes zero. This function never throws.

```
T& operator*() const;
```

> This dereferencing operator returns and dereferences the stored pointer. If the stored pointer is null, invoking this operator results in undefined behavior. When in doubt, make sure that the intrusive_ptr has a non-null pointer. This is done using either the function get or by testing the intrusive_ptr in a Boolean context. The dereferencing operator never throws.

```
T* operator->() const;
```

> This operator returns the stored pointer. Calling this operator when the referenced pointer is null invokes undefined behavior. The operator never throws.

```
T* get() const;
```

> This member function returns the stored pointer. It can be used when a raw pointer is needed, and may be called even when the stored pointer is null. This function never throws.

```
operator unspecified-bool-type() const;
```

This conversion function returns a type that can be used in Boolean expressions, but it is not `operator bool`, because that would allow for other operations that should be prohibited. The conversion allows `intrusive_ptr` to be tested in Boolean contexts—for example, `if (p)`, with p being an instance of `intrusive_ptr`. The returned value is `true` if the `intrusive_ptr` references a non-null pointer; otherwise, it returns `false`. This conversion function never throws.

Free Functions

```
template <class T> T* get_pointer(const intrusive_ptr<T>& p);
```

The function returns `p.get()`, and its purpose is mainly to support generic programming.[10] It may also be used as a coding convention instead of calling the member function `get`, because it can be overloaded to work with raw pointers and third-party smart pointer classes. Some simply prefer calling a free function over accessing a member function.[11] The function never throws.

```
template <class T,class U>
   intrusive_ptr<T> static_pointer_cast(const intrusive_ptr<U>& r);
```

This function returns `intrusive_ptr<T>(static_cast<T*>(r.get()))`. Unlike with `shared_ptr`, you can use `static_cast` safely on pointers to objects stored in `intrusive_ptrs`. However, you may want to use this function for consistent usage of smart pointer casts. `static_pointer_cast` never throws.

---

10. Such functions are known as *shims*. See [12] in the Bibliography.

11. The idea is that the line between operating on the smart pointer and operating on what it points to can be blurred when using smart pointer member functions. For example, p.get() and p->get() have completely different meanings and can be a little difficult to distinguish at a glance, whereas get_pointer(p) and p->get() look nothing alike. Whether that's a problem for you is a matter of taste and experience.

Usage

There are two major differences when using `intrusive_ptr` compared to using `shared_ptr`. The first is that you need to provide the reference counting mechanism. The second is that it becomes legal to treat `this` as a smart pointer,[12] which can sometimes be convenient, as we shall see. Note that in most cases, the right smart pointer to use is the non-intrusive `shared_ptr`.

To use `boost::intrusive_ptr`, include `"boost/intrusive_ptr.hpp"` and then define the two free functions `intrusive_ptr_add_ref` and `intrusive_ptr_release`. These should accept an argument that is a pointer to the type(s) that you want to use with `intrusive_ptr`. Any return value from these two functions is discarded. Often, it makes sense to parameterize these functions, and simply forward to member functions of the managed type to do the work (for example, calling `add_ref` and `release`). If the reference counter becomes zero, `intrusive_ptr_release` should take care of releasing the resource. Here's how you might implement these functions generically:

```
template <typename T> void intrusive_ptr_add_ref(T* t) {
  t->add_ref();
}

template <typename T> void intrusive_ptr_release(T* t) {
  if (t->release()<=0)
    delete t;
}
```

Note that these functions should be defined in the scope of their argument types. This means that if this function is called with arguments from a namespace, the functions should be defined there, too. The reason for this is that the calls are unqualified, which means that argument-dependent lookup is permitted, and there may be cases where more than one version of these functions must be provided, which makes the global namespace a bad place to put them. We'll see an example of where to place these functions later, but first, we need to provide some sort of internal reference counter.

---

12. You cannot do that with `shared_ptr` without special measures, such as `enable_shared_from_this`.

Providing a Reference Counter

Now that the management functions have been defined, we must provide an internal reference count. In this example, the reference count is a private data member that's initialized to zero, and we'll expose `add_ref` and `release` member functions to manipulate it. `add_ref` increments the reference count and `release` decrements it.[13] We could add a third member function to return the current value of the reference count, but it suffices to have `release` return it. The following base class, `reference_counter`, provides a counter and the `add_ref` and `release` member functions, making adding reference counting to a class as easy as using inheritance.

```
class reference_counter {
  int ref_count_;
  public:
    reference_counter() : ref_count_(0) {}

    virtual ~reference_counter() {}

    void add_ref() {
      ++ref_count_;
    }

    int release() {
      return --ref_count_;
    }

  protected:
    reference_counter& operator=(const reference_counter&) {
    // No-op
      return *this;
    }
  private:
    // Copy construction disallowed
    reference_counter(const reference_counter&);
};
```

The reason for making the destructor of `reference_counter` virtual is that the class is publicly inherited, and thus it is possible to `delete` derived classes using a pointer to `reference_counter`. We want this deletion to do the right

---

13. Note that in a multithreaded environment, any operation on the variable holding the reference count needs to be synchronized.

thing—that is, to call the destructor for the derived type. The implementation is straightforward: add_ref increments the reference count and release decrements the current reference count and returns it. To use this reference counter, all that's needed is to derive publicly from it. Here's an example with a class some_class that contains an internal reference count, and intrusive_ptrs that use it.

```cpp
#include <iostream>
#include "boost/intrusive_ptr.hpp"

class some_class : public reference_counter {
public:
  some_class() {
    std::cout << "some_class::some_class()\n";
  }

  some_class(const some_class& other) {
    std::cout << "some_class(const some_class& other)\n";
  }

  ~some_class() {
    std::cout << "some_class::~some_class()\n";
  }
};

int main() {
  std::cout << "Before start of scope\n";
  {
    boost::intrusive_ptr<some_class> p1(new some_class());
    boost::intrusive_ptr<some_class> p2(p1);
  }
  std::cout << "After end of scope \n";
}
```

To demonstrate that the intrusive_ptrs together with the functions intrusive_ptr_add_ref and intrusive_ptr_release do their jobs right, here is the output from running the program:

```
Before start of scope
some_class::some_class()
some_class::~some_class()
After end of scope
```

The `intrusive_ptr` is taking care of business for us. When the first `intrusive_ptr` p1 is created, it is passed a new instance of `some_class`. The `intrusive_ptr` constructor actually takes two arguments. The second is a `bool` that states whether `intrusive_ptr_add_ref` should be called or not. Because the default value of this argument is `true`, when constructing p1, the reference counter for the instance of `some_class` becomes 1. Then, a second `intrusive_ptr`, p2, is constructed. It is copy constructed from p1, and when p2 sees that p1 is referencing a non-null pointer, it calls `intrusive_ptr_add_ref`. The reference count is now 2. Then, the two `intrusive_ptrs` leave scope. First, p2 is destroyed, and the destructor calls `intrusive_ptr_release`. This decrements the reference counter to 1. Then, p1 is destroyed, and the destructor calls `intrusive_ptr_release` again, which causes the reference count to drop to 0; this in turn triggers our implementation of `intrusive_ptr_release` to `delete` the pointer. You'll note that the implementation of `reference_counter` is not thread-safe, and therefore cannot be used in multithreaded applications without adding synchronization.

Rather than relying on a generic implementation of `intrusive_ptr_add_ref` and `intrusive_ptr_release`, we could have these functions operate directly on the base class (here, `reference_counter`). The advantage of this approach is that even if the classes derived from `reference_counter` are defined in other namespaces, `intrusive_ptr_add_ref` and `intrusive_ptr_release` will still be found using ADL (argument dependent lookup). Changing the implementation of `reference_counter` is straightforward.

```
class reference_counter {
  int ref_count_;
  public:
    reference_counter() : ref_count_(0) {}

    virtual ~reference_counter() {}

    friend void intrusive_ptr_add_ref(reference_counter* p) {
      ++p->ref_count_;
    }

    friend void intrusive_ptr_release(reference_counter* p) {
      if (--p->ref_count_==0)
        delete p;
    }

  protected:
```

```
      reference_counter& operator=(const reference_counter&) {
      // No-op
        return *this;
      }
  private:
      // Copy construction disallowed
      reference_counter(const reference_counter&);
};
```

Treating *this* As a Smart Pointer

It's not altogether easy to come up with scenarios where intrusive, reference-counted smart pointers are really *required*. Most, if not all, problems can be solved with non-intrusive smart pointers. However, there is one case in which it's *easier* to use an intrusive reference count: when one needs to return this from a member function, to be stored in another smart pointer. When returning this from a type that's being owned by non-intrusive smart pointers, the result is that two different smart pointers believe that they own the same object, which implies that they will both try to delete it when the time has come to do so. This leads to double deletion, with the probable result that your application will crash. It must somehow be possible to tell the other smart pointer that this resource is already referenced by another smart pointer, and that's exactly what an internal reference counter (implicitly) does. Because the logic of intrusive_ptr indirectly operates on the internal reference count of the objects they refer to, there is no violation of ownership or inconsistencies in the reference counting. The reference count is simply incremented.

Let's take a look at the potential problem first, with an implementation relying on boost::shared_ptr for sharing resource ownership. It's basically the example from earlier in this chapter, when discussing enable_shared_from_this.

```
#include "boost/shared_ptr.hpp"

class A;

void do_stuff(boost::shared_ptr<A> p) {
  // ...
}

class A {
public:
```

```
   call_do_stuff() {
     shared_ptr<A> p(???);
      do_stuff(p);
   }
};

int main() {
  boost::shared_ptr<A> p(new A());
  p->call_do_stuff();
}
```

The class A wants to call the function do_stuff, but the problem is that do_stuff expects a shared_ptr<A>, not a plain pointer to A. So, in A::call_do_stuff, how should the shared_ptr be created? Now, let's rewrite A to make it compatible with intrusive_ptr, by deriving from reference_counter, and let's also add an overloaded version of do_stuff, accepting an argument of type intrusive_ptr<A>.

```
#include "boost/intrusive_ptr.hpp"

class A;

void do_stuff(boost::intrusive_ptr<A> p) {
  // ...
}

void do_stuff(boost::shared_ptr<A> p) {
  // ...
}

class A : public reference_counter {
public:
  void call_do_stuff() {
     do_stuff(this);
   }
};

int main() {
  boost::intrusive_ptr<A> p(new A());
  p->call_do_stuff();
}
```

As you can see, in this version of `A::call_do_stuff`, we are able to send this directly to the function expecting an `intrusive_ptr<A>`, due to the converting constructor of `intrusive_ptr`.

Here's a special treat to end this section: Now that `A` is supporting `intrusive_ptr`, we can actually write code that creates a `shared_ptr` that *wraps* the `intrusive_ptr`, allowing us to call the original version of `do_stuff`, which takes a `shared_ptr<A>` as argument. Assuming that you cannot control the source code for `do_stuff`, this might be a very real problem that you need to solve. Again, the solution awaits in the form of a custom deleter, one that understands that it needs to call `intrusive_ptr_release`. Here's the new version of `A::call_do_stuff`.

```
void call_do_stuff() {
  intrusive_ptr_add_ref(this);
  boost::shared_ptr<A> p(this,&intrusive_ptr_release<A>);
  do_stuff(p);
}
```

An elegant solution indeed. When there are no more `shared_ptr`s left, the custom deleter is invoked, which calls `intrusive_ptr_release`, which in turn decreases the internal reference counter of `A`. Note that if `intrusive_ptr_add_ref` and `intrusive_ptr_release` are implemented to operate on `reference_counter`, you'd create the `shared_ptr` like so:

```
boost::shared_ptr<A> p(this,&intrusive_ptr_release);
```

Supporting Different Reference Counters

We talked earlier about the possibility of supporting different reference counts for different types. This may be necessary when integrating existing classes with different reference-counting mechanisms (third-party classes employing their own version of a reference-counter, for example). Or there may be different requirements for deallocating, such as calling another function rather than `delete`. As mentioned already, the calls to `intrusive_ptr_add_ref` and `intrusive_ptr_release` are unqualified. This means that the scope of the argument (the pointer type) is considered during name lookup, and thus these functions should be defined in the same scope as the type on which they should operate. If you implement generic versions of `intrusive_ptr_add_ref` and intrusive_ptr_release in the global namespace, you make it impossible to create generic versions in other namespaces. For example, if a namespace needs a special version for all of its types, specializations or overloads must be provided for each and every type. Otherwise, the functions in the global namespace introduce an ambiguity. It is therefore not a good idea to provide generic versions in the global namespace, though they are fine in other namespaces.

Because of the way that we have implemented the reference counter, using the base class reference_counter, it is a good idea to have an ordinary function in the global namespace that accepts an argument of type reference_counter*. This still allows us to provide generic overloads inside other namespaces without introducing ambiguities. As an example, consider the classes another_class and derived_class in a namespace called my_namespace.

```cpp
namespace my_namespace {
  class another_class : public reference_counter {
  public:
    void call_before_destruction() const {
      std::cout <<
        "Yes, I'm ready before destruction\n";
    }
  };

  class derived_class : public another_class {};

  template <typename T> void intrusive_ptr_add_ref(T* t) {
    t->add_ref();
  }

  template <typename T> void intrusive_ptr_release(T* t) {
    if (t->release()<=0) {
      t->call_before_destruction();
      delete t;
    }
  }
}
```

Here, we have implemented generic versions of intrusive_ptr_add_ref and intrusive_ptr_release. We must therefore remove the generic versions that we previously put in the global namespace, and replace them with non-templated versions accepting a pointer to reference_counter as their argument. Or, we could omit these functions from the global namespace altogether, to avoid cluttering it. For the two classes `my_namespace::another_class` and `my_namespace::derived_class`, the special version (which calls a member function `call_before_destruction` on its arguments) is called. Other types either have corresponding functions in the namespace where they are defined or use the version in the global namespace, if it exists. Here's a short program to illustrate how this works:

```
int main() {
  boost::intrusive_ptr<my_namespace::another_class>
    p1(new my_namespace::another_class());
  boost::intrusive_ptr<A>
    p2(new good_class());
  boost::intrusive_ptr<my_namespace::derived_class>
    p3(new my_namespace::derived_class());
}
```

First, the `intrusive_ptr` p1 is passed a new instance of `my_namespace::another_class`. When resolving the call to `intrusive_ptr_add_ref`, the compiler finds the version in `my_namespace`, the namespace of the `my_namespace::another_class*` argument. Thus, the generic function, which is provided for types in that namespace, is correctly invoked. This applies when finding `intrusive_ptr_release`, too. Then, the `intrusive_ptr` p2 is created and passed a pointer of type A (the one we created earlier). That type resides in the global namespace, so when the compiler tries to find the best match for the call to `intrusive_ptr_add_ref`, it finds only one, which is the version accepting an argument of type pointer to `reference_counter` (you'll recall that we had to remove the generic version from the global namespace). Because A inherits publicly from `reference_counter`, the implicit conversion succeeds and the correct call is made. Finally, the generic version in `my_namespace` is used for the class `my_namespace::derived_class`; this works exactly like the lookup for `another_class`.

The important lesson here is that when implementing the function `intrusive_ptr_add_ref` and `intrusive_ptr_release`, they should always be defined in the namespace where the types they operate on exist. This makes perfect sense from a design perspective too, keeping related things together, and it helps ensure that the correct version is always called, regardless of whether there are several different implementations to choose from.

Summary

In most situations, you should not use `boost::intrusive_ptr`, because the functionality of shared ownership is readily available in `boost::shared_ptr`, and a non-intrusive smart pointer is more flexible than an intrusive smart pointer. However, there are times when one needs an intrusive reference count, perhaps for legacy code or for integration with third-party classes. When the need arises, `intrusive_ptr` fits the bill, with the same semantics as the other Boost smart pointer classes. By using another of the Boost smart pointers, you ensure a consistent interface for all smart pointer needs, be they intrusive or not. The reference count must be provided by the classes that are used with `intrusive_ptr`. `intrusive_ptr` manages the reference count by making unqualified calls to two functions, `intrusive_ptr_add_ref` and `intrusive_ptr_release`; these functions must properly manipulate the intrusive reference count for `intrusive_ptr`s to work correctly. For all cases where a reference count already exists in the types that are to be used with `intrusive_ptr`, enabling support for `intrusive_ptr` is as easy as implementing those two functions. In some cases, it's possible to create parameterized versions of those functions, and have all types with intrusive reference counts use the same implementation of these functions. In most cases, the best place to declare the functions is in the same namespace as the types they support.

Use `intrusive_ptr` when

- You need to treat `this` as a smart pointer.

- There is existing code that uses or provides an intrusive reference count.

- It is imperative that the size of the smart pointer equals the size of a raw pointer.

weak_ptr

Header: `"boost/weak_ptr.hpp"`

A `weak_ptr` is an observer of a `shared_ptr`. It does not interfere with the ownership of what a `shared_ptr` shares. When a `shared_ptr` that is being observed by a `weak_ptr` must release its resource, it sets the observing `weak_ptr`'s pointer to null. That prevents the weak_ptr from holding a dangling pointer. Why would you need a weak_ptr? There are many situations where one needs to observe and use a shared resource without accepting ownership, such as to break cyclic dependencies, to observe a shared resource without assuming ownership of it, or to avoid dangling pointers. It's possible to construct a shared_ptr from a weak_ptr, thereby gaining access to the shared resource.

This is a partial synopsis for weak_ptr, showing and then briefly discussing the most important functions.

```
namespace boost {

  template<typename T> class weak_ptr {
  public:
    template <typename Y>
      weak_ptr(const shared_ptr<Y>& r);

    weak_ptr(const weak_ptr& r);

    ~weak_ptr();

    T* get() const;
    bool expired() const;
    shared_ptr<T> lock() const;
  };
}
```

Members

```
template <typename Y> weak_ptr(const shared_ptr<Y>& r);
```

This constructor creates a weak_ptr from a shared_ptr, provided there is an implicit conversion from Y* to T*. The new weak_ptr is configured to observe the resource referred to by r. r's reference count remains unchanged. This implies that the resource referenced by r may be deleted despite the existence of the new weak_ptr referring to it. This constructor never throws.

```
weak_ptr(const weak_ptr& r);
```

The copy constructor makes the new `weak_ptr` observe the resource referenced by `shared_ptr r`. The reference count of the `shared_ptr` is unchanged. This constructor never throws.

```
~weak_ptr();
```

The `weak_ptr` destructor, similarly to the constructor, does not change the reference count. If needed, the destructor detaches `*this` as an observer for the shared resource. This destructor never throws.

```
bool expired() const;
```

Returns `true` if the observed resource has "expired," which means that it has been released. If the stored pointer is non-null, `expired` returns `false`. This function never throws.

```
shared_ptr<T> lock() const
```

Returns a `shared_ptr` that refers to the resource that this `weak_ptr` observes, if any. If there is no such pointer (that is, the `weak_ptr` refers to the null pointer), the resulting `shared_ptr` refers to the null pointer. Otherwise, the reference count for the resource referenced by the `shared_ptr` is incremented as usual. This function never throws.

Usage

We begin with an example that shows the basics of `weak_ptr`s, and especially demonstrates how they do not affect the reference counts. Out of necessity, the examples in this subsection include `shared_ptr`s as well, because a `weak_ptr` always needs to be used together with a `shared_ptr`. To use `weak_ptr`, include `"boost/weak_ptr.hpp"`.

```
#include "boost/shared_ptr.hpp"
#include "boost/weak_ptr.hpp"
#include <iostream>
#include <cassert>

class A {};

int main() {
```

```
boost::weak_ptr<A> w;
assert(w.expired());
{
   boost::shared_ptr<A> p(new A());
   assert(p.use_count()==1);
   w=p;
   assert(p.use_count()==w.use_count());
   assert(p.use_count()==1);

   // Create a shared_ptr from the weak_ptr
   boost::shared_ptr<A> p2(w);
   assert(p2==p);
}
assert(w.expired());
boost::shared_ptr<A> p3=w.lock();
assert(!p3);
}
```

The weak_ptr w is default constructed, which means that it initially isn't observing any resource. To test whether or not a weak_ptr is observing a live object, you use the function expired. To start observing, a weak_ptr must be assigned a shared_ptr. In the example, when shared_ptr p is assigned to weak_ptr w, it's asserted that the use counts—that is, the reference count—of p and w are equal. Then, a shared_ptr is constructed from the weak_ptr, which is one of the ways to gain access to the shared resource from a weak_ptr. If the weak_ptr has expired when the shared_ptr is constructed, an exception of type boost::bad_weak_ptr is thrown by shared_ptr's constructor. Moving on, when the shared_ptr p goes out of scope, w is expired. When its member function lock is called to obtain a shared_ptr—the second way of gaining access to the shared resource—an empty shared_ptr is returned. Note that throughout the example, the weak_ptr had no effect on the reference count of the shared object.

Unlike other smart pointers, weak_ptr doesn't provide access to the observed pointer with overloaded operator* and operator->. The reason for this is that all operations on the resource that the weak_ptr is observing must explicitly be made safe; it would be just too easy to inadvertently access an invalid pointer, as weak_ptrs do not affect the reference counter of the shared resource they observe. This is why you must pass the weak_ptr to shared_ptr's constructor, or obtain a shared_ptr by calling weak_ptr::lock. Both of these operations increase the reference count, so after the shared_ptr is created from a weak_ptr, it keeps the shared resource alive, ensuring that it will not be deallocated during the time we want to use it.

A Common Question

Because the ordering of smart pointers doesn't involve the actual *values* their pointers are pointing to but the *pointer values*, a common question with regard to using these smart pointers in Standard Library containers is how to use algorithms with the smart pointers; they typically need to access the values of the actual objects rather than their addresses. For example, how does one call std::sort and make it perform useful sorting? Actually, the problem is hardly any different from storing and operating on regular pointers in containers, but that fact is easily overlooked (probably because storing a raw pointer is so problematic that we tend to avoid doing it). Out of the box, there is no support for comparing the values of smart pointers, but that's easy to amend. A typical need is to use predicates that dereference the smart pointers, so we'll create a reusable predicate that makes it easy to use the Standard Library algorithms with iterators referencing smart pointers—in this case, weak_ptrs.

```cpp
#include <functional>
#include "boost/shared_ptr.hpp"
#include "boost/weak_ptr.hpp"

template <typename Func, typename T>
  struct weak_ptr_unary_t :
    public std::unary_function<boost::weak_ptr<T>,bool> {
  T t_;
  Func func_;

  weak_ptr_unary_t(const Func& func,const T& t)
    : t_(t),func_(func) {}

  bool operator()(boost::weak_ptr<T> arg) const {
    boost::shared_ptr<T> sp=arg.lock();
    if (!sp) {
      return false;
    }
    return func_(*sp,t_);
  }
};

template <typename Func, typename T> weak_ptr_unary_t<Func,T>
  weak_ptr_unary(const Func& func, const T& value) {
    return weak_ptr_unary_t<Func,T>(func,value);
}
```

   The `weak_ptr_unary_t` function object is parameterized on the function to
invoke, and the type of the argument. The fact that the function to invoke is
stored in the function object makes the function object easy to use, which
we shall see shortly. To make the predicate compatible with adapters,
`weak_ptr_unary_t` derives from `std::unary_function`, which makes sure
that the required `typedefs` are present (this is required in order for the Standard
Library adaptors to work with such function objects). The real work is done in
the function call operator, where a `shared_ptr` is created from the `weak_ptr`.
This is necessary to ensure that the resource stays alive during the function call.
Then, the function (or function object) is invoked, passing the argument (dereferenced, so that we get to the actual resource) and the stored value, which was
passed in the constructor for `weak_ptr_unary_t`. This simple function object can
now be used with any applicable algorithms. For convenience, we also defined a
helper function, `weak_ptr_unary`, which deduces the types of the arguments and
returns an appropriate function object.[14] Let's see how we can use this beast.

```cpp
#include <iostream>
#include <string>

#include <vector>
#include <algorithm>
#include "boost/shared_ptr.hpp"
#include "boost/weak_ptr.hpp"

int main() {
  using std::string;
  using std::vector;
  using boost::shared_ptr;
  using boost::weak_ptr;

  vector<weak_ptr<string> > vec;

  shared_ptr<string> sp1(
    new string("An example"));
  shared_ptr<string> sp2(
    new string("of using"));
  shared_ptr<string> sp3(
    new string("smart pointers and predicates"));
  vec.push_back(weak_ptr<string>(sp1));
```

---

14. To make this type generally usable, a lot more programming would be required.

```
vec.push_back(weak_ptr<string>(sp2));
vec.push_back(weak_ptr<string>(sp3));

vector<weak_ptr<string> >::iterator
  it=std::find_if(vec.begin(),vec.end(),
   weak_ptr_unary(std::equal_to<string>(),string("of using")));

if (it!=vec.end()) {
  shared_ptr<string> sp(*++it);
  std::cout << *sp << '\n';
}
}
```

In the example, a `vector` containing `weak_ptrs` is created. The most interesting line of code (yes, it's quite a long one) is where we create a `weak_ptr_unary_t` for use with the `find_if` algorithm.

```
vector<weak_ptr<string> >::iterator it=std::find_if(
  vec.begin(),
  vec.end(),
  weak_ptr_unary(
    std::equal_to<string>(),string("of using")));
```

The function object is created by passing another function object, `std::equal_to`, to the helper function `weak_ptr_unary`, together with the `string` that is to be used for the matching. Because of the fact that `weak_ptr_unary_t` is compatible with adaptors (it is compatible because it inherits from `std::unary_function`), we could compose any type of function object out of it. For instance, we could have searched for the first string *not* matching `"of using"`:

```
vector<weak_ptr<string> >::iterator it=std::find_if(
  vec.begin(),
  vec.end(),
std::not1(
    weak_ptr_unary(
      std::equal_to<string>(),string("of using"))));
```

The Boost smart pointers were specifically designed to work well with the Standard Library. That makes it easy for us to create useful components that help us simplify the usage of these powerful smart pointers. Utilities such as `weak_ptr_unary` aren't needed all that often; there are libraries that provide general binders that do a much better job of that than weak_ptr_unary.[15] These, too, are typically aware of smart pointer semantics, which makes using them completely transparent to use.

Two Idiomatic Ways of Creating a *shared_ptr* from a *weak_ptr*

As you have seen, when you have a weak_ptr that's observing some resource, you'll eventually want to access that resource. To do so, the weak_ptr must be converted to a shared_ptr, because the weak_ptr alone does not allow direct access to the resource. There are two ways of creating a shared_ptr from a weak_ptr: Either pass the weak_ptr to the constructor of shared_ptr or call the weak_ptr member function lock, which returns a shared_ptr. Which to choose depends on whether you consider an empty weak_ptr to be an error or not. The shared_ptr constructor accepting a weak_ptr argument will throw an exception of type bad_weak_ptr if the weak_ptr is empty. It should therefore be used only if an empty weak_ptr constitutes an error. When using the weak_ptr function lock, the returned shared_ptr will be empty if the weak_ptr is empty. This is the right thing to do if you need to test for a valid resource—that is, an empty weak_ptr is expected behavior. Furthermore, when using lock, the idiomatic way to use the resource is to initialize it and test it simultaneously, like so:

```
#include <iostream>
#include <string>
#include "boost/shared_ptr.hpp"
#include "boost/weak_ptr.hpp"

int main() {
  boost::shared_ptr<std::string>
    sp(new std::string("Some resource"));
  boost::weak_ptr<std::string> wp(sp);
  // ...
  if (boost::shared_ptr<std::string> p=wp.lock())
    std::cout << "Got it: " << *p << '\n';
  else
    std::cout << "Nah, the shared_ptr is empty\n";
}
```

---

15. Boost.Bind is just such a library.

As you can see, the `shared_ptr` p is initialized with the result of locking the `weak_ptr` wp. Then p is tested, and only if it is non-empty is the resource accessed. As the `shared_ptr` is only valid in that scope, there is no chance of inadvertently trying to use it outside of the scope where it is valid. The other scenario is when the `weak_ptr` logically must be non-empty. In that case, testing for an empty `shared_ptr` is easy to forget—and because the `shared_ptr` constructor throws an exception when handed an empty `weak_ptr`, this is the way to go.

```cpp
#include <iostream>
#include <string>
#include "boost/shared_ptr.hpp"
#include "boost/weak_ptr.hpp"

void access_the_resource(boost::weak_ptr<std::string> wp) {
  boost::shared_ptr<std::string> sp(wp);
  std::cout << *sp << '\n';
}

int main() {
  boost::shared_ptr<std::string>
    sp(new std::string("Some resource"));
  boost::weak_ptr<std::string> wp(sp);
  // ...
  access_the_resource(wp);
}
```

In this example, the function `access_the_resource` constructs the `shared_ptr` sp from a `weak_ptr`. It doesn't need to test whether the `shared_ptr` is empty or not, because if the `weak_ptr` is empty, an exception of type `bad_weak_ptr` is thrown, and therefore the function leaves scope immediately; catching and handling the error will be handled where it's suitable. This is much better than explicitly testing for an empty `shared_ptr` and then returning. These are the two ways in which to get a `shared_ptr` out of a `weak_ptr`.

Summary

`weak_ptr` is the last piece that we must place on the Boost smart pointer puzzle. The `weak_ptr` abstraction is a very important companion to that of `shared_ptr`. It allows us to break cyclic dependencies. It also handles a very common problem—that of the dangling pointer. When sharing a resource, it is common that some of the users of that resource must not take part in its lifetime management. This cannot be handled using raw pointers, because when the last shared_ptr is destroyed, it takes the shared resource with it. Had raw pointers been used to refer to that resource, there would be no way of knowing whether the resource still exists. If it doesn't, accessing it wreaks havoc. With weak_ptrs, the information that the shared resource has been destroyed is propagated to all weak_ptrs observing it, which means that no one can inadvertently access an invalid pointer. It's like a special case of the Observer pattern; when the resource is destroyed, those who have expressed interest in knowing about it are informed.

Use weak_ptr to

- Break cyclic dependencies

- Use a shared resource without sharing ownership

- Avoid dangling pointers

Smart_ptr Summary

This chapter has introduced the Boost smart pointers, a contribution to the C++ community that can hardly be overestimated. For a smart pointer library to be successful, it must take into consideration and correctly handle a great number of factors. I'm sure you have seen quite a number of smart pointers, and you might have even been involved in their creation, so you are aware of the effort involved to get things right. Not many smart pointers are as smart as they should be, and that makes the value of a proven library such as Boost.Smart_ptr immense.

Being such a central component of software engineering, the smart pointers in Boost have obviously received a lot of attention and thorough review. It is therefore hard to give credit to all who deserve it. Many have contributed valuable opinions and have been part of shaping the current smart pointer library. However, a few exceptional people and efforts must be mentioned here:

- Greg Colvin, the father of auto_ptr, also suggested counted_ptr, which later became what we now call shared_ptr.

- Beman Dawes revived the discussion about smart pointers and proposed that the original semantics as suggested by Greg Colvin be considered.

- Peter Dimov redesigned the smart pointer classes, adding thread safety, intrusive_ptr, and weak_ptr.

It is intriguing that such a well-known concept continues to evolve. There will undoubtedly be more progress in the domain of smart pointers or maybe, smart resources, but just as important is the quality of smart pointers that are used *today*. It's survival of the fittest, and that's why people are using Smart_ptr. The Boost smart pointers are a fine, assorted selection of delicious software chocolate, and I eat them regularly (you should, too). We'll soon see some of them become part of the C++ Standard Library, as they have been accepted into the Library Technical Report.

Library 2
Conversion

How Does the Conversion Library Improve Your Programs?

- Understandable, maintainable, and consistent polymorphic conversions

- Static downcasting using safer constructs than `static_cast`

- Range-preserving numeric conversions that ensure correct value logic and less time debugging

- Correct and reusable lexical conversions that lead to less time coding

The versatility of C++ is one of the primary reasons for its success, but sometimes also a formidable source of headaches because of the complexity of certain parts of the language. For instance, the rules for numeric conversions and type promotions are far from trivial. Other conversions are trivial, but tedious; how many times do we need to write a safe function[1] for converting between `string`s and `int`s, `double`s and `string`s, and so on? Conversions can be problematic in every library and program you write, and that's how and why the Conversion library can help. It provides facilities that prevent dangerous conversions and simplify recurring conversion tasks.

The Conversion library consists of four *cast functions* that provide better type safety (`polymorphic_cast`), better efficiency with preserved type safety (`polymorphic_downcast`), range-checked numeric conversions (`numeric_cast`), and lexical conversions (`lexical_cast`). These cast-like functions share the

---

1. To avoid using `sprintf` and its ilk.

semantics of the C++ cast operators. Like the C++ cast operators, these functions have an important quality that, together with type safety, sets them apart from C-style casts: They unambiguously state the programmer's intent.[2] The importance of the code we write goes far further than its implementation and present behavior. More important is to clearly convey our intents when writing it. This library makes it somewhat easier by extending our C++ vocabulary.

polymorphic_cast

Header: `"boost/cast.hpp"`

Polymorphic conversions in C++ are performed via `dynamic_cast`. A feature of `dynamic_cast`, which is sometimes also the cause of erroneous code, is that it behaves differently depending on the type with which it is used. `dynamic_cast` throws an exception—`std::bad_cast`—if the conversion is not possible when used on a reference type. The reason for the exception is simple. There is no such thing as a null reference in C++, so either the conversion succeeds and the result is a valid reference or it fails and you get an exception instead. Of course, when using `dynamic_cast` to convert a pointer type, failure is indicated by returning the null pointer.

`dynamic_cast`'s different behavior depending on whether pointer or reference types are used is a valuable property, because it allows the programmer to express intent. Typically, if a failed conversion doesn't constitute a logical error, the pointer conversion is used, and if it is an error, the reference version is used. Unfortunately, the difference is quite subtle—it boils down to an asterisk or an ampersand—and it isn't always a natural choice. What if a failed cast to a pointer type is an error? To make that clear by having an exception thrown automatically, and to make the code consistent, Boost offers `polymorphic_cast`. It *always* throws a `std::bad_cast` exception if the conversion fails.

In *The C++ Programming Language 3rd Edition*, Stroustrup has the following to say about `dynamic_cast` with pointer types, and the fact that it can return the null pointer:

---

2. They can also be overloaded, which sometimes makes them superior to the C++ cast operators.

"Explicit tests against 0 can be—and therefore occasionally will be—accidentally omitted. If that worries you, you can write a conversion function that throws an exception in case of failure."

polymorphic_cast is precisely that conversion function.

Usage

polymorphic_cast is used just like dynamic_cast, except (pun intended) that it always throws a std::bad_cast on failure to convert. Another feature of polymorphic_cast is that it is a function, and can be overloaded, if necessary. As a natural extension to our C++ vocabulary, it makes code clearer and casts less error prone. To use it, include the header "boost/cast.hpp". The function is parameterized on the type to convert to, and accepts one argument to be converted.

```
template <class Target, class Source>
  polymorphic_cast(Source* p);
```

It should be mentioned that there is no version of polymorphic_cast for reference types. The reason for this is that the implementation would do exactly what dynamic_cast already does, and there is no need for polymorphic_cast to duplicate existing functionality of the C++ language. The following example shows the syntactic similarity with dynamic_cast.

Downcast and Crosscast

There are two typical scenarios when using dynamic_cast or polymorphic_cast is appropriate: when downcasting from a base class to a derived class or when crosscasting, which means casting from one base class to another. The following example shows both types of casts using polymorphic_cast. There are two base classes, base1 and base2, and a class derived that inherits publicly from both of the base classes.

```
#include <iostream>
#include <string>
#include "boost/cast.hpp"
```

```cpp
class base1 {
public:
  virtual void print() {
    std::cout << "base1::print()\n";
  }

  virtual ~base1() {}
};

class base2 {
public:

  void only_base2() {
    std::cout << "only_base2()\n";
  }

  virtual ~base2() {}
};

class derived : public base1, public base2 {
public:

  void print() {
    std::cout << "derived::print()\n";
  }

  void only_here() {
    std::cout << "derived::only_here()\n";
  }
  void only_base2() {
    std::cout << "Oops, here too!\n";
  }
};

int main() {
  base1* p1=new derived;

 p1->print();

  try {
    derived* pD=boost::polymorphic_cast<derived*>(p1);
    pD->only_here();
    pD->only_base2();
```

```
      base2* pB=boost::polymorphic_cast<base2*>(p1);
      pB->only_base2();

  }
  catch(std::bad_cast& e) {
    std::cout << e.what() << '\n';
  }

  delete p1;
}
```

To show how `polymorphic_cast` works, the first thing we did was to create an instance of `derived` and manipulate it through various pointers to the base and derived classes. The one function that will work out-of-the-box for `p1` is `print`, which is a virtual function in `base1` and `derived`. We then use a *downcast* to be able to call `only_here`, available only in `derived`:

```
derived* pD=boost::polymorphic_cast<derived*>(p1);
pD->only_here();
```

Note that if the `polymorphic_cast` fails, a `std::bad_cast` exception is thrown, so the code is protected by a `try`/`catch` block. This behavior is exactly the same as for `dynamic_cast` using reference types. The pointer `pD` is then used to call the function `only_base2`. The function is a non-virtual function in `base2`, but is also provided by `derived`, which hides the version in `base2`. Thus, we need to perform a crosscast to get a pointer to `base2` to call `base2::only_base2` rather than `derived::only_base2`.

```
base2* pB=boost::polymorphic_cast<base2*>(p1);
pB->only_base2();
```

Again, if the conversion fails, an exception is thrown. This example shows the ease with which error handling is performed when using `polymorphic_cast` if failed conversions are considered errors. There is no need to test for null pointers or to propagate an error out of the function explicitly. As we shall see shortly, `dynamic_cast` sometimes adds unnecessary complexity for this type of code; it may even lead to undefined behavior.

dynamic_cast Versus polymorphic_cast

To see the difference between these complementary casts,[3] let's put them head to head in a race against complexity. We'll reuse the classes base1, base2, and derived from the previous example. You'll note that the tests for a valid pointer when employing dynamic_cast on pointer types are both tedious and repetitious, which makes the tests unfortunate candidates for being omitted by stressed programmers.

```cpp
void polymorphic_cast_example(base1* p) {
  derived* pD=boost::polymorphic_cast<derived*>(p);
  pD->print();

  base2* pB=boost::polymorphic_cast<base2*>(p);
  pB->only_base2();
}

void dynamic_cast_example(base1* p) {
  derived* pD=dynamic_cast<derived*>(p);
  if (!pD)
    throw std::bad_cast();
  pD->print();

  base2* pB=dynamic_cast<base2*>(p);
  if (!pB)
    throw std::bad_cast();

  pB->only_base2();

}

int main() {
  base1* p=new derived;
  try {
    polymorphic_cast_example(p);
    dynamic_cast_example(p);
  }
  catch(std::bad_cast& e) {
    std::cout << e.what() << '\n';
  }
  delete p;
}
```

---

3. Technically, dynamic_cast is a cast operator, whereas polymorphic_cast is a function template.

The two functions, `polymorphic_cast_example` and `dynamic_cast_example`, perform exactly the same work but in different ways. The difference is that wherever a `dynamic_cast` involving pointers is performed, we must remember to test the returned pointer to see if it is null. In our example, this designates an error, which should result in an exception of type `bad_cast` being thrown.[4] When using `polymorphic_cast`, the error handling is localized to the exception handler for `std::bad_cast`, which means that we do not need to worry about testing any returned values from casting between types. In this trivial example, it's not that hard to remember to test for validity of the returned pointer, but it still requires more work than when using `polymorphic_cast`. Add a couple of hundred lines of code, and two or three programmers performing maintenance in the function, and the risk of a forgotten test, or failure to throw the appropriate exception, increases drastically.

polymorphic_cast Isn't Always the Right Choice

If a failed polymorphic pointer cast is not an error, you should use `dynamic_cast` rather than `polymorphic_cast`. For example, this is often the case when one uses `dynamic_cast` to *test* for certain types. Using exception handling to try conversions to several types makes for inefficient, hard-to-read code. It is this behavior of `dynamic_cast` that is its real strength. When using both `polymorphic_cast` and `dynamic_cast`, you can capture your intent very clearly. Even without `polymorphic_cast`, if people know about the different ways that `dynamic_cast` works, it is still possible to achieve the same level of safety, as is shown in the following example.

```
void failure_is_error(base1* p) {

  try {
    some_other_class& soc=dynamic_cast<some_other_class&>(*p);
    // Use soc
  }
  catch(std::bad_cast& e) {
    std::cout << e.what() << '\n';
  }
}

void failure_is_ok(base1* p) {
```

---

4. Of course, the returned pointer must always be tested anyway, unless one is absolutely certain that the conversion will not fail.

```
if (some_other_class* psoc=
    dynamic_cast<some_other_class*>(p)) {
    // Use psoc
}
}
```

In this example, the pointer p is dereferenced[5] and the target type of the conversion is a reference to some_other_class. This invokes the throwing version of dynamic_cast. The second part of the example uses the non-throwing version by converting to a pointer type. Whether you see this as a clear and concise statement of the code's intent depends upon your experience. Veteran C++ programmers will understand the last example perfectly well. Will all of those reading the code be sufficiently familiar with the workings of dynamic_cast, or is it possible that they'll be unaware of the fact that it works differently depending on whether the type being converted is a pointer or reference? Will you or a maintenance programmer always remember to test for the null pointer? Will a maintenance programmer realize that dereferencing the pointer is necessary to get the exception if the conversion fails? Do you really want to write the same logic every time you need this behavior? Sorry for this rhetoric—its intent is to make it painfully obvious that polymorphic_cast makes a stronger, clearer statement than dynamic_cast when a conversion failure should result in an exception. It either succeeds, producing a valid pointer, or it fails, throwing an exception. Simple rules are easier to remember.

We haven't looked at how you can overload polymorphic_cast to account for unusual conversion needs, but it should be noted that it's possible. When would you want to change the default behavior of a polymorphic cast? One example is for handle/body-classes, where the rules for downcasting may be different from the default, or should be disallowed altogether.

Summary

It is imperative to remember that others need to maintain the code we write. That means that we have to make sure that the code and its intent are clear and understandable. In part, this can be accomplished by annotating the code, but it's much easier for everyone if the code is self-explanatory. polymorphic_cast documents the intent of code more clearly than dynamic_cast when an exception is expected for failed (pointer) conversions, and it makes for shorter code. If a failed

---

5. If the pointer p is null, the example results in undefined behavior because it will dereference a null pointer.

conversion isn't considered an error, `dynamic_cast` should be used instead, which makes use of `dynamic_cast` clearer, too. Using `dynamic_cast` as the only means of expressing these different purposes is error prone and less clear. The difference between the throwing and non-throwing version is too subtle for many programmers.

When to use `polymorphic_cast` and `dynamic_cast`:

- When a polymorphic cast failure is expected, use `dynamic_cast<T*>`. It makes clear that the failure is not an error.

- When a polymorphic cast must succeed in order for the logic to be correct, use `polymorphic_cast<T*>`. It makes clear that a conversion failure is an error.

- When performing polymorphic casts to reference types, use `dynamic_cast`.

polymorphic_downcast

Header: `"boost/cast.hpp"`

Sometimes `dynamic_cast` is considered too inefficient (measured, I'm sure!). There is runtime overhead for performing `dynamic_cast`s. To avoid that overhead, it is tempting to use `static_cast`, which doesn't have such performance implications. `static_cast` for downcasts can be dangerous and cause errors, but it is faster than `dynamic_cast`. If the extra speed is required, we must make sure that the downcasts are safe. Whereas `dynamic_cast` tests the downcasts and returns the null pointer or throws an exception on failure, `static_cast` just performs the necessary pointer arithmetic and leaves it up to the programmer to make sure that the conversion is valid. To be sure that `static_cast` is safe for downcasting, you must make sure to test every conversion that will be performed. `polymorphic_downcast` tests the cast with `dynamic_cast`, but only in debug builds; it then uses `static_cast` to perform the conversion. In release mode, only the `static_cast` is performed. The nature of the cast implies that you know it can't possibly fail, so there is no error handling, and no exception is ever thrown. So what happens if a `polymorphic_downcast` fails in a non-debug build? Undefined behavior. Your computer may melt. The Earth may stop spinning. You may float above the clouds. The only thing you can safely assume is that bad things will happen to your program. If a `polymorphic_downcast` fails in a debug build, it asserts on the null pointer result of `dynamic_cast`.

Before considering how to speed up a program by exchanging `polymorphic_downcast` for `dynamic_cast`, review the design. Optimizations on casts are likely indicators of a design problem. If the downcasts are indeed needed and proven to be performance bottlenecks, `polymorphic_downcast` is what you need. You can only find erroneous casts in testing, not production (release builds), and if you've ever had to listen to a screaming customer on the other end of the phone, you know that catching errors in testing is rather important and makes life a lot easier. Even more likely is that you've *been* the customer from time to time, and know firsthand how annoying it is to find and report someone else's problems. So, use `polymorphic_downcast` if needed, but tread carefully.

Usage

`polymorphic_downcast` is used in situations where you'd normally use `dynamic_cast` but don't because you're sure which conversions will take place, that they will all succeed, and that you need the improved performance it brings. *Nota bene*: Be sure to test all possible combinations of types and casts using `polymorphic_downcast`. If that's not possible, do not use `polymorphic_downcast`; use `dynamic_cast` instead. When you decide to go ahead and use `polymorphic_downcast`, include `"boost/cast.hpp"`.

```cpp
#include <iostream>
#include "boost/cast.hpp"

struct base {
  virtual ~base() {};
};

struct derived1 : public base {
  void foo() {
    std::cout << "derived1::foo()\n";
  }
};

struct derived2 : public base {
  void foo() {
    std::cout << "derived2::foo()\n";
  }
```

```
};

void older(base* p) {
  // Logic that suggests that p points to derived1 omitted
  derived1* pd=static_cast<derived1*>(p);
  pd->foo(); // <-- What will happen here?
}

void newer(base* p) {
  // Logic that suggests that p points to derived1 omitted
  derived1* pd=boost::polymorphic_downcast<derived1*>(p);
  // ^-- The above cast will cause an assertion in debug builds
  pd->foo();
}

int main() {
      derived2* p=new derived2;
      older(p); // <-- Undefined
      newer(p); // <-- Well defined in debug build
}
```

The static_cast in the function older will succeed,[6] and as bad luck would have it, the existence of a member function foo lets the error (probably, but again, no guarantees hold here) slip until someone with an error report in one hand and a debugger in the other starts looking into some strange behavior. When the pointer is downcast using static_cast to a derived1*, the compiler has no option but to trust the programmer that the conversion is valid. However, the pointer passed to older is in fact pointing to an instance of derived2. Thus, the pointer pd in older actually points to a completely different type, which means that anything can happen. That's the risk one takes when using a static_cast to downcast. The conversion will always "succeed" but the pointer may not be valid.

In the call to function newer, the "better static_cast," polymorphic_downcast not only catches the error, it is also kind enough to pinpoint the location of the error by asserting. Of course, that's true only for debug builds, where the cast is tested by a dynamic_cast. Letting an invalid conversion through to release will cause grief. In other words, you get added safety for debug builds, but that doesn't necessarily mean that you've tried all possible conversions.

---

6. At least it will compile.

Summary

Performing downcasts using static_cast is dangerous in many situations. You should almost never do it, but if the need does arise, some additional safety can be bought by using polymorphic_downcast. It adds tests in debug builds, which can help find conversion errors, but you must test all possible conversions to make its use safe.

- If you are downcasting and need the speed of static_cast in release builds, use polymorphic_downcast; at least you'll get assertions for errors during testing.

- If it's not possible to cover all possible casts in testing, do not use polymorphic_downcast.

Remember that this is an optimization, and you should only apply optimizations after profiling demonstrates the need for them.

numeric_cast

Header: "boost/cast.hpp"

Conversions between integral types can often produce unexpected results. For example, a long can typically hold a much greater range of values than a short, so what happens when assigning a long to a short and the long's value is outside of short's range? The answer is that the result is implementation defined (a nice term for "you can never know for sure"). Signed to unsigned conversions between same size integers are fine, so long as the signed value is positive, but what happens if the signed value is negative? It turns into a large unsigned value, which is indeed a problem if that was not the intention. numeric_cast helps ensure valid conversions by testing whether the range is preserved and by throwing an exception if it isn't.

Before we can fully appreciate numeric_cast, we must understand the rules that govern conversions and promotions of integral types. The rules are many and sometimes subtle—they can trap even the experienced programmer. Rather than stating all of the rules[7] and then carry on, I'll give you examples of

---

7. The C++ Standard covers promotions and conversions for numeric types in §4.5-4.9.

conversions that are subject to undefined or surprising behavior, and explain which rules the conversions adhere to.

When assigning to a variable from one of a different numeric type, a *conversion* occurs. This is perfectly safe when the destination type can hold any value that the source can, but is unsafe otherwise. For example, a char generally cannot hold the maximum value of an int, so when an assignment from int to char occurs, there is a good chance that the int value cannot be represented in the char. When the types differ in the range of values they can represent, we must make sure that the actual value to convert is in the valid range of the destination type. Otherwise, we enter the land of *implementation-defined behavior*; that's what happens when a value outside of the range of possible values is assigned to a numeric type.[8] Implementation-defined behavior means that the implementation is free to do whatever it wants to; different systems may well have totally different behavior. numeric_cast can ensure that the conversions are valid and legal or they will not be allowed.

Usage

numeric_cast is a function template that looks like a C++ cast operator and is parameterized on both the destination and source types. The source type can be implicitly deduced from the function argument. To use numeric_cast, include the header "boost/cast.hpp". The following two conversions use numeric_cast to safely convert an int to a char, and a double to a float.

```
char c=boost::numeric_cast<char>(12);
float f=boost::numeric_cast<float>(3.001);
```

One of the most common numeric conversion problems is assigning a value from a type with a wider range than the one being assigned to. Let's see how numeric_cast can help.

Assignment from a Larger to a Smaller Type

When assigning a value from a larger type (for example, long) to a smaller type (for example, short), there is a chance that the value is too large or too small to be represented in the destination type. If this happens, the result is (yes, you've

---

8. Unsigned arithmetic notwithstanding; it is well defined for these cases.

guessed it) implementation-defined. We'll talk about the potential problems with unsigned types later; let's just start with the signed types. There are four built-in signed integral types in C++:

- `signed char`

- `short int (short)`

- `int`

- `long int (long)`

There's not much one can say with absolute certainty about which type is larger[9] than others, but typically, the listing is in increasing size, with the exception that `int` and `long` often hold the same range of values. They're all distinct types, though, even if they're the same size. To see the sizes on your system, use either `sizeof(T)` or `std::numeric_limits<T>::max()` and `std::numeric_limits<T>::min()`.

When assigning one signed integral type to another, the C++ Standard says:

> *"If the destination type is signed, the value is unchanged if it can be represented in the destination type (and bitfield width); otherwise, the value is implementation-defined."*[10]

The following piece of code gives an example of how these implementation-defined values are often the result of seemingly innocent assignments, and finally how they are avoided with the help of `numeric_cast`.

```
#include <iostream>
#include "boost/cast.hpp"
#include "boost/limits.hpp"

int main() {
   std::cout << "larger_to_smaller example\n";

   // Conversions without numeric_cast
   long l=std::numeric_limits<short>::max();

   short s=l;
   std::cout << "s is: " << s << '\n';
```

---

9. Of course, the ranges of signed and unsigned types are different even if the types have the same size.

10. See §4.7.3 of the C++ Standard.

```
    s=++l;
    std::cout << "s is: " << s << "\n\n";

    // Conversions with numeric_cast
    try {
      l=std::numeric_limits<short>::max();
      s=boost::numeric_cast<short>(l);
      std::cout << "s is: " << s << '\n';
      s=boost::numeric_cast<short>(++l);
      std::cout << "s is: " << s << '\n';
    }
    catch(boost::bad_numeric_cast& e) {
      std::cout << e.what() << '\n';
    }
}
```

Utilizing `std::numeric_limits`, the `long` l is initialized to the maximum value that a `short` can possibly hold. That value is assigned to the `short` s and printed. After that, l is incremented by one, which means that it now holds a value that cannot be represented by a `short`; it is outside the range of values that a `short` can represent. After assigning from the new value of l to s, s is printed again. What's the value, you might ask? Well, because the assignment results in implementation-defined behavior, that depends upon the platform. On my system, with my compiler, it turns out that the result is a large negative value, which implies that the value has been wrapped. There's no telling[11] what it will be on your system without running the preceding code. Next, the same operations are performed again, but this time using `numeric_cast`. The first cast succeeds, because the value is within range. The second, however, fails, and the result is that an exception of type `bad_numeric_cast` is thrown. The output of the program is as follows.

```
larger_to_smaller example
s is: 32767
s is: -32768

s is: 32767
bad numeric cast: loss of range in numeric_cast
```

A benefit that might be even more important than dodging the implementation-

---

11. Although the behavior and value demonstrated here is very common on 32-bit platforms.

defined value is that `numeric_cast` helps us avoid errors that are otherwise very hard to trap. The strange value could be passed on to other parts of the application, perhaps working in some cases, but almost certainly yielding the wrong result. Of course, this only happens for certain values, and if those values seldom occur, the error will be very hard to track down. Such errors are insidious because they happen only for some values rather than all of the time.

Loss of precision or range is not unusual, and if you aren't absolutely certain that a value too large or too small for the destination type will never be assigned, `numeric_cast` is the tool for you. You can even use `numeric_cast` when it's unnecessary; the maintenance programmer may not have the same insight as you do. Note that although we have covered only signed types here, the same principles apply to unsigned integral types, too.

Special Case—Unsigned Integral Type As Destination

Unsigned integral types have a very interesting property—any numeric value can be legally assigned to them! There is no notion of positive or negative overflow when it comes to unsigned types. They are reduced modulo the number that is one greater than the largest value of the destination type. Say what? An example in code might make it clearer.

```
#include <iostream>
#include "boost/limits.hpp"

int main() {
  unsigned char c;
  long l=std::numeric_limits<unsigned char>::max()+14;

  c=l;
  std::cout << "c is:          " << (int)c << '\n';
  long reduced=l%(std::numeric_limits<unsigned char>::max()+1);
  std::cout << "reduced is: " << reduced << '\n';
}
```

The output of running the program follows:

```
c is:        13
reduced is: 13
```

The example assigns a value that is certainly greater than what an unsigned char can hold, and then that same value is calculated. The workings of the assignment is shown in this line:

```
long reduced=1%(std::numeric_limits<unsigned char>::max()+1);
```

This behavior is often referred to as *value wrapping*. If you want to use this property of unsigned integral types, there is no need to use numeric_cast in those situations. Furthermore, numeric_cast won't accept it. numeric_cast's intent is to catch errors, and this is considered an error because it is the result of a typical user misunderstanding. If the destination type cannot represent the value that is being assigned, a bad_numeric_cast exception is thrown. Just because unsigned integer arithmetic is well defined doesn't make the programmer's error less fatal.[12] For numeric_cast, the important aspect is to preserve the actual value.

Mixing Signed and Unsigned Integral Types

It's easy to have fun[13] when mixing signed and unsigned types, especially when performing arithmetic operations. Plain assignments offer some clever pitfalls, too. The most common problem is assigning a negative value to an unsigned type. The result is almost certainly not what was intended. Another issue is when assigning from an unsigned type to a signed type of the same size. Somehow, it seems to be easy to forget that the unsigned type can hold higher values than the signed counterpart. It's even easier to forget the types involved in an expression or function call. Here's an example that shows how these common errors are caught by numeric_cast.

```
#include <iostream>
#include "boost/limits.hpp"
#include "boost/cast.hpp"

int main() {
  unsigned int ui=std::numeric_limits<unsigned int>::max();
  int i;

  try {
    std::cout << "Assignment from unsigned int to signed int\n";
```

---

12. The point: If you really want value wrapping, don't use numeric_cast.

13. This is a highly subjective matter, of course, and your mileage may vary.

```
      i=boost::numeric_cast<int>(ui);
  }
  catch(boost::bad_numeric_cast& e) {
     std::cout << e.what() << "\n\n";
  }

  try {
     std::cout << "Assignment from signed int to unsigned int\n";
     i=-12;
     ui=boost::numeric_cast<unsigned int>(i);
  }
  catch(boost::bad_numeric_cast& e) {
     std::cout << e.what() << "\n\n";
  }
}
```

The output clearly shows that the errors were trapped as expected.

```
Assignment from unsigned int to signed int
bad numeric cast: loss of range in numeric_cast
Assignment from signed int to unsigned int
bad numeric cast: loss of range in numeric_cast
```

The basic rule to follow is simple: Whenever a type conversion is performed between different types, make the conversion safe by using numeric_cast.

Floating Point Types

numeric_cast does not help with loss of precision when converting between floating point types. The reason is that the conversions between float, double, and long double aren't susceptible to the implicit conversions of integer types. It is important to remember that because it is easy to think that the following would result in an exception being thrown.

```
double d=0.123456789123456;
float f=0.123456;

try {
  f=boost::numeric_cast<float>(d);
}
  catch(boost::bad_numeric_cast& e) {
     std::cout << e.what();
}
```

No exception will be thrown when running this code. The conversion from `double` to `float` results in a loss of precision on most implementations, although it's not guaranteed by the C++ Standard. All we know for sure is that a `double` has *at least* the precision of a `float`.

What about conversions from floating point types to integer types? When a floating point type is converted to an integer type, it is truncated; the fractional part is discarded. `numeric_cast` performs the same checking on the truncated value and destination type range as it would for two integral types.

```cpp
double d=127.123456789123456;
char c;
std::cout << "char type maximum: ";
std::cout << (int)std::numeric_limits<char>::max() << "\n\n";

c=d;
std::cout << "Assignment from double to char: \n";
std::cout << "double: " << d << "\n";
std::cout << "char:   " << (int)c << "\n";

std::cout << "Trying the same thing with numeric_cast:\n";

try {
  c=boost::numeric_cast<char>(d);
  std::cout << "double: " << d;
  std::cout << "char:   " << (int)c;
}
  catch(boost::bad_numeric_cast& e) {
    std::cout << e.what();
}
```

Doing range checks to ensure valid assignments like the preceding ones is a daunting task. Although the rules seem simple, there are many combinations that must be considered. For example, a test for floating point to integral assignment could look like this:

```cpp
template <typename INT, typename FLOAT>
  bool is_valid_assignment(FLOAT f) {
    return std::numeric_limits<INT>::max() >=
      static_cast<INT>(f);
  }
```

Even though I just mentioned that the fractional part is discarded when a floating point type is converted, it's easy to miss the error in this implementation. This is the nature of conversions and promotions of arithmetic types. Omitting the `static_cast` makes the test work correctly, because the result of `numeric_limits<INT>::max` then is converted to the floating point type.[14] If the floating point value is converted to an integral type, it is truncated; in other words, the bug in this function is that any fractional part is lost.

Summary

`numeric_cast` offers efficient, range-checked conversions between arithmetic types. For those cases where the destination type can hold all values that the source type can, there is no efficiency penalty for using `numeric_cast`. It only has impact when the destination type can hold only a subset of the values of the source type. When a conversion fails, `numeric_cast` signals the failure by throwing an exception of type `bad_numeric_cast`. As there are so many intricate rules governing conversions between numeric types, ensuring correctness is vital.

When to use `numeric_cast`:

- When assigning/comparing unsigned and signed types

- When assigning/comparing integral types of different sizes

- When assigning a function return type to a numeric variable, to protect against future changes to the function

Notice a pattern here? Mimicking existing language and library names and behavior is a powerful technique for simplifying learning and usage, but it also requires a lot of thought. Augmenting the built-in C++ casts is a walk along a narrow road; straying comes at a high price. Making something follow the syntactic and semantic rules of the language implies responsibility. In fact, for novices, there might not be any difference at all between built-in casts and functions that look like casts, so if the behavior is incorrect it can wreak havoc. `numeric_cast` has the similar syntax and semantics of `static_cast`, `dynamic_cast`, and `reinterpret_cast`. If it looks and behaves like a cast, it is a cast, and this particular one is a nice addition to that family.

---

14. As a result of the usual arithmetic conversions.

lexical_cast

Header: `"boost/lexical_cast.hpp"`

Lexical conversions are performed in virtually all applications. We convert strings to numeric values and vice versa. Many user-defined types can be converted to strings or created from strings. It is all too common to write the code for these conversions each time you need it, which suggests that it is very much suited for a reusable implementation. That's `lexical_cast`'s purpose. Think of `lexical_cast` as using a `std::stringstream` as an interpreter between the string and other representation of a value. That means that it will work for any source with an appropriate output `operator<<` and any target with an appropriate `operator<<`. That's true for all of the built-in types and many user-defined types (UDTs).

Usage

`lexical_cast` makes a conversion between types look like any other type-converting cast. Of course, there must be a conversion function somewhere to make it work, but conceptually, it can be thought of as a cast. Rather than calling one of a number of conversion routines, or even coding the conversion locally, `lexical_cast` does that job for any types that meet its requirements. The source type must be OutputStreamable and the destination type must be InputStreamable. In addition, both types need to be CopyConstructible, and the target also DefaultConstructible and Assignable. OutputStreamable means that there's an `operator<<` defined for the type, and InputStreamable mandates an `operator>>`. This is true for many types, including the built-in types and the string classes from the Standard Library. To use `lexical_cast`, include `"boost/lexical_cast.hpp"`.

Putting *lexical_cast* to Work

I won't bore you by producing conversion code manually to show how much code `lexical_cast` saves you, because I'm sure you've written these conversions yourself, and quite probably done so more than once. Instead, the example just uses `lexical_cast` for a number of common (lexical) type conversions.

```
#include <iostream>
#include <string>
#include "boost/lexical_cast.hpp"

int main() {
  // string to int
  std::string s="42";
  int i=boost::lexical_cast<int>(s);

  // float to string
  float f=3.14151;
  s=boost::lexical_cast<std::string>(f);

  // literal to double
  double d=boost::lexical_cast<double>("2.52");

  // Failed conversion
  s="Not an int";
  try {
    i=boost::lexical_cast<int>(s);
  }
  catch(boost::bad_lexical_cast& e) {
    // The lexical_cast above will fail,
    // and we'll end up here
  }
}
```

This example shows only a few of many scenarios where lexical conversion are performed, and I think you'll agree that it usually takes a few more lines of code than this to get the job done. Whenever there's uncertainty that the conversion is valid, the lexical_cast should be protected by a try/catch block, as you see in the preceding example. You'll note that there is no way of controlling the formatting of these conversions; if you need that level of control, use std::stringstream!

If you were to manually convert between types, you'd need to handle the conversions and possible failures in different ways for different types. This is not only inconvenient; it also stands in the way of any attempt to perform the conversions in generic code. We'll see how lexical_cast can help with that in just a moment.

The conversions in the example are fairly simple to do by hand, and although lexical_cast makes it look that much simpler, there's a chance that you missed the beauty and elegance of this cast. But it's there. Consider again the simple requirements that need to be fulfilled for any class to work with lexical_cast. Think about the fact that a conversion can be done in one line for all of those classes meeting the requirements. Combine this with the fact that the implementation relies on the Standard Library's stringstream to do the grunt work,[15] and you can see that lexical_cast is more than a convenient way of performing lexical conversions; it's also a display of the art of programming in C++.

Generic Programming with *lexical_cast*

As a simple example of using lexical_cast for solving generic programming tasks, consider what it would take to create a to_string function. The function would accept any type of argument (adhering to certain requirements, of course) and return a string representing the value. Users of the Standard Library would no doubt be able to do this in a few lines of code, with the help of std::stringstream. In this case, we'll just use lexical_cast for most of the implementation, with just a forwarding function and some error handling.

```cpp
#include <iostream>
#include <string>
#include "boost/lexical_cast.hpp"

template <typename T> std::string to_string(const T& arg) {
  try {
    return boost::lexical_cast<std::string>(arg);
  }
  catch(boost::bad_lexical_cast& e) {
    return "";
  }
}

int main() {
  std::string s=to_string(412);
  s=to_string(2.357);
}
```

This handy function is not only easy to implement, it also adds value, elegantly enabled by virtue of lexical_cast.

---

15. Actually, there are optimizations that avoid the overhead of using std::stringstream for some conversions. Indeed, you can customize its behavior for your own types, if necessary.

Enabling Classes for Use with *lexical_cast*

Because `lexical_cast` only requires that `operator<<` and `operator>>` be suitably defined for the types it operates on, it's straightforward to add support for lexical conversions to user-defined types. A simple UDT that can be both the target and source when used with `lexical_cast` might look like this:

```cpp
class lexical_castable {
public:
  lexical_castable() {};
  lexical_castable(const std::string s) : s_(s) {};

  friend std::ostream operator<<
    (std::ostream& o, const lexical_castable& le);
  friend std::istream operator>>
    (std::istream& i, lexical_castable& le);

private:
  virtual void print_(std::ostream& o) const {
    o << s_ <<"\n";
  }

  virtual void read_(std::istream& i) const {
    i >> s_;
  }

  std::string s_;
};

std::ostream operator<<(std::ostream& o,
  const lexical_castable& le) {
  le.print_(o);
  return o;
}

std::istream operator>>(std::istream& i, lexical_castable& le) {
  le.read_(i);
  return i;
}
```

The `lexical_castable` class can now be used like so:

```
int main(int argc, char* argv[]) {
  lexical_castable le;
  std::cin >> le;

  try {
    int i = boost::lexical_cast<int>(le);
  }
  catch(boost::bad_lexical_cast&) {
    std::cout << "You were supposed to enter a number!\n";
  }
}
```

Of course, the input and output operators allow the class to be used with other streams as well. If you're using IOStreams from the Standard Library, or another library that uses `operator<<` and `operator>>`, you probably have many classes that are ready for `lexical_cast` in place. These do not have to be modified at all. Just lexically cast them!

Summary

`lexical_cast` is a reusable and reasonably efficient tool for lexical conversions, those between string and other types. With its combination of functionality and elegance, it is a great example of what a creative programmer can do.[16] Rather than implementing small conversion functions whenever the need arises, or worse, implementing that logic directly in other functions, a generic tool like `lexical_cast` should be used. It helps make the code clearer and allows programmers to focus on solving the problem at hand.

When to use `lexical_cast`:

- For conversions from string types to numeric types

- For conversions from numeric types to string types

- For all lexical conversions that are supported by your user-defined types

---

16. I've always felt—presumptuously, I know—that we, The Programmers, work simultaneously with mathematics, physics, engineering, architecture, sculpturing, and a few other arts and disciplines. This is daunting, but also endlessly rewarding.

Conversion Summary

In this chapter, you have learned about the Boost.Conversion library, starting with `polymorphic_cast`. The rationale for `polymorphic_cast` is code clarity and safety—clarity, because it gives us increased flexibility in stating our intent in code, and safety, because it's safer than its companion `dynamic_cast<T*>`, because tests of the resulting pointer are easily forgotten.

You then looked at safe optimizations, using `polymorphic_downcast`, which adds `dynamic_cast`-like safety in debug builds, but uses `static_cast` for the conversion. This makes it safer than `static_cast` alone.

`numeric_cast` helped with some of the thorny issues related to numeric conversions. Again, code clarity was improved and we stayed clear of both undefined and implementation-defined behavior.

Finally, there was `lexical_cast`. No more repetitive conversion functions. That's why it's been proposed for inclusion in the next revision of the C++ Standard Library. It is a tool that is very handy for converting different streamable data types.

If you were to read the implementation for these casts, you'd agree that none of them are very complicated. Still, it took insight, vision, and knowledge to recognize the need for them and to implement them correctly, portably, and efficiently. Not all people realize that there is something amiss when using `dynamic_cast`. Not many know the intricacies of integral type conversion and promotion. The Boost conversion "casts" include all of that knowledge and are well crafted and tested; they are excellent candidates for your use.

Library 3
Utility

How Does the Utility Library Improve Your Programs?

- Compile time assertions with BOOST_STATIC_ASSERT

- Safe destruction with checked_delete and checked_array_delete

- Prohibition of copying with noncopyable

- Retrieval of object addresses when operator& is overloaded through addressof

- Controlled participation of overloads and specializations with enable_if and disable_if

There are some utilities that just don't constitute a library in their own right, and are therefore grouped together with other entities. This is what Boost.Utility is, a collection of useful tools with no better home. They are useful enough to warrant inclusion in Boost, yet they are too small to deserve their own library. This chapter covers some of Boost.Utility's most fundamental and widely applicable tools.

We'll start with BOOST_STATIC_ASSERT, a facility for asserting integral constant expressions at compile time. Then, we'll see what happens when you delete an object through a pointer to an incomplete type—that is, when the layout of the object being destroyed is unknown. checked_delete makes that discussion more interesting. We'll also see how noncopyable prevents a class from ever being copied, which is arguably the most important topic of this chapter. Then, we'll check out `addressof`, which defeats the ill doings of menacing programmers[1] who overload `operator&`. Finally, we shall examine `enable_if`, which is really useful for controlling whether function overloads and template specializations are considered during name lookup or not.

BOOST_STATIC_ASSERT

Header: `"boost/static_assert.hpp"`

Performing assertions at runtime is something that you probably do regularly, and for good reasons. It is an excellent way of testing preconditions, postconditions, and invariants. There are many variations for performing runtime assertions, but how do you assert at compile time? Of course, the only way to do that is to have the compiler generate an error, and while that is quite trivial (I've inadvertently done it many thousand times), it's not obvious how to get meaningful information into the error message. Furthermore, even if you find a way on one compiler, it's a lot harder to do it portably. This is the rationale for `BOOST_STATIC_ASSERT`. It can be used at different scopes, as we shall see.

Usage

To start using static assertions, include the header `"boost/static_assert.hpp"`. This header defines the macro[2] `BOOST_STATIC_ASSERT`. For the first demonstration of its usage, we'll see how it is used at class scope. Consider a parameterized class that requires that the types with which it is instantiated are of integral type. We'd rather not provide specializations for all of those types, so what we need is to assert, at compile time, that whatever type our class is being parameterized on is indeed an integral type. Now, we're going to get a little bit ahead of ourselves by using another Boost library for testing the type—Boost.Type_traits. We'll use a predicate called `is_integral`, which performs a compile time evaluation of its argument and, as you might guess from its name, indicates whether that type is an integral type.

---

1. If you feel that I'm out of line here, please send me your most compelling use cases for overloading `operator&`.

2. Yes, it's a macro. They too can be useful, you know.

```
#include <iostream>

#include "boost/type_traits.hpp"
#include "boost/static_assert.hpp"

template <typename T> class only_compatible_with_integral_types {
  BOOST_STATIC_ASSERT(boost::is_integral<T>::value);
};
```

With this assertion, trying to instantiate the class `only_compatible_with_integral_types` with a type that is not an integral type causes a failure at compile time. The output depends on the compiler, but it is surprisingly consistent on most compilers.

Suppose we tried to instantiate the class like this:

```
only_compatible_with_integral_types<double> test2;
```

The compiler output will look something like this:

```
Error: use of undefined type
  'boost::STATIC_ASSERTION_FAILURE<false>'
```

At class scope, you can ensure certain requirements for the class: For a template like this, the parameterizing type is an obvious example. You could also use assertions for other assumptions that the class makes, such as the size of certain types and such.

BOOST_STATIC_ASSERT at Function Scope

`BOOST_STATIC_ASSERT` can also be used at function scope. For example, consider a function that is parameterized on a non-type template parameter—let's assume an `int`—and the parameter can accept values between 1 and 10. Rather than asserting that this precondition holds at runtime, we can enforce it at compile time using a static assertion.

```
template <int i> void accepts_values_between_1_and_10() {
  BOOST_STATIC_ASSERT(i>=1 && i<=10);
}
```

Users of this function can never instantiate it with values outside of the permitted range. The requirement on the expression in the assertion is, of course, that it be purely a compile time expression—that is, the arguments and operators in the expression must all be known to the compiler. BOOST_STATIC_ASSERT is not, by any means, confined to use in parameterized functions; we can just as easily test requirements in any function. For example, if a function makes platform dependent assumptions, asserting that these hold is often necessary.

```
void expects_ints_to_be_4_bytes() {
  BOOST_STATIC_ASSERT(sizeof(int)==4);
}
```

Summary

Static assertions like the ones you've seen here are becoming as common in C++ as their runtime companion assert. This is, at least in part, due to the "metaprogramming revolution," where much of a program's computation is performed at compile time. The only way to express compile time assertions is by having the compiler issue an error. To make the assertions usable, the error messages must convey the necessary information, but that's hard to do portably (in fact, it's hard to do at all). This is what BOOST_STATIC_ASSERT does, by providing consistent output for compile time assertions on a wide range of compilers. It can be used at namespace, class, and function, scope.

Use BOOST_STATIC_ASSERT when:

- A condition can be expressed at compile time

- Requirements on types are expressible at compile time

- You need to assert a relation of two or more constant integral values

checked_delete

Header: `"boost/checked_delete.hpp"`

When deleting an object through a pointer, the result is typically dependent on whether the type being deleted is known at the time of the deletion. There are hardly ever compiler warnings when delete-ing a pointer to an incomplete type, but it can cause all kinds of trouble, because the destructor may not be invoked. This, in turn, means that cleanup code won't be performed. checked_delete is in effect a static assertion that the class type is known upon destruction, enforcing the constraint that the destructor will be called.

Usage

checked_delete is a template function residing in the boost namespace. It is used for deleting dynamically allocated objects—and there's a companion used for dynamically allocated arrays called checked_array_delete. The functions accept one argument; the pointer or array to be deleted. Both of these functions require that the types they delete be known at the time they are destroyed (that is, when they are passed to the functions). To use the functions, include the header "boost/checked_delete.hpp". When utilizing the functions, simply call them where you would otherwise call delete. The following program forward declares a class, some_class, that is never defined. Any compiler would allow a pointer to some_class to be deleted (more on this later), but checked_delete does not compile until a definition of some_class is available.

```
#include "boost/checked_delete.hpp"

class some_class;

some_class* create() {
  return (some_class*)0;
}

int main() {
  some_class* p=create();
  boost::checked_delete(p2);
}
```

When trying to compile this program, the instantiation of the function checked_delete<some_class> fails because some_class is an incomplete type. Your compiler will say something like this:

```
checked_delete.hpp: In function 'void
boost::checked_delete(T*) [with T = some_class]':
checked_sample.cpp:11:   instantiated from here
boost/checked_delete.hpp:34: error: invalid application of 'sizeof' to
an incomplete type
```

```
boost/checked_delete.hpp:34: error: creating array with
size zero ('-1')
boost/checked_delete.hpp:35: error: invalid application of
'sizeof' to an incomplete type
boost/checked_delete.hpp:35: error: creating array with
size zero ('-1')
boost/checked_delete.hpp:32: warning: 'x' has incomplete type
```

The first part of the preceding error message clearly spells out the problem: that checked_delete has encountered an incomplete type. But when and how are incomplete types problems in our code? The following section talks about exactly that.

What's the Problem, Anyway?

Before we really start enjoying the benefits of checked_delete, let's make sure that we understand the problem in full. If you try to delete a pointer to an incomplete type[3] with a non-trivial destructor,[4] the result is undefined behavior. How can that come about? Let's look at an example.

```
// deleter.h

class to_be_deleted;

class deleter {
public:
  void delete_it(to_be_deleted* p);
};

// deleter.cpp
#include "deleter.h"

void deleter::delete_it(to_be_deleted* p) {
  delete p;
}

// to_be_deleted.h
```

---

3. An incomplete type is one that has been declared but not defined.

4. That's Standardese for saying that the class, one or more of its direct bases, or one or more of its non-static data members has a user-defined destructor.

```
#include <iostream>
class to_be_deleted
{
public:
  ~to_be_deleted() {
    std::cout <<
      "I'd like to say important things here, please.";
  }
};

// Test application
#include "deleter.h"
#include "to_be_deleted.h"

int main() {
  to_be_deleted* p=new to_be_deleted;

  deleter d;
  d.delete_it(p);
}
```

The preceding code tries to delete a pointer to an incomplete type, to_be_deleted, resulting in undefined behavior. Notice that to_be_deleted is forward declared in deleter.h; that deleter.cpp includes deleter.h and not to_be_deleted.h: and that to_be_deleted.h defines a non-trivial destructor for to_be_deleted. It can be easy to get into this kind of trouble, especially when using smart pointers. What we need is a way to ensure that a type is complete when calling delete, and that's just what checked_delete does.

checked_delete to the Rescue

The previous example shows that it's feasible to get into trouble when deleting incomplete types without realizing it, and not all compilers even emit a warning when it happens. When writing generic code, avoiding that situation is imperative. To rewrite the example to make use of checked_delete, you just need to change the delete p to checked_delete(p).

```
void deleter::do_it(to_be_deleted* p) {
  boost::checked_delete(p);
}
```

`checked_delete` is basically a static assertion that the class type is complete, which is accomplished like so:

```
template< typename T > inline void checked_delete(T * x) {
  typedef char type_must_be_complete[sizeof(T)];
  delete x;
}
```

The idea here is to create an array of `char`, with the number of array elements being equal to the size of `T`. If `checked_delete` is instantiated with a type `T` that is incomplete, the compilation fails, because `sizeof(T)` returns 0, and it's illegal to create an (automatic) array with 0 elements. You could also have used `BOOST_STATIC_ASSERT` for asserting this.

```
BOOST_STATIC_ASSERT(sizeof(T));
```

This utility is very handy when writing templates that must ensure that they are instantiated only with complete types. There is also a corresponding "checked deleter" for arrays, called `checked_array_delete`, which works just like `checked_delete`.

```
to_be_deleted* p=new to_be_deleted[10];
boost::checked_array_delete(p);
```

Summary

When a dynamically allocated object is deleted, it is imperative that its destructor is called. If the type is incomplete—that is, it has been declared but not defined—the destructor will probably never be called. This is a potentially disastrous situation, so avoiding it is paramount. For class templates and functions, the risk is greater than for other types, because there's no telling in advance which types will be used with it. When using `checked_delete` and `checked_array_delete`, the problem of deleting incomplete types is removed. There is no runtime overhead compared to a direct call to `delete`, so the extra safety brought forth by `checked_delete` comes virtually without a price.

Use `checked_delete` when you need to ensure that types are complete when calling `delete`.

noncopyable

Header: `"boost/utility.hpp"`

The compiler is often a very good friend of the programmer, but not always. One example of its friendliness is the way that it automatically provides copy construction and assignment for our classes, should we decide not to do so ourselves. This can lead to some unpleasant surprises, if the class isn't meant to be copied (or assigned to) in the first place. When that's the case, we need to tell clients of this class explicitly that copy construction and assignment are prohibited. I'm not talking about comments in the code, but about denying access to the copy constructor and copy assignment operator. Fortunately, the compiler-generated copy constructor and copy assignment operator are not usable when the class has bases or data members that aren't copyable or assignable. `boost::noncopyable` works by prohibiting access to its copy constructor and assignment operator and then being used as a base class.

Usage

To make use of `boost::noncopyable`, have the noncopyable classes derive privately from it. Although public inheritance works, too, this is a bad practice. Public inheritance says IS-A (denoting that the derived class also IS-A base) to people reading the class declaration, but stating that a class IS-A `noncopyable` seems a bit far fetched. Include `"boost/utility.hpp"` when deriving from `noncopyable`.

```
#include "boost/utility.hpp"

class please_dont_make_copies : boost::noncopyable {};

int main() {
  please_dont_make_copies d1;
  please_dont_make_copies d2(d1);
  please_dont_make_copies d3;
  d3=d1;
  }
```

The preceding example does not compile. The attempted copy construction of `d2` fails because the copy constructor of `noncopyable` is private. The attempted

assignment of d1 to d3 fails because the copy assignment operator of
noncopyable is private. The compiler should give you something similar to
the following output:

```
noncopyable.hpp: In copy constructor
' please_dont_make_copies::please_dont_make_copies (const
please_dont_make_copies&)':
boost/noncopyable.hpp:27: error: '
  boost::noncopyable::noncopyable(const boost::noncopyable&)' is
  private
noncopyable.cpp:8: error: within this context
boost/noncopyable.hpp: In member function 'please_dont_make_copies&
  please_dont_make_copies::operator=(const please_dont_make_copies&)':
boost/noncopyable.hpp:28: error: 'const boost::noncopyable&
  boost::noncopyable::operator=(const boost::noncopyable&)' is private
noncopyable.cpp:10: error: within this context
```

We'll examine how this works in the following sections. It's clear that copying
an assignment is prohibited when deriving from noncopyable. This can also
be achieved by defining the copy constructor and copy assignment operator
privately—let's see how to do that.

Making Classes Noncopyable

Consider again the class please_dont_make_copies, which, for some reason,
should never be copied.

```
class please_dont_make_copies {
public:
  void do_stuff() {
    std::cout <<
      "Dear client, would you please refrain from copying me?";
  }
};
```

Because the compiler generates a copy constructor and an assignment operator,
there's nothing about this class that prohibits copying or assignment.

```
please_dont_make_copies p1;
please_dont_make_copies p2(p1);
please_dont_make_copies p3;
p3=p2;
```

We could fix this mess by declaring the copy constructor and copy assignment operator private or protected, and by adding a default constructor (which would no longer be generated by the compiler).

```cpp
class please_dont_make_copies {
public:
  please_dont_make_copies() {}

  void do_stuff() {
    std::cout <<
      "Dear client, would you please refrain from copying me?";
  }
private:
  please_dont_make_copies(const please_dont_make_copies&);
  please_dont_make_copies& operator=
    (const please_dont_make_copies&);
};
```

That works very well, but it isn't as immediately apparent to please_dont_make_copies' clients that it is noncopyable. Seeing noncopyable instead makes the class more obviously noncopyable with less typing.

Using *noncopyable*

The class boost::noncopyable is intended to be used as a private base class, which effectively turns off copy construction and copy assignment operations. Using the previous example, here's how the code would look when using noncopyable:

```cpp
#include "boost/utility.hpp"

class please_dont_make_copies : boost::noncopyable {
public:
  void do_stuff() {
    std::cout << "Dear client, you just cannot copy me!";
  }
};
```

There's no need to declare the copy constructor or copy assignment operator. Because we've derived from noncopyable, the compiler won't generate them either, which disables copying and copy assignment. Terseness can lend clarity, especially for such basic and distinct concepts such as this. For a client reading the code, it is immediately apparent that this class cannot be copied, or copy assigned, because `boost::noncopyable` appears at the very start of the class definition. One last note: Do you recall that the default access control for classes is private? That means that inheritance is private by default, too. You could make this fact even more obvious by spelling it out like this:

```
class please_dont_make_copies : private boost::noncopyable {
```

It all depends on the audience; some programmers find such redundant information annoying and distracting, whereas others appreciate the clarification. It's up to you to decide which way is right for your classes, and your programmers. Either way, using `noncopyable` is definitely better than "forgetting" the copy constructor and the copy assignment operator, and it's also clearer than privately declaring them.

Remember the Big Three

As we have seen, `noncopyable` provides a convenient way of disabling copying and copy assignment for a class. But when do we need to do that? Which are the circumstances that demand a user-defined copy constructor or copy assignment operator in the first place? There is a general answer to this question, one that just about always is correct: Whenever you need to define one of the destructor, the copy constructor, or the copy assignment operator, you also need to define the remaining two.[5] These three interoperate in important ways, and when one exists, the others typically must, too. Let's assume that one of your classes has a member that is a pointer. You have defined a destructor for proper deallocation, but you haven't bothered defining a copy constructor or a copy assignment operator. This means that there are at least two potential defects in your code, which are easy to trigger.

```
class full_of_errors {
   int* value_;
public:
   full_of_errors() {
     value_=new int(13);
   }
```

---

5. The name Law of the Big Three comes from C++ FAQs (see [2] in the Bibliography for details).

```
~full_of_errors() {
    delete value_;
  }
};
```

Using this class, there are at least three ways of producing errors that aren't obvious if one neglects to consider the copy constructor and the assignment operator that the compiler has graciously augmented the class with.

```
full_of_errors f1;
full_of_errors f2(f1);
full_of_errors f3=f2;
full_of_errors f4;
f4=f3;
```

Note that the two equivalent ways of invoking the copy constructor here are on the second and third lines. They both call the synthesized copy constructor, although the syntax is different. The final error is on the last line, where the copy assignment operator makes sure that the same pointer is used and deleted by at least two instances of full_of_errors. Doing things correctly, we would have realized the need for copy assignment and copy construction right away, when we defined our destructor. Here's what should have been done:

```
class not_full_of_errors {
    int* value_;
public:
    not_full_of_errors() {
        value_=new int(13);
    }

    not_full_of_errors(const not_full_of_errors& other) :
        value_(new int(*other.value_)) {}

    not_full_of_errors& operator=
        (const not_full_of_errors& other) {
        *value_=*other.value_;
        return *this;
    }

    ~not_full_of_errors() {
        delete value_;
    }
};
```

So, whenever one of the big three—copy constructor, (virtual) destructor, and copy assignment operator—is manually defined in a class, think long and hard before deciding that the remaining two are unnecessary. And, remember to use `boost::noncopyable` if there is to be no copying at all!

Summary

There are many types for which we need to prohibit copying and copy assignment. However, declaring the copy constructor and copy assignment operator private is often neglected for such types, and responsibility for knowing that copying doesn't make sense is transferred to clients of the type. Even when types ensure that they cannot be copied or assigned, using private copy constructors and copy assignment operators, it isn't always clear to the client that this is the case. Of course, the compiler kindly informs those who try, but it may not be apparent where the error is coming from. Either way, the best we can do is to be explicit about it, and deriving from `noncopyable` makes a clear statement. It is immediately in view when scanning the declaration of the type. When compiling, an error message almost certainly includes the name *noncopyable*. And it also saves some typing, which is a killer argument for some.

Use `noncopyable` when:

- Copying and copy assignment of types is not allowed

- Prohibition of copying and assignment should be as explicit as possible

addressof

Header: `"boost/utility.hpp"`

When taking the address of a variable, we typically depend on the returned value to be, well, the address of the variable. However, it's technically possible to overload `operator&`, which means that evildoers may be on a mission to wreak havoc on your address-dependent code. `boost::addressof` is provided to get the address anyway, regardless of potential uses and misuses of operator overloading. By using some clever internal machinery, the template function `addressof` ensures that it gets to the actual object and its address.

Usage

To always be sure to get the real address of an object, use `boost::addressof`. It is defined in `"boost/utility.hpp"`. It is used where `operator&` would otherwise be used, and it accepts an argument that is a reference to the type whose address should be taken.

```cpp
#include "boost/utility.hpp"

class some_class {};

int main() {
  some_class s;
  some_class* p=boost::addressof(s);
}
```

Before seeing more details on how to use `addressof`, it is helpful to understand why and how `operator&` may not actually return the address of an object.

Quick Lesson for Evildoers

If you really, really, really need to overload `operator&`, or just want to experiment with the potential uses of operator overloading, it's actually quite easy. When overloading `operator&`, the semantics are always different from what most users (and functions!) expect, so don't do it just to be cute; do it for a very good reason or not at all. That said, here's a code-breaker for you:

```cpp
class codebreaker {
public:
  int operator&() const {
    return 13;
  }
};
```

With this class, anyone who tries to take the address of an instance of `codebreaker` is handed the magical number 13.

```cpp
template <typename T> void print_address(const T& t) {
  std::cout << "Address: " << (&t) << '\n';
}
```

```
int main() {
  codebreaker c;
  print_address(c);
}
```

It's not hard to do this, but are there good arguments for ever doing it in real code? Probably not, because it cannot be made safe except when using local classes. The reason for this is that while it is legal to take the address of an incomplete type, it is undefined behavior to do so on an incomplete class with a user-defined operator&. Because we cannot guarantee that this won't happen, we're better off not overloading operator&.

Quick Remedy for Others

Even when operator& is supplied by the class, it is possible to get to the real address of instances of the class. addressof performs some clever work[6] behind the scenes to get to the bottom of the address issue, regardless of any operator& chicanery. If you adjust the function (print_address) to make use of addressof, you'll get what we came here for:

```
template <typename T> void print_address(const T& t) {
  std::cout << "&t: " << (&t) << '\n';
  std::cout << "addressof(t): " << boost::addressof(t) << '\n';
}
```

When invoked, the function gives this output (or similar, because the exact address differs depending upon your system).

```
&t: 13
addressof(t):  0012FECB13
```

That's more like it! If there are scenarios where you know, or suspect, that operator& is provided by a class but you need to be really sure that you get the actual address (which is unlikely for an overloaded operator& or why else would it be overloaded in the first place?), use addressof.

---

6. Also known as an ingenious hack.

Summary

There are not many potent arguments for overloading operator&,[7] but because it is possible, some people do it anyway. When writing code that relies on retrieving the actual address of objects, addressof can help by ensuring that the real address is returned. When writing generic code, there is no way of telling which types will be operated upon, so if the address of parameterized types needs to be taken, use addressof.

Use addressof when you must retrieve the actual address of an object, regardless of the semantics for operator&.

enable_if

Header: "boost/utility/enable_if.hpp"

Sometimes, we wish to control whether a certain function, or class template specialization, can take part in the set of available overloads/specializations for overload resolution. For example, consider an overloaded function where one version is an ordinary function taking an int argument, and the other is a templated version that requires that the argument of type T has a nested type called type. They might look like this:

```
void some_func(int i) {
  std::cout << "void some_func(" << i << ")\n";
}

template <typename T> void some_func(T t) {
  typename T::type variable_of_nested_type;
  std::cout <<
    "template <typename T> void some_func(" << t << ")\n";
}
```

Now, imagine what happens when you call some_func somewhere in your code. If the type of the argument is int, the first version is called. Assuming that the type is something other than int, the second (templated) version is called.

---

7. Custom hardware device drivers notwithstanding.

This is fine, as long as that type has a nested type named `type`, but if it doesn't, this code does not compile. Is this really a problem? Well, consider what happens when another integral type is used, like `short`, or `char`, or `unsigned long`.

```cpp
#include <iostream>

void some_func(int i) {
  std::cout << "void some_func(" << i << ")\n";
}

template <typename T> void some_func(T t) {
  typename T::type variable_of_nested_type;
  std::cout <<
    "template <typename T> void some_func(" << t << ")\n";
}

int main() {
  int i=12;
  short s=12;

  some_func(i);
  some_func(s);
}
```

When compiling this program, you will get something like the following output from the frustrated compiler:

```
enable_if_sample1.cpp: In function 'void some_func(T)
  [with T = short int]':
enable_if_sample1.cpp:17:   instantiated from here
enable_if_sample1.cpp:8: error:
  'short int' is not a class, struct, or union type

Compilation exited abnormally with code 1 at Sat Mar 06 14:30:08
```

There it is. The template version of `some_func` has been chosen as the best overload, but the code in that version is not valid for the type `short`. How could we have avoided this? Well, we would have liked to only enable the template version of `some_func` for types with a nested type named type, and to ignore it for those without it. We can do that. The easiest way, which is not always an option in real life, is to change the return type of the template version like so:

```
template <typename T> typename T::type* some_func(T t) {
  typename T::type variable_of_nested_type;
  std::cout <<
    "template <typename T> void some_func(" << t << ")\n";
  return 0;
}
```

If you haven't yet studied *SFINAE (substitution failure is not an error)*,[8] chances are that you have a perplexed look on your face right now. When compiling with this update, our example compiles cleanly. The `short` is promoted to `int`, and the first version is called. The reason for this surprising behavior is that the template version of `some_func` isn't included in the overload resolution set anymore. It's excluded because when the compiler sees that the return type of the function requires that `type` be a nested type of the template type `T` (lots of types here), it knows that `short` doesn't fit the bill, so it removes the function template from the overload resolution set. This is what Daveed Vandevorde and Nicolai Josuttis have taught us to refer to as *SFINAE*, and it means that rather than producing a compiler error, that function simply is not considered as a valid overload for the type in question. If the type has such a nested type, though, it will be part of the overload set.

```
class some_class {
public:
  typedef int type;
};

int main() {
  int i=12;
  short s=12;

  some_func(i);
  some_func(s);
  some_func(some_class());
}
```

The output when running this program is as follows:

```
void some_func(12)
void some_func(12)
template <typename T> void some_func(T t)
```

---

8. See [3] in the Bibliography.

This works, but it's not a pretty sight. In this scenario, we had the luxury of playing with a `void` return type, which we could use for other purposes. If that hadn't been the case, we could have added another argument to the function and given it a default value.

```
template <typename T>
  void some_func(T t,typename T::type* p=0) {
  typename T::type variable_of_nested_type;
  std::cout << "template <typename T> void some_func(T t)\n";
}
```

This version also uses SFINAE to disqualify itself from use with invalid types. The problem with both of these solutions is that they're really ugly, we have made them a part of the public interface, and they only work in some scenarios. Boost offers a much cleaner solution, which is both syntactically nicer and offers a much wider range of functionality than our earlier ad hoc solutions.

Usage

To use `enable_if` and `disable_if`, include `"boost/utility/enable_if.hpp"`. For the first example, we'll disable the second version of `some_func` if the type of the argument is integral. Type information such as whether a type is integral is available in another Boost library, `Boost.Type_traits`. The `enable_if` and `disable_if` templates both accept a predicate controlling whether to enable or disable the function, respectively.

```
#include <iostream>
#include "boost/utility/enable_if.hpp"
#include "boost/type_traits.hpp"

void some_func(int i) {
  std::cout << "void some_func(" << i << ")\n";
}

template <typename T> void some_func(
  T t,typename boost::disable_if<
    boost::is_integral<T> >::type* p=0) {
    typename T::type variable_of_nested_type;
    std::cout << "template <typename T> void some_func(T t)\n";
}
```

Although this is similar to what we did before, it's expressing something that we couldn't have done as easily using our direct approach, and this also has the advantage of documenting important information about the function in its signature. When reading this, it is clear that the function requires that the type T is *not* an integral type. It would be even better if we could enable it (and document it accordingly) only for types with a nested type, type, and we can do that if we use another library, Boost.Mpl.[9] Check this out:

```
#include <iostream>
#include "boost/utility/enable_if.hpp"
#include "boost/type_traits.hpp"
#include "boost/mpl/has_xxx.hpp"

BOOST_MPL_HAS_XXX_TRAIT_DEF(type)

void some_func(int i) {
  std::cout << "void some_func(" << i << ")\n";
}

template <typename T> void some_func(T t,
  typename boost::enable_if<has_type<T> >::type* p=0) {
    typename T::type variable_of_nested_type;
    std::cout << "template <typename T> void some_func(T t)\n";
}
```

This is very cool indeed! We are now disabling the template version of some_func when there is no nested type, type, in T, and we explicitly document that this is a requirement for the function in its signature. The trick here is to use a very nifty feature of Boost.Mpl that can test whether a certain nested type (or typedef) exists in an arbitrary type T. Using the macro invocation, BOOST_MPL_HAS_XXX_TRAIT_DEF(type), we define a new trait called has_type, which we use in the function some_func as the predicate for enable_if. If the predicate yields true, the function is part of the overload set; if it yields false, it is excluded.

It's also possible to wrap the return type rather than add an extra (defaulted) argument. The equivalent of our latest and greatest some_func, but using enable_if in the return type, looks like this.

9. Boost.Mpl is beyond the scope of this book. Visit http://www.boost.org for more information on Mpl. Also, get your hands on David Abrahams's and Aleksey Gurtovoy's book, *C++ Template Metaprogramming*!

```
template <typename T> typename
boost::enable_if<has_type<T>,void>::type
  some_func(T t) {
    typename T::type variable_of_nested_type;
    std::cout << "template <typename T> void some_func(T t)\n";
}
```

If you need to return the type that you need to enable or disable on, using
`enable_if` and `disable_if` on the return type makes more sense than adding a
defaulted argument. Also, there is a chance that someone actually provides a
value instead of that default argument, which breaks the code. Sometimes,
class template specializations need to be enabled or disabled, and `enable_if`/
`disable_if` work for those cases too. The difference is that for class templates,
we must give the primary template some special treatment—an additional template parameter. Consider a class template with a member function `max` that
returns an `int`:

```
template <typename T> class some_class {
public:
  int max() const {
    std::cout << "some_class::max() for the primary template\n";
    return std::numeric_limits<int>::max();
  }
};
```

Suppose we decide that for all arithmetic types (integral types and floating
point types), there should be a specialization available that returns `max` as the
maximum value that the type can hold. We'll thus need `std::numeric_limits`
for the template type `T`, and we want all other types to use the primary template.
To make this work, we must add a template parameter to the primary template,
which has a default type of `void` (this means that users don't have to deal explicitly with this type). This results in the following primary template:

```
template <typename T,typename Enable=void> class some_class {
public:
  int max() const {
    std::cout << "some_class::max() for the primary template\n";
    return std::numeric_limits<int>::max();
  }
};
```

We've now paved the way for providing a more specialized version, to be enabled if the type is arithmetic. That trait is available via the Boost.Type_traits library. Here's the specialization:

```
template <typename T> class some_class<T,
  typename boost::enable_if<boost::is_arithmetic<T> >::type> {
public:
  T max() const {
    std::cout << "some_class::max() with an arithmetic type\n";
    return std::numeric_limits<T>::max();
  }
};
```

This version is only enabled when instantiated with a type that is arithmetic—that is, when the trait is_arithmetic yields true. This works because boost::enable_if<false>::type is void, matching the primary template specialization. The following program tests these templates with various types:

```
#include <iostream>
#include <string>
#include <limits>
#include "boost/utility/enable_if.hpp"
#include "boost/type_traits.hpp"

// Definition of the template some_class omitted

int main() {
  std::cout << "Max for std::string: " <<
    some_class<std::string>().max() << '\n';
  std::cout << "Max for void: " <<
    some_class<void>().max() << '\n';
  std::cout << "Max for short: " <<
    some_class<short>().max() << '\n';
  std::cout << "Max for int: " <<
    some_class<int>().max() << '\n';
  std::cout << "Max for long: " <<
    some_class<long>().max() << '\n';
  std::cout << "Max for double: " <<
    some_class<double>().max() << '\n';
}
```

We'd expect the first two uses of `some_class` to instantiate the primary template, and the rest to instantiate the specialization for arithmetic types. Running the program shows that this is indeed the case.

```
some_class::max() for the primary template
Max for std::string: 2147483647
some_class::max() for the primary template
Max for void: 2147483647
some_class::max() with an arithmetic type
Max for short: 32767
some_class::max() with an arithmetic type
Max for int: 2147483647
some_class::max() with an arithmetic type
Max for long: 2147483647
some_class::max() with an arithmetic type
Max for double: 1.79769e+308
```

That's all there is to it! Enabling and disabling overloaded functions and template specializations has heretofore required some tricky programming, which most who read the code would not fully understand. By using `enable_if` and `disable_if`, the solution becomes easier to code and read, and automatically captures the type requirements right in the declaration. In the preceding example, we use the template `enable_if`, which expects that the condition has a nested definition called `value`. This is true for most metaprogramming-enabled types, but it certainly isn't for integral constant expressions, for example. When there is no nested type called `value`, use `enable_if_c` instead, which expects an integral constant expression. Naively using the trait `is_arithmetic` and extracting its value directly, we could have written the enabling condition for `some_class`, like so:

```cpp
template <typename T> class some_class<T,
   typename boost::enable_if_c<
     boost::is_arithmetic<T>::value>::type> {
public:
  T max() const {
    std::cout << "some_class::max() with an arithmetic type\n";
    return std::numeric_limits<T>::max();
  }
};
```

There is no fundamental difference between `enable_if` and `enable_if_c`. It's only the expectation of a nested type value that sets them apart.

Summary

The C++ language feature known as SFINAE is important. Without it, a lot of new code would break existing code, and some types of function overloads (and template specializations) would simply not be possible. To directly make use of SFINAE in a controlled way to enable or disable certain functions or types for overload resolution is complicated. It also makes for hard-to-read code. Using `boost::enable_if` is an elegant way of simultaneously stating that an overload is only eligible when certain conditions apply. The same argument holds for `disable_if`, which is used to state the opposite—that an overload is not applicable if the condition holds true. There is promise of even more practical uses of SFINAE, and this library also serves as a very nice introduction of the topic. This chapter has omitted the lazy versions of `enable_if` and `disable_if` (named `lazy_enable_if` and `lazy_disable_if`), but I'll give them a brief mention here. The lazy versions are used to avoid instantiating types that may not be available (depending on the value of the condition).

Use `enable_if` when:

- You need to add or remove a function to the overload set depending on some condition

- You need to add or remove a class template specialization from the set of specializations depending on some condition

Utility Summary

This chapter has demonstrated some useful utility classes that can greatly simplify our daily life. `BOOST_STATIC_ASSERT` asserts at compile time, which is very helpful both for testing preconditions and enforcing other requirements. For generic programming, `checked_delete` is extremely helpful in detecting erroneous usage, which in turn can save a lot of time reading terribly verbose error messages and studying code that seems just fine. We have also covered `addressof`, which is a handy tool for getting to the real address of an object, regardless of what `operator&` says. We also saw how `enable_if` and `disable_if` can control which functions participate in overload resolution and learned what SFINAE means!

We talked about the base class `noncopyable`. By providing both a useful idiom and straightforward usage that catches the eye of anyone reading the code, it definitely deserves to be used regularly. The omission of a copy constructor and assignment operator in classes that need them, whether through the need for customized copying/assignment or the prohibition thereof, is all too common in code, costing lots of frustration, time, and money.

This is one of the shortest chapters in the book, and I suspect that you've read through it fairly quickly. It pays you back fast, too, if you start using these utilities right away. There are other utilities in Boost.Utility, which I haven't covered here. You might want to surf over to the Boost Web site and have a look at the online documentation to see what other handy tools there would suit you well in your current work.

Library 4
Operators

How Does the Operators Library Improve Your Programs?

- Provides a complete set of comparison operators

- Provides a complete set of arithmetic operators

- Provides a complete set of operators for iterators

Among the operators defined in C++, there are a number of related sets. When you encounter a class with one operator from one of these sets, you typically expect to find the others, too. For instance, when a class provides `operator==`, you expect to find `operator!=` and probably `operator<`, `operator<=`, `operator>`, and `operator>=`. Sometimes, a class only provides `operator<` in order to define an ordering so objects of that class can be used in associative containers, but that often leaves class users wanting more. Likewise, a class with value semantics that provides `operator+` but not `operator+=` or `operator-` is limiting its potential uses. When you define one operator from a set for your class, you should typically provide the remaining operators from that set to avoid surprises. Unfortunately, it is cumbersome and error prone to augment a class with the many operators needed to support comparisons or arithmetic, and iterator classes must provide certain sets of operators according to the iterator category they model just to function correctly.

Besides the tedium of defining the number of operators needed, their semantics must be correct to meet users' expectations. Otherwise, the class is, for all practical purposes, unusable. We can relieve ourselves from doing it all by hand, though. As you know, some of the operators are typically implemented in terms of others, such as implementing `operator+` in terms of `operator+=`, and that suggests that some automation of this task is possible. In fact, that is the purpose of Boost.Operators. By allowing you to define only a subset of the required comparison or arithmetic operators, and then defining the rest for you based upon those you provide, Boost.Operators enforces the correct operator semantics, and reduces your chance of making mistakes.

An additional value of the Operators library is the explicit naming of concepts that apply for different operations, such as *addable* for classes supporting `operator+` and `operator+=`, *shiftable* for classes supporting `operator<<` and `operator>>`, and so on. This is important for two reasons: A consistent naming scheme aids understanding; and these concepts, and the classes named after them, can be part of class interfaces, clearly documenting important behaviors.

How Does Operators Fit with the Standard Library?

When using the Standard Library containers and algorithms, one typically supplies at least some relational operators (most commonly `operator<`) to enable sorting, and thus also storage of the type in sorted, associative containers. A common practice is to define only the bare minimum of the required operators, which has the unfortunate side effect of making the class less complete, and harder to understand. On the other hand, when defining a full set of operators, there is a risk of introducing defective semantics. In these cases, the Operators library helps to make sure that the classes behave correctly, and adhere to the requirements of both the Standard Library and the users of the type. Finally, for types that define arithmetic operators, there are a number of operators that are well suited to be implemented in terms of other operators, and Boost.Operators is of great use here, too.

Operators

Header: `"boost/operators.hpp"`

There are a number of base classes that comprise the Operators library. Each class contributes operators according to the concept it names. You use them by inheriting from them—multiply inheriting if you need the services of more than one. Fortunately, there are some composite concepts defined in Operators obviating the need to multiply inherit for many common cases. The following synopses describe some of the most commonly used Operator classes, the concepts they represent, and the demands they place on classes derived from them. In some cases, the requirements for the actual concepts are not the same as the requirements for the concept base classes when using Operators. For example, the concept *addable* requires that there be an operator `T operator+(const T& lhs,const T& rhs)` defined, but the Operators base class `addable` instead requires a member function, `T operator+=(const T& other)`. Using this member function, the base class `addable` augments the derived class with `operator+`. Throughout the synopses, the concepts are always stated first, followed by the type requirements for classes deriving from them. Rather than repeating all of the concepts in this library, I have selected a few important ones; you'll find the full reference at www.boost.org, of course.

less_than_comparable

The `less_than_comparable` concept requires the following semantics for a type `T`.

```
bool operator<(const T&,const T&);
bool operator>(const T&,const T&);
bool operator<=(const T&,const T&);
bool operator>=(const T&,const T&);
```

When deriving from `boost::less_than_comparable`, the derived class (`T`) must provide the equivalent of

```
bool operator<(const T&, const T&);
```

Note that the return type need not be exactly `bool`, but it must be implicitly convertible to `bool`. For the concept *LessThanComparable* found in the C++ Standard, `operator<` is required, so classes derived from `less_than_comparable` need to comply with that requirement. In return, `less_than_comparable` implements the three remaining operators in terms of `operator<`.

equality_comparable

The `equality_comparable` concept requires the following semantics for a type `T`.

```
bool operator==(const T&,const T&);
bool operator!=(const T&,const T&);
```

When deriving from `boost::equality_comparable`, the derived class (T) must provide the equivalent of

```
bool operator==(const T&,const T&);
```

Again, the return type needn't be `bool`, but it must be a type implicitly convertible to `bool`. For the concept *EqualityComparable* in the C++ Standard, `operator==` is required, so derived classes from `equality_comparable` need to comply with that requirement. The class `equality_comparable` equips T with `bool operator!=(const T&,const T&)`.

addable

The `addable` concept requires the following semantics for a type T.

```
T operator+(const T&,const T&);
T operator+=(const T&);
```

When deriving from `boost::addable`, the derived class (T) must provide the equivalent of

```
T operator+=(const T&);
```

The return type must be implicitly convertible to T. The class `addable` equips T with `T operator+(const T&,const T&)`.

subtractable

The `subtractable` concept requires the following semantics for a type T.

```
T operator-(const T&,const T&);
T operator+=(const T&);
```

When deriving from `boost::subtractable`, the derived class (T) must provide the equivalent of

```
T operator-=(const T&,const T&);
```

The return type must be implicitly convertible to T. The class `subtractable` equips T with `T operator-(const T&,const T&)`.

orable

The `orable` concept requires the following semantics for a type `T`.

```
T operator|(const T&,const T&);
T operator|=(const T&,const T&);
```

When deriving from `boost::orable`, the derived class (`T`) must provide the equivalent of

```
T operator|=(const T&,const T&);
```

The return type must be implicitly convertible to `T`. The class `orable` equips `T` with `T operator|(const T&,const T&)`.

andable

The `andable` concept requires the following semantics for a type `T`.

```
T operator&(const T&,const T&);
T operator&=(const T&,const T&);
```

When deriving from `boost::andable`, the derived class (`T`) must provide the equivalent of

```
T operator&=(const T&,const T&);
```

The return type must be implicitly convertible to `T`. The class `andable` equips `T` with `T operator&(const T&,const T&)`.

incrementable

The `incrementable` concept requires the following semantics for a type `T`.

```
T& operator++(T&);
T operator++(T&,int);
```

When deriving from `boost::incrementable`, the derived class (`T`) must provide the equivalent of

```
T& operator++(T&);
```

The return type must be implicitly convertible to T. The class `incrementable` equips T with `T operator++(T&,int)`.

decrementable

The `decrementable` concept requires the following semantics for a type T.

```
T& operator--(T&);
T operator--(T&,int);
```

When deriving from `boost::decrementable`, the derived class (T) must provide the equivalent of

```
T& operator--(T&);
```

The return type must be implicitly convertible to T. The class `decrementable` equips T with `T operator--(T&,int)`.

equivalent

The `equivalent` concept requires the following semantics for a type T.

```
bool operator<(const T&,const T&);
bool operator==(const T&,const T&);
```

When deriving from `boost::equivalent`, the derived class (T) must provide the equivalent of

```
bool operator<(const T&,const T&);
```

The return type must be implicitly convertible to `bool`. The class `equivalent` equips T with `T operator==(const T&,const T&)`. Note that equivalence and equality are, by definition, different beasts; two objects that are *equivalent* aren't necessarily *equal*. However, for the purposes of the `equivalent` concept, they are the same.

Dereferencing Operators

Especially useful for iterators, these two concepts, `dereferenceable` and `indexable`, cover two cases of dereferencing: `*t`, where t is an iterator that supports dereferencing (and all iterators obviously do), and indexing, `t[x]`, where t is a type that supports indexing through the subscript operator, and x is of an integral type. These two are used together with a higher-level abstraction, grouped iterator operators, which builds on both these dereferencing operators and the simple arithmetic operators.

dereferenceable

The `dereferenceable` concept requires the following semantics for a type T, assuming that T is the operand, R is the reference type, and P is a pointer type (for example, T is an iterator type, R is a reference to the iterator's `value_type`, and P is a pointer to the iterator's `value_type`).

```
P operator->() const;
R operator*() const;
```

When deriving from `boost::dereferenceable`, the derived class (T) must provide the equivalent of

```
R operator*() const;
```

Additionally, the unary `operator&` for R must be implicitly convertible to P. This means that R doesn't actually need to be the reference type—it can just as well be a proxy class. The class `dereferenceable` equips T with
`P operator->() const`.

indexable

The `indexable` concept requires the following semantics for a type T, assuming that T is the operand, R is the reference type, P is a pointer type, and D is the `difference_type` (for example, T is an iterator type, R is a reference to the iterator's `value_type`, P is a pointer to the iterator's `value_type`, and D is the `difference_type`).

```
R operator[](D) const;
R operator+(const T&,D);
```

When deriving from `boost::indexable`, the derived class (T) must provide the equivalent of

```
R operator+(const T&,D);
```

The class `indexable` equips T with `R operator[](D) const`.

Composite Arithmetic Operators

The concepts we've seen thus far represent primitive functionality. However, there are higher level, or composite, concepts that combine several primitive concepts or even add a primitive concept to another composite concept. For example, a class is `totally_ordered` if it is both `less_than_comparable` and `equality_comparable`. These groups are useful both because they reduce the amount of code that needs to be written and that they explicitly name important, commonly used concepts. Because they merely represent the combination of concepts already covered, these composite concepts are most easily represented in a table showing the primitive concepts on which they are built. For example, if a class inherits from `totally_ordered`, it must implement the operators required for `less_than_comparable` (`bool operator<(const T&, const T&)`) and for `equality_comparable` (`bool operator==(const T&, const T&)`).

Composite Concept	Constituent Concepts
totally_ordered	less_than_comparable equality_comparable
additive	addable subtractable
multiplicative	multipliable dividable
integer_multiplicative	multiplicative modable
arithmetic	additive multiplicative
integer_arithmetic	additive integer_multiplicative
bitwise	andable orable xorable
unit_steppable	incrementable decrementable
shiftable	left_shiftable right_shiftable
ring_operators	additive multipliable

Composite Concept	Constituent Concepts
ordered_ring_operators	ring_operators totally_ordered
field_operators	ring_operators dividable
ordered_field_operators	field_operators totally_ordered
euclidian_ring_operators	ring_operators dividable modable
ordered_ euclidian_ring_operators	euclidean_ring_operators totally_ordered

Usage

To start using the Operators library, implement the applicable operator(s) for your class, include `"boost/operators.hpp"`, and derive from one or more of the Operator base classes (they have the same names as the concepts they help implement), which all reside in namespace `boost`. Note that the inheritance doesn't have to be public; private inheritance works just as well. In this usage section, we look at several examples of using the different concepts, and also take a good look at how arithmetic and relational operators work, both in C++ and conceptually. For the first example of usage, we'll define a class, `some_class`, with an `operator<`. We decide that the equivalence relation implied by `operator<` should be made available through `operator==`. This can be accomplished by inheriting from `boost::equivalent`.

```
#include <iostream>
#include "boost/operators.hpp"

class some_class : boost::equivalent<some_class> {
  int value_;
public:
  some_class(int value) : value_(value) {}

  bool less_than(const some_class& other) const {
    return value_<other.value_;
  }
};
```

```
bool operator<(const some_class& lhs, const some_class& rhs) {
  return lhs.less_than(rhs);
}

int main() {
  some_class s1(12);
  some_class s2(11);

  if (s1==s2)
    std::cout << "s1==s2\n";
  else
    std::cout << "s1!=s2\n";
}
```

The `operator<` is implemented in terms of the member function `less_than`. The requirement for the `equivalent` base class is that `operator<` be present for the class in question. When deriving from `equivalent`, we pass the derived class—that is, `some_class`—as a template parameter. In `main`, the `operator==` that is graciously implemented for us by the Operators library is used. Next, we'll take a look at `operator<` again, and see what other relations can be expressed in terms of *less than*.

Supporting Comparison Operators

A relational operator that we commonly implement is less than—that is, `operator<`. We do so to support storage in associative containers and sorting. However, it is exceedingly common to supply *only* that operator, which can be confusing to users of the class. For example, most people know that negating the result of `operator<` yields `operator>=`.[1] Less than can also be used to calculate greater than, and so on. So, clients of a class supporting the less than relation have good cause for expecting that the operators that must also (at least implicitly) be supported are also part of the class interface. Alas, if we just add the support for `operator<` and omit the others, the class isn't as usable as it could, and should, be. Here's a class that's been made compliant with the sorting routines of the Standard Library containers.

```
class thing {
  std::string name_;
public:
```

---

1. Although too many seem to think that it yields `operator>`!

```
thing() {}
explicit thing(const std::string& name):name_(name) {}

friend bool operator<(const thing& lhs, const thing& rhs) {
  return lhs.name_<rhs.name_;
  }
};
```

This class supports sorting, and it can be stored in associative containers, but it may not meet the expectations of the client! For example, if a client needs to know whether `thing` a is greater than `thing` b, the client might write code like this:

```
// is a greater than b?
if (b<a) {}
```

Although this is just as correct, it doesn't convey the intent of the code clearly, which is almost as important as the correctness. If the client needs to know whether a is less than or equal to b, he would have to do this:

```
// is a less than, or equal to, b?
if (!(b<a)) {}
```

Again, the code is quite correct, but it will confuse people; the intent is certainly unclear to most casual readers. It becomes even more confusing when introducing the notion of equivalence, which we support (otherwise our class couldn't be stored in associative containers).

```
// is a equivalent to b?
if (!(a<b) && !(b<a)) {}
```

Please note that equivalence is a different relation than equality, a topic which is expanded upon in a later section. All of the aforementioned relational properties are typically expressed differently in C++, namely through the operators that explicitly perform the tests. The preceding examples should look like this (perhaps with the exception of equivalence, but we'll let it pass for now):

```
if (a>b) {}
if (a<=b) {}
if (a==b) {}
```

The comments are now redundant, because the code says it all. As is, this code doesn't compile, because the `thing` class doesn't support `operator>`, `operator<=`, or `operator==`. But, as these operators (except `operator==`) can always be expressed for types that implement the `less_than_comparable` concept, the Operators library can help us out. All we need to do is to have `thing` derive from `boost::less_than_comparable`, like so:

```
class thing : boost::less_than_comparable<thing> {
```

This gives you all the operators that can be implemented in terms of `operator<`, and so, by just specifying a base class, the `thing` class now works as one would expect it to. As you can see, when deriving `thing` from a class in the Operators library, we must also pass `thing` as a template parameter to that base class. This technique is discussed in the following section. Note that `operator==` is not defined for classes supporting `less_than_comparable`, but there is another concept that we can use for that one, namely `equivalent`. Deriving from `boost::equivalent` adds `operator==`, but it should be duly noted that `operator==` is now defined in terms of an *equivalence relation*, which in turn does *not* define equality. Equivalence implies a strict weak ordering.[2] Our final version of the class `thing` looks like this:

```
class thing :
  boost::less_than_comparable<thing>,
  boost::equivalent<thing> {

  std::string name_;
public:
  thing() {}
  explicit thing(const std::string& name):name_(name) {}

  friend bool operator<(const thing& lhs,const thing& rhs) {
    return lhs.name_<rhs.name_;
  }
};
```

This version only defines a single operator in `thing`'s definition, which keeps the definition concise, and by virtue of the inheritance from `less_than_comparable` and `equivalent`, it provides quite an impressive set of useful operators.

---

2. If you're wondering what a strict weak ordering is, skip ahead to the next section, but don't forget to return here later!

```
bool operator<(const thing&,const thing&);
bool operator>(const thing&,const thing&);
bool operator<=(const thing&,const thing&);
bool operator>=(const thing&,const thing&);
bool operator==(const thing&,const thing&);
```

I'm sure you've seen many classes that provide a multitude of operators. Such class definitions can be difficult to read because there are so many operator functions declared/implemented. By inheriting from the concept classes in `operators`, you provide the same interface but do so more clearly and with much less code. Mentioning these concepts in the class definition makes it obvious for a reader familiar with `less_than_comparable` and `equivalent` that the class supports the aforementioned relational operations.

The Barton-Nackman Trick

In the two examples we've seen of inheriting from operator base classes, a strange-looking construct feeds the derived class to its base class. This is a well-known technique that is referred to as either the Barton-Nackmann trick[3] or the Curiously Recurring Template Pattern.[4] The problem that this technique solves is that of a cyclic dependency. Consider implementing a generic class that provides `operator==` for other classes that define `operator<`. Incidentally, this is a concept known as `equivalent` in this library (and mathematics, of course). Now, it is clear that any class utilizing an implementation providing such services needs to know about the enabling class—let's call it `equivalent` after the concept it helps implement. However, it's just as clear that `equivalent` needs to know about the class for which it should define `operator==`! This is a cyclic dependency, and at first glance, there's no easy way out. However, if we make `equivalent` a class template, and add a template parameter that designates the class for which to define `operator==`, we have effectively injected the dependent type—which is the derived class—into the scope of `equivalent`. This example demonstrates the use of this idea.

```
#include <iostream>

template <typename Derived> class equivalent {
```

---

3. "Invented" by John Barton and Lee Nackmann.

4. "Invented" by James Coplien.

```
public:
  friend bool operator==(const Derived& lhs,const Derived& rhs) {
    return !(lhs<rhs) && !(rhs<lhs);
  }
};

class some_class : equivalent<some_class> {
  int value_;
public:
  some_class(int value) : value_(value) {}
  friend bool operator<(const some_class& lhs,
    const some_class& rhs) {
    return lhs.value_<rhs.value_;
  }
};

int main() {
  some_class s1(4);
  some_class s2(4);

  if (s1==s2)
    std::cout << "s1==s2\n";
}
```

The base class—equivalent—accepts a template argument that is the type for which it defines operator==. It implements this operator in a generic fashion by using operator< for the parameterizing type. Then, the class some_class, wishing to utilize the services of equivalent, derives from it and passes itself as equivalent's template parameter. Therefore, the resulting operator== is defined for the type some_class, implemented in terms of some_class's operator<. That's all there is to the Barton-Nackmann trick. This is a simple yet immensely useful pattern, quite beautiful in its elegance.

Strict Weak Ordering

I have already mentioned *strict weak orderings* twice in this book, and if you're not familiar with what they are, this brief digression should help. A strict weak ordering is a relation between two objects. First, let's get a bit theoretical and then we can make it more concrete. For a function f(a,b) that implements a strict weak ordering, with a and b being two objects of the same type, we say that a and b are equivalent if f(a,b) is false and f(b,a) is false. This means that a does not precede b, and b does not precede a. We can thus consider them to be equivalent. Furthermore, f(a,a) must always yield false[5] and if f(a,b) is true, then f(b,a) must be false.[6] Also, if f(a,b) and f(b,c) is true, then so is f(a,c).[7] Finally, if f(a,b) is false and f(b,a) is false, and if f(b,c) is false and f(c,b) is false, then f(a,c) is false and f(c,a) is false.[8]

Applying the preceding to our previous example (with the class thing) can help clarify the theory. The less than comparison for things is implemented in terms of less than for std::string. This, in turn, is a lexicographical comparison. So, given a thing a containing the string "First," a thing b containing the string "Second," and a thing c containing the string "Third," let's assert the earlier definitions and axioms.

```cpp
#include <cassert>
#include <string>
#include "boost/operators.hpp"

// Definition of class thing omitted

int main() {
   thing a("First");
   thing b("Second");
   thing c("Third");

   // assert that a<b<c
   assert(a<b && a<c && !(b<a) && b<c && !(c<a) && !(c<b));

   // Equivalence
   thing x=a;
   assert(!(x<a) && !(a<x));

   // Irreflexivity
   assert(!(a<a));

   // Antisymmetry
   assert((a<b)==!(b<a));
```

---

5. This is irreflexivity.

6. This is antisymmetry.

7. This is transitivity.

8. This is transitivity of equivalence.

```
// Transitivity
assert(a<b && b<c && a<c);

// Transitivity of equivalence
thing y=x;
assert( (!(x<a) && !(a<x)) &&
   (!(y<x) && !(x<y)) &&
   (!(y<a) && !(a<y)));
}
```

Now, all of these `asserts` hold, because `std::string` implements a strict weak ordering.[9] Just as `operator<` should define a strict weak ordering, so should `operator>`. Later on, we'll look at a very concrete example of what happens when we fail to acknowledge the difference between equivalence (which is required for a strict weak ordering) and equality (which is not).

Avoid Object Bloating

In the previous example, our class derived from two base classes: `less_than_comparable<thing>` and `equivalent<thing>`. Depending on your compiler, you may pay a price for this multiple inheritance; `thing` may be much larger than it needs to be. The standard permits a compiler to use the *empty base optimization* to make a base class that contains no data members, no virtual functions, and no duplicated base classes, to take zero space in derived class objects, and most modern compilers perform that optimization. Unfortunately, using the Operators library often leads to inheriting from multiple classes and few compilers apply the empty base optimization in that case. To avoid the potential object size bloating, Operators supports a technique known as *base class chaining*. Every operator class accepts an optional, additional template parameter, from which it derives. By having one concept class derive from another, which derives from another, which derives from another...(you get the idea), the multiple inheritance is eliminated. This alternative is easy to use. Rather than inheriting from several base classes, simply chain the classes together, like so.

---

9. In fact, `std::string` defines a total ordering, which is a strict weak ordering with the additional requirement that equivalence and equality are identical.

```
// Before
boost::less_than_comparable<thing>,boost::equivalent<thing>
// After
boost::less_than_comparable<thing,boost::equivalent<thing> >
```

This method removes the inheritance from multiple empty base classes, which may not trigger your compiler's empty base optimization, in favor of derivation from a chain of empty base classes, increasing the chance of triggering the empty base optimization and reducing the size of the derived classes. Experiment with your compiler to see what benefits you can gain from this technique. Note that there is a limit to the length of the base class chain that depends upon the compiler. There's also a limit to the length of the chain a human can grok! That means that classes that need to derive from many operator classes may need to group them. Better yet, use the composite concepts already provided by the Operators library.

The difference in size between using base class chaining and multiple inheritance on a popular compiler[10] that doesn't perform the empty base class optimization for multiple inheritance is quite large for my tests. Using base class chaining ensures that the size of types is not negatively affected, whereas with multiple inheritance, the size grows by 8 bytes for a trivial type (admittedly, 8 additional bytes isn't typically a problem for most applications). If the size of the wrapped type is very small, the overhead caused by multiple inheritance is potentially more than is tolerable. Because it is so easy, consider using base class chaining all the time!

Operators and Different Types

Sometimes, an operator involves more than one type. For example, consider a string class that supports concatenation from character arrays through `operator+` and `operator+=`. The Operators library helps here too, by way of the two-argument versions of the operator templates. In the case of the string class, there is probably a conversion constructor available that accepts a `char*`, but as we shall see, that doesn't solve all of the problems for this class. Here's the string class that we'll use.

---

10. I say this both because there's no need for calling names, and because everyone already knows that I'm talking about Microsoft's old compiler (their new one rocks).

```
class simple_string {
public:
  simple_string();

  explicit simple_string(const char* s);
  simple_string(const simple_string& s);

  ~simple_string();

  simple_string& operator=(const simple_string& s);

  simple_string& operator+=(const simple_string& s);
  simple_string& operator+=(const char* s);

  friend std::ostream&
    operator<<(std::ostream& os,const simple_string& s);
};
```

As you can see, we've already added two versions of `operator+=` for
`simple_string`. One accepts a `const simple_string&`, and the other accepts
a `const char*`. As is, our class supports usage like this.

```
simple_string s1("Hello there");
simple_string s2(", do you like the concatenation support?");
s1+=s2;
s1+=" This works, too";
```

Although the preceding works as intended, we still haven't provided the binary
`operator+`, an omission that the class' users definitely won't be pleased with.
Note that for our `simple_string`, we could have opted to enable concatenation
by omitting the explicit conversion constructor. However, doing so would involve
an extra (unnecessary) copy of the character buffer, and the only savings would
be the omission of an operator.

```
// This won't compile
simple_string s3=s1+s2;
simple_string s4=s3+" Why does this class behave so strangely?";
```

Now let's use the Operators library to supply the missing operators for the class.
Note that there are actually three missing operators.

```
simple_string operator+(const simple_string&,const simple_string&);
simple_string operator+(const simple_string& lhs, const char* rhs);
simple_string operator+(const char* lhs, const simple_string& rhs);
```

When defining operators manually, it's easy to forget one of the overloads for taking one `const simple_string&` and one `const char*`. When using the Operators library, you can't forget, because the library is implementing the missing operators for you! What we want for `simple_string` is the *addable* concept, so we simply derive `simple_string` from `boost::addable<simple_string>`.

```
class simple_string : boost::addable<simple_string> {
```

In this case, however, we also want the operators that allow mixing `simple_strings` and `const char*s`. To do this, we must specify two types—the result type, `simple_string`, and the second argument type, `const char*`. We'll utilize base class chaining to avoid increasing the size of the class.

```
class simple_string :
  boost::addable<simple_string,
    boost::addable2<simple_string,const char*> > {
```

This is all that's needed for supporting the full set of operators that we aimed for! As you can see, we used a different operator class: `addable2`. If you're using a compiler that supports partial template specialization, you don't have to qualify the name; use `addable` instead of `addable2`. There are also versions of the classes with the suffix "1" provided for symmetry. It may increase the readability to always be explicit about the number of arguments, which gives us the following derivation for `simple_string`.

```
class simple_string :
  boost::addable1<simple_string,
    boost::addable2<simple_string,const char*> > {
```

Choose between them according to taste, and if your compiler supports partial template specialization, the simplest choice is to omit the suffixes altogether.

```
class simple_string :
  boost::addable<simple_string,
    boost::addable<simple_string,const char*> > {
```

The Difference Between Equality and Equivalence

When defining relational operators for classes, it's important to make the distinction between equality and equivalence. An equivalence relation is required in order to use the associative containers, and it defines a strict weak ordering through the concept *LessThanComparable*.[11] This relation makes the least assumptions, and poses as few requirements as possible, for types that are to be used with the Standard Library containers. However, the difference between equality and equivalence can sometimes be confusing, and it is important to understand the difference. When a class supports the concept *LessThanComparable*, it typically also supports the notion of equivalence. If two elements are compared, and neither is less than the other, we can consider them to be equivalent. However, equivalence doesn't necessarily mean equal. For example, it may be reasonable to omit certain characteristics from a less than relation, but consider them for equality.[12] To illustrate this, let's look at a class, `animal`, which supports both an equivalence relation and an equality relation.

```
class animal : boost::less_than_comparable<animal,
boost::equality_comparable<animal> > {
  std::string name_;
  int age_;
public:
  animal(const std::string& name,int age)
    :name_(name),age_(age) {}

  void print() const {
    std::cout << name_ << " with the age " << age_ << '\n';
  }

  friend bool operator<(const animal& lhs, const animal& rhs) {
    return lhs.name_<rhs.name_;
  }

  friend bool operator==(const animal& lhs, const animal& rhs) {
    return lhs.name_==rhs.name_ && lhs.age_==rhs.age_;
  }

};
```

Notice the difference between the implementation of `operator<` and that of `operator==`. Only the animal's name is part of the less than relation, whereas

---

11. Capitalized concepts like *LessThanComparable* come straight from the C++ Standard. All of the concepts in Boost.Operators use lowercase names.

12. Which implies a strict weak ordering, but not a total ordering.

comparison of both the name and the age comprise the equality test. There is nothing wrong with this approach, but it can have interesting ramifications. Let's now put this class into action by storing some elements of the class in a `std::set`. Just like other associative containers, `set` only relies on the concept *LessThanComparable*. In the sample code that follows, we create four animals that are all different, and then try to insert them into a `set`, all while pretending we don't know that there is a difference between equality and equivalence.

```cpp
#include <iostream>
#include <string>
#include <set>
#include <algorithm>
#include "boost/operators.hpp"
#include "boost/bind.hpp"

int main() {
  animal a1("Monkey", 3);
  animal a2("Bear", 8);
  animal a3("Turtle", 56);
  animal a4("Monkey", 5);

  std::set<animal> s;
  s.insert(a1);
  s.insert(a2);
  s.insert(a3);
  s.insert(a4);

  std::cout << "Number of animals: " << s.size() << '\n';
  std::for_each(s.begin(),s.end(),boost::bind(&animal::print,_1));
  std::cout << '\n';

  std::set<animal>::iterator it(s.find(animal("Monkey",200)));
  if (it!=s.end()) {
    std::cout << "Amazingly, there's a 200 year old monkey "
      "in this set!\n";
    it->print();
  }

  it=std::find(s.begin(),s.end(),animal("Monkey",200));
  if (it==s.end()) {
    std::cout << "Of course there's no 200 year old monkey "
      "in this set!\n";
  }
}
```

Running the program produces the following, utterly nonsensical, output.

```
Number of animals: 3
Bear with the age 8
Monkey with the age 3
Turtle with the age 56

Amazingly, there's a 200 year old monkey in this set!
Monkey with the age 3
Of course there's no 200 year old monkey in this set!
```

The problem is not the age of the monkey—it very seldom is—but the failure to distinguish between two related concepts. First, when the four `animals` (`a1`, `a2`, `a3`, `a4`) are inserted into the `set`, the second monkey, `a4`, is actually not inserted at all, because `a1` and `a4` are *equivalent*. The reason is that `std::set` uses the expression `!(a1<a4) && !(a4<a1)` to decide whether there is already a matching element. Because the result of that expression is `true` (our `operator<` doesn't include the age), the insertion fails.[13] Then, when we ask the set to search for a 200 year old monkey using `find`, it supposedly locates such a beast. Again, this is because of the equivalence relation for `animal`, which relies on `animal`'s `operator<` and thus, doesn't care about age. We use `find` again to locate the monkey in the set (`a1`), but then, to decide whether it matches, we call on `operator==` and find that the monkeys *don't* match. It's not hard to understand the difference between equality and equivalence when looking at these monkeys, but it is imperative to know which one is applicable for a given context.

Arithmetic Types

The Operators library is especially useful when defining arithmetic types. There are many operators that must be defined for an arithmetic type, and doing it manually is a daunting, tedious task, with plenty of opportunity for errors or omissions. The concepts that are defined by the Operators library make it easy to define only the bare minimum of operators for a class, and have the rest supplied automagically. Consider a class that is to support addition and subtraction. Assume that this class uses a built-in type for its implementation. Now add the appropriate operators and be sure that they work with not only instances of that

---

13. A set, by definition, does not contain duplicates.

class, but also with the built-in types that are convertible to the implementation type. You'll need to provide 12 different addition and subtraction operators. The easier (and safer!) approach, of course, is to use the two-argument form of the `addable` and `subtractable` classes. Now suppose you need to add the set of relational operators, too. You could probably add the 10 operators needed yourself, but by now you know that the easiest thing is to use `less_than_comparable` and `equality_comparable`. Having done so, you'd have 22 operators for the cost of 6. However, you might also note that these concepts are common for value type classes. Indeed, instead of using those four classes, you could just use `additive` and `totally_ordered`.

We'll start by deriving from all four of the concept classes: `addable`, `subtractable`, `less_than_comparable`, and `equality_comparable`. The class, `limited_type`, just wraps a built-in type and forwards any operation to that type. It limits the number of available operations, providing just the relational operators and those for addition and subtraction.

```
#include "boost/operators.hpp"

template <typename T> class limited_type :
  boost::addable<limited_type<T>,
    boost::addable<limited_type<T>,T,
      boost::subtractable<limited_type<T>,
        boost::subtractable<limited_type<T>,T,
          boost::less_than_comparable<limited_type<T>,
            boost::less_than_comparable<limited_type<T>,T,
              boost::equality_comparable<limited_type<T>,
                boost::equality_comparable<limited_type<T>,T >
> > > > > > > {

  T t_;
public:
  limited_type():t_() {}
  limited_type(T t):t_(t) {}

  T get() {
    return t_;
  }

  // For less_than_comparable
  friend bool operator<(
      const limited_type<T>& lhs,
      const limited_type<T>& rhs) {
```

```
    return lhs.t_<rhs.t_;
  }

  // For equality_comparable
  friend bool operator==(
      const limited_type<T>& lhs,
      const limited_type<T>& rhs) {
    return lhs.t_==rhs.t_;
  }

  // For addable
  limited_type<T>& operator+=(const limited_type<T>& other) {
    t_+=other.t_;
    return *this;
  }

  // For subtractable
  limited_type<T>& operator-=(const limited_type<T>& other) {
    t_-=other.t_;
    return *this;
  }
};
```

This is a good example of how easy the implementation becomes when using the Operators library. Implementing the few operators that must be implemented to get support for the full set of operators is typically not that hard, and the class becomes much more understandable and maintainable than would otherwise have been the case. (Even if implementing those operators is hard, you can concentrate on getting just those few right.) The only potential problem with the class is the derivation from eight different operator classes which, when using base class chaining, is not as readable as one would like. We can greatly simplify our class by using composite concepts instead.

```
template <typename T> class limited_type :
  boost::additive<limited_type<T>,
    boost::additive<limited_type<T>,T,
      boost::totally_ordered<limited_type<T>,
        boost::totally_ordered<limited_type<T>,T > > > > {
```

This is much nicer, and it does save some typing, too.

Use Operators Only When Operators Should Be Used

It may seem really obvious that operators should be used only when appropriate, but for some reason there is a certain "coolness factor" about operators that seems to tempt some people to add them even when their semantics are unclear. There are many scenarios requiring operators, such as when there is a relation between instances of a type, or when creating an arithmetic type. But there are also less clear-cut cases, where one needs to consider the expectations of clients of the class, and where perceived ambiguity might make a member function a better choice.

Operators have been plied into unusual service over the years. Concatenating strings with addition operators and I/O with shift operators are two common examples where the operators do not necessarily have a mathematical meaning, but have been used for other semantic purposes. Some have questioned the use of the subscript operator for accessing elements in a `std::map`. (Others, of course, think it's perfectly natural. And they are right.) Sometimes, using operators for tasks other than their role with built-in types makes sense. Other times, it can go horribly wrong, causing confusion and ambiguities. When you choose to overload operators with meanings that deviate from those of the built-in types, you must do so carefully. You must ensure that the meaning is obvious and that the precedence is correct. That was the reason for choosing the shift operators for I/O in the IOStreams library. The operators clearly suggested moving something one direction or the other and the precedence of the shift operators put them lower than most others. If you create a class representing a car, some might find `operator-=` convenient. However, what might that operator mean to clients? Some might think it was used to account for gasoline used while driving. Others might think that it was used to account for depreciation of the car's value (an accountant, of course). Adding that operator is wrongheaded because it doesn't have a clear purpose, whereas a member function can name the operation providing clarity. Don't add operators just because it makes for "cool" coding. Add them because it makes sense, be sure to add all the operators that apply, and be sure to use the Boost.Operators library!

Understanding How It Works

We'll now take a look at how this library works, to further your understanding of how to use it properly. For Boost.Operators, it's not a hard thing to do. Let's see how to implement support for `less_than_comparable`. You need to know the type for which you'll add support, and you need to augment that type with operators that use one or more operators supplied for that type. less_than_ comparable requires that we provide operator<, operator>, operator<=, and operator>=. Of these, by now, you know how to implement operator>, operator<=, and operator>= in terms of operator<. Here's how one might implement it.

```
template <class T>
class less_than1
{
public:
   friend bool operator>(const T& lhs,const T& rhs)   {
      return rhs<lhs;
   }

   friend bool operator<=(const T& lhs,const T& rhs) {
      return !(rhs<lhs);
   }

   friend bool operator>=(const T& lhs,const T& rhs) {
      return !(lhs<rhs);
   }
};
```

For operator>, you just need to switch the order of the arguments. For operator<=, observe that a<=b means that b is not less than a. Thus, the implementation is to call operator< with the arguments in reverse order and negate the result. For operator>=, there's the similar observation that a>=b also means that a is not less than b. Thus, the implementation just negates the result of calling operator<. This is a working example: You could use it directly and it would do the right thing. However, it would be nice to also have a version that supports comparisons between T and compatible types, which is simply a case of adding more overloads. For symmetry, you need to allow either type to be on the left side of the operation. (This is easy to forget when adding operators manually; one tends to only see clearly the fact that the right side must accept the other type. Of course, your two-type version of less_than wouldn't make such silly mistakes, right?)

```
template <class T,class U>
class less_than2
{
public:
```

```
    friend bool operator<=(const T& lhs,const U& rhs) {
      return !(lhs>rhs);
    }

    friend bool operator>=(const T& lhs,const U& rhs) {
      return !(lhs<rhs);
    }

    friend bool operator>(const U& lhs,const T& rhs) {
      return rhs<lhs;
    }

    friend bool operator<(const U& lhs,const T& rhs)  {
      return rhs>lhs;
    }

    friend bool operator<=(const U& lhs,const T& rhs) {
      return !(rhs<lhs);
    }

    friend bool operator>=(const U& lhs,const T& rhs) {
      return !(rhs>lhs);
    }
};
```

There it is! Two fully functioning `less_than` classes. Of course, to match the functionality of `less_than_comparable` in the Operators library, we must somehow get rid of the suffix stating how many types are used. What we really want is *one* version, or at least one name. If you are working with a compiler that supports partial template specialization, you're in luck, because it's basically a three-liner to make this happen. But, there are still a number of programmers who don't have that luxury, so we'll do it the hard way, and avoid partial specialization altogether. First, we know that we need something called `less_than`, which is to be a template accepting one or two argument types. We also know that the second type should be optional, which we can accomplish by adding a default type that we know users won't pass to the template.

```
struct dummy {};
template <typename T,typename U=dummy> class less_than {};
```

We need some mechanism for selecting the correct version of `less_than` (`less_than1` or `less_than2`); we can do this without partial template specialization by using an auxiliary class that is parameterized on one type, with a nested template `struct` that accepts an additional type. Then, using full special-ization, we can make sure that whenever the type `U` is `dummy`, `less_than1` is selected.

```
template <typename T> struct selector {
  template <typename U> struct type {
    typedef less_than_2<U,T> value;
  };
};
```

The preceding version creates a type definition called `value`, which is a correct instantiation of the `less_than2` template that we've created.

```
template<> struct selector<dummy> {
  template <typename U> struct type {
    typedef less_than1<U> value;
  };
};
```

The fully specialized `selector` creates a `typedef` for the other version, `less_than1`. To make it easier for the compiler, we'll create another auxiliary class with the sole responsibility of collecting the correct type and storing it in the suitably named typedef `type`.

```
template <typename T,typename U> struct select_implementation {
  typedef typename selector<U>::template type<T>::value type;
};
```

The syntax is not so pleasing to the eye, because of the nested parameterized `struct` in the `selector` class, but as clients of this class don't have to read this part of the code, that's really not a big issue. Now that we have all the ingredi-ents that we need to select a correct implementation, we finalize the class by deriving `less_than` from `select_implementation<T,U>::type`, which evalu-ates to either `less_than1` or `less_than2`, depending on whether the user has supplied one or two types to our class.

```
template <typename T,typename U=dummy> class less_than :
  select_implementation<T,U>::type {};
```

That's it! We now have a fully working version of `less_than`, which users can use in the easiest possible way due to the extra effort we spent in adding a mechanism for detecting and selecting the correct version of the implementation. We also know exactly how `operator<` can be used to create the remaining operators that are applicable for any type that is `less_than_comparable`. Doing the same for the other operators is just a matter of being meticulous and understanding how different operators work together to form new concepts.

The Things That Remain

We haven't yet spoken about the remaining part of the Operators library, the iterator helpers. I won't show example code for those, because you'll mainly want to use them when defining iterator types, and that needs additional explanation that does not fit in this chapter or in this book. However, I mention them here because if you are defining iterator types without the help of Boost.Iterators, you most definitely want to use these helpers. The dereference operators help define the correct operators regardless of whether you are using a proxy class. They are also useful when defining smart pointers, which typically also require defining both `operator->` and `operator*`. The iterator helpers group together concepts that are required for the different types of iterators. For example, a random access iterator needs to be `bidirectional_iterable`, `totally_ordered`, `additive`, and `indexable`. When defining new iterator types, which should preferably be done with the help of the Boost.Iterator library, the Operators library can help.

Operators Summary

Providing the correct set of relational and arithmetic operators for user-defined classes is vital and provides significant challenges to get right. With the use of the Operators library, this task is greatly simplified, and correctness and symmetry come almost for free. In addition to the help that the library offers in defining the full sets of operators, the naming and definitions of the concepts that a class can support is made explicit in the definition of the class (and by the Operators library!). In this chapter, we have seen several examples of how using this library improves programming with operators by simplification and ensured correctness. It is a sad fact that providing important relational and arithmetic operators for user-defined types is often overlooked, and part of the reason is that there is so much work involved to get it right. This is no longer the case, and Boost.Operators is the reason why.

An important consideration when providing relational and arithmetic operators is to make sure that they are warranted in the first place. When there is an ordering relation between types, or for numeric types, this is always the case, but for other types of classes, operators may not convey intent clearly. Operators are almost always syntactic sugar, and the importance of syntactic sugar must never be underestimated. Unfortunately, operators are also seductive. Use them wisely, for they wield vast power. When you choose to add operators to a class, the Boost.Operators library increases the quality and efficiency of your work. The conclusion is that you should augment your classes with operators only after careful thought, and use the Operators library whenever you get the chance!

The Operators library is the result of contributions from several people. It was started by David Abrahams, and has since received valuable additions from Jeremy Siek, Aleksey Gurtovoy, Beman Dawes, and Daryle Walker. As is the case for most Boost libraries, innumerable other people have been involved in making this library what it is today.

Library 5
Regex

How Does the Regex Library Improve Your Programs?

- Brings support for regular expressions to C++

- Improves the robustness of input validation

Regular expressions are very often used in text processing. For example, there are a number of validation tasks that are suitable for regular expressions. Consider an application that requires the input to consist only of numbers. Another program might require a specific format, such as three digits, followed by a character, then two more digits. You could validate ZIP Codes, credit card numbers, Social Security numbers, or just about anything else; and using regular expressions to do the validation is straightforward. Another typical area where regular expressions excel are text substitutions—that is, replacing some text with other text. Suppose you need to change the spelling of the word *colour* to *color* throughout a number of documents. Again, regular expressions provide the best means to do that—including remembering to make the changes also for *Colour* and *COLOUR*, and for the plural form *colours*, the verb *colourize*, and so forth. Yet another use case for regular expressions is in formatting of text.

Many popular programming languages—Perl is a prime example—have built-in support for regular expressions, but that's not the case with C++. Also, the C++ Standard is silent when it comes to regexes. Boost.Regex is a very complete and effective library for incorporating regular expressions in C++ programs, and it even includes several different syntaxes that are used in widespread tools such as Perl, grep, and Emacs. It is one of the most renowned C++ libraries for working with regular expressions, and is both easy to use and incredibly powerful.

How Does Regex Fit with the Standard Library?

There is currently no support for regular expressions in the C++ Standard
Library. This is unfortunate, as there are numerous uses for regular expressions,
and users are sometimes deterred from using C++ for writing applications that
need support for regular expressions. Boost.Regex fills that void in the standard,
and it has been proposed for inclusion in a future version of the C++ Standard.
Boost.Regex has been accepted for the upcoming Library Technical Report.

Regex

Header: `"boost/regex.hpp"`

A regular expression is encapsulated in an object of type `basic_regex`. We will
look closer at the options for how regular expressions are compiled and parsed in
subsequent sections, but let's first take a cursory look at `basic_regex` and the
three important algorithms that are the bulk of this library.

```
namespace boost {
  template <class charT,
              class traits=regex_traits<charT> >
  class basic_regex {
  public:
    explicit basic_regex(
      const charT* p,
      flag_type f=regex_constants::normal);

    bool empty() const;

    unsigned mark_count() const;

    flag_type flags() const;
  };

  typedef basic_regex<char> regex;
  typedef basic_regex<wchar_t> wregex;
}
```

Members

```
explicit basic_regex (
  const charT* p,
  flag_type f=regex_constants::normal);
```

This constructor accepts a character sequence that contains the regular expression, and an argument denoting which options to use for the regular expression—for example, whether it should ignore case. If the regular expression in p isn't valid, an exception of type bad_expression, or regex_error, is thrown. Note that these two exceptions mean the same thing; at the time of this writing, the change from the current name bad_expression has not yet been made, but the next version of Boost.Regex will change it to regex_error.

```
bool empty() const;
```

This member is a predicate that returns true if the instance of basic_regex does not contain a valid regular expression—that is, it has been assigned an empty character sequence.

```
unsigned mark_count() const;
```

mark_count returns the number of marked subexpressions in the regex. A marked subexpression is a part of the regular expression enclosed within parentheses. The text that matches a subexpression can be retrieved after calling one of the regular expression algorithms.

```
flag_type flags() const;
```

Returns a bitmask containing the option flags that are set for this basic_regex. Examples of flags are icase, which means that the regular expression is ignoring case, and JavaScript, indicating that the syntax for the regex is the one used in JavaScript.

```
typedef basic_regex<char> regex;
typedef basic_regex<wchar_t> wregex;
```

Rather than declaring variables of type basic_regex, you'll typically use one of these two typedefs. These two, regex and wregex, are shorthands for the two character types, similar to how string and wstring are shorthands for `basic_string<char>` and `basic_string<wchar_t>`. This similarity is no coincidence, as a `regex` is, in a way, a container for a special type of string.

Free Functions

```
template <class charT,class Allocator,class traits >
  bool regex_match(
    const charT* str,
    match_results<const charT*,Allocator>& m,
    const basic_regex<charT,traits >& e,
    match_flag_type flags = match_default);
```

`regex_match` determines whether a regular expression (the argument `e`) matches the whole character sequence `str`. It is mainly used for validating text. Note that the regular expression must match everything in the parsed sequence, or the function returns `false`. If the sequence is successfully matched, `regex_match` returns `true`.

```
template <class charT,class Allocator, class traits>
  bool regex_search(
    const charT* str,
    match_results<const charT*,Allocator>& m,
    const basic_regex<charT,traits >& e,
    match_flag_type flags = match_default);
```

`regex_search` is similar to `regex_match`, but it does not require that the whole character sequence be matched for success. You use `regex_search` to find a subsequence of the input that matches the regular expression `e`.

```
template <class traits,class charT>
  basic_string<charT> regex_replace(
    const basic_string<charT>& s,
    const basic_regex<charT,traits >& e,
    const basic_string<charT>& fmt,
    match_flag_type flags = match_default);
```

`regex_replace` searches through a character sequence for all matches of the regular expression `e`. Every time the algorithm makes a successful match, it formats the matched string according to the argument `fmt`. By default, any text that is not matched is unchanged—that is, the text is part of the output but is not altered.

There are several overloads for all of these three algorithms: one accepting a `const charT*` (`charT` is the character type), another accepting a `const basic_string<charT>&`, and one overload that takes two bidirectional iterators as input arguments.

Usage

To begin using Boost.Regex, you need to include the header `"boost/regex.hpp"`. Regex is one of the two libraries (the other one is Boost.Signals) covered in this book that need to be separately compiled. You'll be glad to know that after you've built Boost—this is a one-liner from the command prompt—linking is automatic (for Windows-based compilers anyway), so you're relieved from the tedium of figuring out which lib file to use.

The first thing you need to do is to declare a variable of type `basic_regex`. This is one of the core classes in the library, and it's the one that stores the regular expression. Creating one is simple; just pass a string to the constructor containing the regular expression you want to use.

```
boost::regex reg("(A.*)");
```

This regular expression contains three interesting features of regular expressions. The first is the enclosing of a subexpression within parentheses—this makes it possible to refer to that subexpression later on in the same regular expression or to extract the text that matches it. We'll talk about this in detail later on, so don't worry if you don't yet see how that's useful. The second feature is the *wildcard* character, the dot. The wildcard has a very special meaning in regular expressions; it matches any character. Finally, the expression uses a repeat, `*`, called the Kleene star, which means that the preceding expression may match zero or more times. This regular expression is ready to be used in one of the algorithms, like so:

```
bool b=boost::regex_match(
  "This expression could match from A and beyond.",
  reg);
```

As you can see, you pass the regular expression and the string to be parsed to the algorithm `regex_match`. The result of calling the function is `true` if there is an exact match for the regular expression; otherwise, it is `false`. In this case, the result is `false`, because `regex_match` only returns `true` when all of the input data is successfully matched by the regular expression. Do you see why that's not the case for this code? Look again at the regular expression. The first character is a capital `A`, so that's obviously the first character that could ever match the expression. So, a part of the input—`"A and beyond."`—does match the expression, but it does not exhaust the input. Let's try another input string.

```
bool b=boost::regex_match(
  "As this string starts with A, does it match? ",
  reg);
```

This time, `regex_match` returns `true`. When the regular expression engine matches the `A`, it then goes on to see what should follow. In our regex, `A` is followed by the wildcard, to which we have applied the Kleene star, meaning that any character is matching any number of times. Thus, the parsing starts to consume the rest of the input string, and matches all the rest of the input.

Next, let's see how we can put regexes and `regex_match` to work with data validation.

Validating Input

A common scenario where regular expressions are used is in validating the format of input data. Applications often require that input adhere to a certain structure. Consider an application that accepts input that must come in the form "*3 digits, a word, any character, 2 digits or the string "N/A," a space, then the first word again.*" Coding such validations manually is both tedious and error prone, and furthermore, these formats are typically exposed to changing requirements; before you know it, some variation of the format needs to be supported, and your carefully crafted parser suddenly needs to be changed and debugged. Let's assemble a regular expression that can validate such input correctly. First, we need an expression that matches exactly 3 digits. There's a special shortcut for digits, `\d`, that we'll use. To have it repeated 3 times, there's a special kind of repeat called the *bounds operator*, which encloses the bounds in curly braces. Putting these two together, here's the first part of our regular expression.

```
boost::regex reg("\\d{3}");
```

Note that we need to escape the escape character, so the shortcut `\d` becomes `\\d` in our string. This is because the compiler consumes the first backslash as an escape character; we need to escape the backslash so a backslash actually appears in the regular expression string.

Next, we need a way to define a word—that is, a sequence of characters, ended by any character that is not a letter. There is more than one way of accomplishing this, but we will do it using the regular expression features character classes (also called character sets) and ranges. A character class is an expression enclosed in square brackets. For example, a character class that matches any one of the characters a, b, and c, looks like this: [abc]. Using a range to accomplish the same thing, we write it like so: [a-c]. For a character class that encompasses all characters, we could go slightly crazy and write it like [abcdefghijklmnopqrstuvwxyzABCDEFGHIJKLMNOPQRSTUVWXYZ], but we won't; we'll use ranges instead: [a-zA-Z]. It should be noted that using ranges like this can make one dependent on the locale that is currently in use, if the basic_regex::collate flag is turned on for the regular expression. Using these tools and the repeat +, which means that the preceding expression can be repeated, but must exist at least once, we're now ready to describe a word.

```
boost::regex reg("[a-zA-Z]+");
```

That regular expression works, but because it is so common, there is an even simpler way to represent a word: \w. That operator matches all word characters, not just the ASCII ones, so not only is it shorter, it is better for internationalization purposes. The next character should be exactly one of *any character*, which we know is the purpose of the dot.

```
boost::regex reg(".");
```

The next part of the input is *2 digits or the string "N/A."* To match that, we need to use a feature called *alternatives*. Alternatives match one of two or more subexpressions, with each alternative separated from the others by |. Here's how it looks:

```
boost::regex reg("(\\d{2}|N/A)");
```

Note that the expression is enclosed in parentheses, to make sure that the full expressions are considered as the two alternatives. Adding a space to the regular expression is simple; there's a shortcut for it: \s. Putting together everything we have so far gives us the following expression:

```
boost::regex reg("\\d{3}[a-zA-Z]+.(\\d{2}|N/A)\\s");
```

Now things get a little trickier. We need a way to validate that the next word in the input data exactly matches the first word (the one we capture using the expression [a-zA-Z]+). The key to accomplish this is to use a *back reference*, which is a reference to a previous subexpression. For us to be able to refer to the expression [a-zA-Z]+, we must first enclose it in parentheses. That makes the expression ([a-zA-Z]+) the first subexpression in our regular expression, and we can therefore create a back reference to it using the index 1.

That gives us the full regular expression for *"3 digits, a word, any character, 2 digits or the string "N/A," a space, then the first word again"*:

```
boost::regex reg("\\d{3}([a-zA-Z]+).(\\d{2}|N/A)\\s\\1");
```

Good work! Here's a simple program that makes use of the expression with the algorithm regex_match, validating two sample input strings.

```
#include <iostream>
#include <cassert>
#include <string>
#include "boost/regex.hpp"

int main() {
  // 3 digits, a word, any character, 2 digits or "N/A",
  // a space, then the first word again
  boost::regex reg("\\d{3}([a-zA-Z]+).(\\d{2}|N/A)\\s\\1");

  std::string correct="123Hello N/A Hello";
  std::string incorrect="123Hello 12 hello";

  assert(boost::regex_match(correct,reg)==true);
  assert(boost::regex_match(incorrect,reg)==false);
}
```

The first string, 123Hello N/A Hello, is correct; 123 is 3 digits, followed by any character (a space), Hello is a word, then another space, and finally the word Hello is repeated. The second string is incorrect, because the word Hello is not repeated exactly. By default, regular expressions are case-sensitive, and the back reference therefore does not match.

One of the keys in crafting regular expressions is successfully decomposing the problem. When looking at the final expression that you just created, it can seem quite intimidating to the untrained eye. However, when decomposing the expression into smaller components, it's not very complicated at all.

Searching

We shall now take a look at another of Boost.Regex's algorithms, `regex_search`. The difference from `regex_match` is that `regex_search` does not require that all of the input data matches, but only that part of it does. For this exposition, consider the problem of a programmer who expects to have forgotten one or two calls to `delete` in his program. Although he realizes that it's by no means a foolproof test, he decides to count the number of occurrences of *new* and *delete* and see if the numbers add up. The regular expression is very simple; we have two alternatives, new and delete.

```
boost::regex reg("(new)|(delete)");
```

There are two reasons for us to enclose the subexpressions in parentheses: one is that we must do so in order to form the two groups for our alternatives. The other reason is that we will want to refer to these subexpressions when calling `regex_search`, to enable us to determine which of the alternatives was actually matched. We will use an overload of `regex_search` that also accepts an argument of type `match_results`. When `regex_search` performs its matching, it reports subexpression matches through an object of type `match_results`. The class template `match_results` is parameterized on the type of iterator that applies to the input sequence.

```
template <class Iterator,
    class Allocator=std::allocator<sub_match<Iterator> >
    class match_results;

typedef match_results<const char*> cmatch;
typedef match_results<const wchar_t> wcmatch;
typedef match_results<std::string::const_iterator> smatch;
typedef match_results<std::wstring::const_iterator> wsmatch;
```

We will use `std::string`, and are therefore interested in the `typedef smatch`, which is short for `match_results<std::string::const_iterator>`. When `regex_search` returns `true`, the reference to `match_results` that is passed to the function contains the results of the subexpression matches. Within `match_results`, there are indexed `sub_matches` for each of the subexpressions in the regular expression. Let's see what we have so far that can help our confused programmer assess the calls to `new` and `delete`.

```
boost::regex reg("(new)|(delete)");
boost::smatch m;
std::string s=
  "Calls to new must be followed by delete. \
  Calling simply new results in a leak!";

if (boost::regex_search(s,m,reg)) {
  // Did new match?
  if (m[1].matched)
    std::cout << "The expression (new) matched!\n";
  if (m[2].matched)
    std::cout << "The expression (delete) matched!\n";
}
```

The preceding program searches the input string for new or delete, and reports which one it finds first. By passing an object of type smatch to regex_search, we gain access to the details of *how* the algorithm succeeded. In our expression, there are two subexpressions, and we can thus get to the subexpression for new by the index 1 of match_results. We then hold an instance of sub_match, which contains a Boolean member, matched, that tells us whether the subexpression participated in the match. So, given the preceding input, running this code would output "The expression (new) matched!\n". Now, you still have some more work to do. You need to continue applying the regular expression to the remainder of the input, and to do that, you use another overload of regex_search, which accepts two iterators denoting the character sequence to search. Because std::string is a container, it provides iterators. Now, for each match, you must update the iterator denoting the beginning of the range to refer to the end of the previous match. Finally, add two variables to hold the counts for new and delete. Here's the complete program:

```
#include <iostream>
#include <string>
#include "boost/regex.hpp"

int main() {
  // Are there equally many occurrences of
  // "new" and "delete"?
  boost::regex reg("(new)|(delete)");
  boost::smatch m;
  std::string s=
    "Calls to new must be followed by delete. \
    Calling simply new results in a leak!";
```

```
int new_counter=0;
int delete_counter=0;
std::string::const_iterator it=s.begin();
std::string::const_iterator end=s.end();

while (boost::regex_search(it,end,m,reg)) {
  // New or delete?
  m[1].matched ? ++new_counter : ++delete_counter;
  it=m[0].second;
}

if (new_counter!=delete_counter)
  std::cout << "Leak detected!\n";
else
  std::cout << "Seems ok...\n";
}
```

Note that the program always sets the iterator `it` to `m[0].second`. `match_results[0]` returns a reference to the submatch that matched the whole regular expression, so we can be sure that the end of that match is always the correct location to start the next run of `regex_search`. Running this program outputs "Leak detected!", because there are two occurrences of `new`, and only one of `delete`. Of course, one variable could be deleted twice, there could be calls to `new[]` and `delete[]`, and so forth.

By now, you should have a good understanding of how subexpression grouping works. It's time to move on to the final algorithm in Boost.Regex, one that is used to perform substitutions.

Replacing

The third in the family of Regex algorithms is `regex_replace`. As the name implies, it's used to perform text substitutions. It searches through the input data, finding all matches to the regular expression. For each match of the expression, the algorithm calls `match_results::format` and outputs the result to an output iterator that is passed to the function.

In the introduction to this chapter, I gave you the example of changing the British spelling of *colour* to the U.S. spelling of *color*. Changing the spelling without using regular expressions is very tedious, and extremely error prone. The problem is that there might be different capitalization, and a lot of words that are affected—for example, colourize. To properly attack this problem, we need to split the regular expression into three subexpressions.

```
boost::regex reg("(Colo)(u)(r)",
  boost::regex::icase|boost::regex::perl);
```

We have isolated the villain—the letter u—in order to surgically remove it from any matches. Also note that this regex is case-insensitive, which we achieve by passing the format flag `boost::regex::icase` to the constructor of `regex`. Note that you must also pass any other flags that you want to be in effect. A common user error when setting format flags is to omit the ones that `regex` turns on by default, but that don't work—you must always apply all of the flags that should be set.

When calling `regex_replace`, we are expected to provide a format string as an argument. This format string determines how the substitution will work. In the format string, it's possible to refer to subexpression matches, and that's precisely what we need here. You want to keep the first matched subexpression, and the third, but let the second (u), silently disappear. The expression $N, where N is the index of a subexpression, expands to the match for that subexpression. So our format string becomes `"$1$3"`, which means that the replacement text is the result of the first and the third subexpressions. By referring to the subexpression matches, we are able to retain any capitalization in the matched text, which would not be possible if we were to use a string literal as the replacement text. Here's a complete program that solves the problem.

```
#include <iostream>
#include <string>
#include "boost/regex.hpp"

int main() {
  boost::regex reg("(Colo)(u)(r)",
    boost::regex::icase|boost::regex::perl);

  std::string s="Colour, colours, color, colourize";

  s=boost::regex_replace(s,reg,"$1$3");
  std::cout << s;
}
```

The output of running this program is "`Color, colors, color, colorize`". `regex_replace` is enormously useful for applying substitutions like this.

A Common User Misunderstanding

One of the most common questions that I see related to Boost.Regex is related to the semantics of `regex_match`. It's easy to forget that all of the input to `regex_match` must match the regular expression. Thus, users often think that code like the following should yield `true`.

```
boost::regex reg("\\d*");
bool b=boost::regex_match("17 is prime",reg);
```

Rest assured that this call never results in a successful match. All of the input must be consumed for `regex_match` to return `true`! Almost all of the users asking why this doesn't work should use `regex_search` rather than `regex_match`.

```
boost::regex reg("\\d*");
bool b=boost::regex_search("17 is prime",reg);
```

This most definitely yields `true`. It is worth noting that it's possible to make `regex_search` behave like `regex_match`, using special buffer operators. `\A` matches the start of a buffer, and `\z` matches the end of a buffer, so if you put `\A` first in your regular expression, and `\z` last, you'll make `regex_search` behave exactly like `regex_match`—that is, it must consume all input for a successful match. The following regular expression always requires that the input be exhausted, regardless of whether you are using `regex_match` or `regex_search`.

```
boost::regex reg("\\A\\d*\\Z");
```

Please understand that this does not imply that `regex_match` should not be used; on the contrary, it should be a clear indication that the semantics we just talked about—that all of the input must be consumed—are in effect.

About Repeats and Greed

Another common source of confusion is the greediness of repeats. Some of the repeats—for example, + and *—are *greedy*. This means that they will consume as much of the input as they possibly can. It's not uncommon to see regular expressions such as the following, with the intent of capturing a digit after a greedy repeat is applied.

```
boost::regex reg("(.*)(\\d{2})");
```

This regular expression succeeds, but it might not match the subexpressions that you think it should! The expression .* happily eats everything that following subexpressions don't match. Here's a sample program that exhibits this behavior:

```
int main() {
  boost::regex reg("(.*)(\\d{2})");
  boost::cmatch m;
  const char* text = "Note that I'm 31 years old, not 32.";
  if(boost::regex_search(text,m, reg)) {
    if (m[1].matched)
      std::cout << "(.*) matched: " << m[1].str() << '\n';
    if (m[2].matched)
      std::cout << "Found the age: " << m[2] << '\n';
  }
}
```

In this program, we are using another parameterization of match_results, through the type cmatch. It is a typedef for match_results<const char*>, and the reason we must use it rather than the type smatch we've been using before is that we're now calling regex_search with a string literal rather than an object of type std::string. What do you expect the output of running this program to be? Typically, users new to regular expressions first think that both m[1].matched and m[2].matched will be true, and that the result of the second subexpression will be "31". Next, after realizing the effects of greedy repeats—that they consume as much input as possible—they tend to think that only the first subexpression can be true—that is, the .* has successfully eaten *all* of the input. Finally, new users come to the conclusion that the expression will match both subexpressions, but that the second expression will match the *last* possible sequence. Here, that means that the first subexpression will match "Note that I'm 31 years old, not" and the second will match "32".

So, what do you do when you actually want is to use a repeat and the *first* occurrence of another subexpression? Use non-greedy repeats. By appending ? to the repeat, it becomes non-greedy. This means that the expression tries to find the *shortest* possible match that doesn't prevent the rest of the expression from matching. So, to make the previous regex work correctly, we need to update it like so.

```
boost::regex reg("(.*?)(\\d{2})");
```

If we change the program to use this regular expression, both `m[1].matched` and `m[2].matched` will still be `true`. The expression `.*?` consumes as little of the input as it can, which means that it stops at the *first* character 3, because that's what the expression needs in order to successfully match. Thus, the first subexpression matches "`Note that I'm`" and the second matches "`31`".

A Look at *regex_iterator*

We have seen how to use several calls to `regex_search` in order to process all of an input sequence, but there's another, more elegant way of doing that, using a `regex_iterator`. This iterator type enumerates all of the regular expression matches in a sequence. Dereferencing a `regex_iterator` yields a reference to an instance of `match_results`. When constructing a `regex_iterator`, you pass to it the iterators denoting the input sequence, and the regular expression to apply. Let's look at an example where we have input data that is a comma-separated list of integers. The regular expression is simple.

```
boost::regex reg("(\\d+),?");
```

Adding the repeat `?` (match zero or one times) to the end of the regular expression ensures that the last digit will be successfully parsed, even if the input sequence does not end with a comma. Further, we are using another repeat, `+`. This repeat ensures that the expression matches one or more times. Now, rather than doing multiple calls to `regex_search`, we create a `regex_iterator`, call the algorithm `for_each`, and supply it with a function object to call with the result of dereferencing the iterator. Here's a function object that accepts any form of `match_results` due to its parameterized function call operator. All work it performs is to add the value of the current match to a total (in our regular expression, the first subexpression is the one we're interested in).

```
class regex_callback {
  int sum_;
public:
  regex_callback() : sum_(0) {}

  template <typename T> void operator()(const T& what) {
    sum_+=atoi(what[1].str().c_str());
  }
```

```
    int sum() const {
        return sum_;
    }
};
```

You now pass an instance of this function object to `std::for_each`, which results in an invocation of the function call operator for every dereference of the iterator `it`—that is, it is invoked every time there is a match of a subexpression in the regex.

```
int main() {
    boost::regex reg("(\\d+),?");
    std::string s="1,1,2,3,5,8,13,21";

    boost::sregex_iterator it(s.begin(),s.end(),reg);
    boost::sregex_iterator end;

    regex_callback c;
    int sum=for_each(it,end,c).sum();
}
```

As you can see, the past-the-end iterator passed to `for_each` is simply a default-constructed instance of `regex_iterator`. Also, the type of `it` and `end` is `boost::sregex_iterator`, which is a `typedef` for `regex_iterator<std::string::const_iterator>`. Using `regex_iterator` this way is a much cleaner way of matching multiple times than what we did previously, where we manually had to advance the starting iterator and call `regex_search` in a loop.

Splitting Strings with *regex_token_iterator*

Another iterator type, or to be more precise, an iterator adaptor, is `boost::regex_token_iterator`. It is similar to `regex_iterator`, but may also be employed to enumerate each character sequence that does not match the regular expression, which is useful for splitting strings. It is also possible to select which subexpressions are of interest, so that when dereferencing the `regex_token_iterator`, only the subexpressions that are "subscribed to" are returned. Consider an application that receives input data where the entries are separated using a forward slash. Anything in between constitutes an item that the application needs to process. With `regex_token_iterator`, splitting the strings is easy. The regular expression is very simple.

```
boost::regex reg("/");
```

The regex matches the separator of items. To use it for splitting the input, simply pass the special index -1 to the constructor of `regex_token_iterator`. Here is the complete program:

```
int main() {
  boost::regex reg("/");
  std::string s="Split/Values/Separated/By/Slashes,";
  std::vector<std::string> vec;
  boost::sregex_token_iterator it(s.begin(),s.end(),reg,-1);
  boost::sregex_token_iterator end;
  while (it!=end)
    vec.push_back(*it++);

  assert(vec.size()==std::count(s.begin(),s.end(),'/')+1);
  assert(vec[0]=="Split");
}
```

Similar to `regex_iterator`, `regex_token_iterator` is a template class parameterized on the iterator type for the sequence it wraps. Here, we're using `sregex_token_iterator`, which is a `typedef` for `regex_token_iterator` `<std::string::const_iterator>`. Each time the iterator `it` is dereferenced, it returns the current `sub_match`, and when the iterator is advanced, it tries to match the regular expression again. These two iterator types, `regex_iterator` and `regex_token_iterator`, are very useful; you'll know that you need them when you are considering to call `regex_search` multiple times!

More Regular Expressions

You have already seen quite a lot of regular expression syntax, but there's still more to know. This section quickly demonstrates the uses of some of the remaining functionality that is useful in your everyday regular expressions. To begin, we will look at the whole set of repeats; we've already looked at *, +, and bounded repeats using {}. There's one more repeat, and that's ?. You may have noted that it is also used to declare non-greedy repeats, but by itself, it means that the expression must occur zero or one times. It's also worth mentioning that the bounded repeats are very flexible; here are three different ways of using them:

```
boost::regex reg1("\\d{5}");
boost::regex reg2("\\d{2,4}");
boost::regex reg3("\\d{2,}");
```

The first regex matches exactly 5 digits. The second matches 2, 3, or 4 digits. The third matches 2 or more digits, without an upper limit.

Another important regular expression feature is to use negated character classes using the metacharacter ^. You use it to form character classes that match any character that is not part of the character class; the complement of the elements you list in the character class. For example, consider this regular expression.

```
boost::regex reg("[^13579]");
```

It contains a negated character class that matches any character that is not one of the odd numbers. Take a look at the following short program, and try to figure out what the output will be.

```
int main() {
  boost::regex reg4("[^13579]");
  std::string s="0123456789";
  boost::sregex_iterator it(s.begin(),s.end(),reg4);
  boost::sregex_iterator end;

  while (it!=end)
    std::cout << *it++;
}
```

Did you figure it out? The output is "02468"—that is, all of the even numbers. Note that this character class does not only match even numbers—had the input string been "AlfaBetaGamma," that would have matched just fine too.

The metacharacter we've just seen, ^, serves another purpose too. It is used to denote the beginning of a line. The metacharacter $ denotes the end of a line.

Bad Regular Expressions

A bad regular expression is one that doesn't conform with the rules that govern regexes. For example, if you happen to forget a closing parenthesis, there's no way the regular expression engine can successfully compile the regular expression. When that happens, an exception of type bad_expression is thrown. As I mentioned before, this name will change in the next version of Boost.Regex, and in the version that's going to be added to the Library Technical Report. The exception type `bad_expression` will be renamed to `regex_error`.

If all of your regular expressions are hardcoded into your application, you may be safe from having to deal with bad expressions, but if you're accepting user input in the form of regexes, you must be prepared to handle errors. Here's a program that prompts the user to enter a regular expression, followed by a string to be matched against the regex. As always, when there's user input involved, there's a chance that the input will be invalid.

```cpp
int main() {
  std::cout << "Enter a regular expression:\n";
  std::string s;
  std::getline(std::cin, s);
  try {
    boost::regex reg(s);
    std::cout << "Enter a string to be matched:\n";

    std::getline(std::cin,s);

    if (boost::regex_match(s,reg))
      std::cout << "That's right!\n";
    else
      std::cout << "No, sorry, that doesn't match.\n";
  }
  catch(const boost::bad_expression& e) {
    std::cout <<
      "That's not a valid regular expression! (Error: " <<
      e.what() << ") Exiting...\n";
  }
}
```

To protect the application and the user, a `try/catch` block ensures that if `boost::regex` throws upon construction, an informative message will be printed, and the application will shut down gracefully. Putting this program to the test, let's begin with some reasonable input.

```
Enter a regular expression:
\d{5}
Enter a string to be matched:
12345
That's right!
```

Now, here's grief coming your way, in the form of a very poor attempt at a regular expression.

```
Enter a regular expression:
(\w*))
That's not a valid regular expression! (Error: Unmatched ( or \()
Exiting...
```

An exception is thrown when the `regex reg` is constructed, because the regular expression cannot be compiled. Consequently, the `catch` handler is invoked, and the program prints an error message and exits. There are only three places where you need to be aware of potential exceptions being thrown. One is when constructing a regular expression, similar to the example you just saw; another is when assigning regular expressions to a `regex`, using the member function `assign`. Finally, the regex iterators and the algorithms can also throw exceptions—if memory is exhausted or if the complexity of the match grows too quickly.

Regex Summary

That regular expressions are useful and important is not disputed, and this library brings terrific regex power to C++. Traditionally, users have had few choices besides using the POSIX C APIs for regular expressions. For text-processing validation tasks, regular expressions are much more scalable and reliable than hand-crafted parsers. For searching and replacing, there are a number of problems that are very elegantly solved using regular expressions, but virtually impossible to solve without them.

Boost.Regex is a powerful library so it has not been possible to cover all of it in this chapter. Similarly, the great expressiveness and range of application of regular expressions necessarily means that this chapter offers little more than an introduction to them. These topics could easily fill a separate book. To learn more, study the online documentation for Boost.Regex and pick up a book on regular expressions (consult the Bibliography for suggestions). Despite the power of Boost.Regex, and the breadth and depth of regular expressions, even complete neophytes can use regular expressions effectively with this library. For programmers who have selected other programming languages due to C++'s lack of support for regular expressions, welcome home.

Boost.Regex is not the only regular expression library available for C++ programmers, but it is certainly one of the best. It's easy to use and fast as lightning when matching your regular expressions. Use it as often as you can.

The author of Boost.Regex is Dr. John Maddock.

Part II
Containers and Data Structures

This part of the book covers the libraries Boost.Any, Boost.Variant, and Boost.Tuple. They are all containers in some sense, although they have virtually nothing in common with the Standard Library container types. These are all extremely useful libraries, which many others and I use to solve programming problems most every day. The problems they solve are not really covered by either C++ or the C++ Standard Library, and they are thus very important additions to our library toolbox. It's interesting to ponder how much the availability of basic data structures affect how we program, and even how we design. Without existing structures, we craft our own, and typically do so with significant consideration for the solution domain, which limits the reusability of our work. That's a common theme for all types of programming, of course, and the tradeoff is between genericity and basically just getting the job done. The value of flexible libraries that addresses both the issues we have at hand, and most issues we are likely to encounter at a later time, is substantial. These libraries also extend our C++ vocabulary in some sense, and the more users the libraries have, the larger the community that speaks these words. I am convinced that each of the libraries in this chapter deserves a place in every C++ professional's toolbox.

Library 6
Any

How Does the Any Library Improve Your Programs?

- Typesafe storage and safe retrieval of arbitrary types

- A means to store heterogeneous types in Standard Library containers

- Types are being passed through layers that need not know anything about the types

The Any library provides a type, `any`, that allows for storage of any type for later retrieval without loss of type safety. It is like a variant type on steroids: It will hold any type, but you have to know the type to retrieve the value. There are times when you need to store unrelated types in the same container. There are times when certain code only cares about conveying data from one point to another without caring about the data's type. At face value, it is easy to do those things. They can be done with an indiscriminate type such as `void*`. They can be done using a discriminated union. There are numerous variant types available that rely on some type tag mechanism. Unfortunately, all of these suffer from a lack of type safety, and only in the most controlled situations should we ever purposely defeat the type system. The Standard Library containers are parameterized on the type they contain, which poses a seemingly impossible challenge for storing elements of heterogeneous types in them. Fortunately, the cure doesn't have to be spelled `void*`, because the Any library allows you to store objects of different types for later retrieval. There is no way to get to the contained value without knowing its exact type, and thus, type safety is preserved.

When designing frameworks, it isn't possible to know in advance about the types that will be used together with the framework classes. A common approach is to require the clients of the framework to adapt a certain interface, or inherit from base classes provided by the framework. This is reasonable, because the framework probably needs to communicate with various higher-level classes in order to be useful. There are, however, situations where the framework stores or otherwise accepts types that it doesn't need to (or can) know anything about. Rather than violating the type system and go with the `void*` approach, the framework can use `any`.

How Does Any Fit with the Standard Library?

One important property of Any is that it provides the capability to store objects of heterogeneous types in Standard Library containers. It is also a sort of variant data type, which is something sorely needed, and currently missing, in the C++ Standard Library.

Any

Header: `"boost/any.hpp"`

The class `any` allows typesafe storage and retrieval of arbitrary types. Unlike indiscriminate types, `any` preserves the type, and actually does not let you near the stored value without knowing the correct type. Of course, there are means for querying for the type, and testing alternatives for the contained value, but in the end, the caller must know the exact type of the value in an `any` object, or `any` denies access. Think of `any` as a locked safe. Without the proper key, you cannot get in. `any` requires the following of the types it stores:

- *CopyConstructible*—It must be possible to copy the type.

- *Non-throwing destructor*—As all destructors should be!

- *Assignable*—For the strong exception guarantee (types that aren't assignable can still be used with `any`, but without the strong guarantee).

This is the public interface of `any`:

```cpp
namespace boost {

  class any {
  public:
    any();
    any(const any&);

    template<typename ValueType>
     any(const ValueType&);

    ~any();

    any& swap(any &);
    any& operator=(const any&);

    template<typename ValueType>
     any& operator=(const ValueType&);

    bool empty() const;
    const std::type_info& type() const;
  };
}
```

Members

`any();`

> The default constructor creates an empty instance of `any`—that is, an `any` that doesn't contain a value. Of course, there is no way of retrieving the value of an empty `any`, because no value exists.

`any(const any& other);`

> Creates a distinct copy of an existing `any` object. The value that is contained in `other` is copied and stored in `this`.

`template<typename ValueType> any(const ValueType&);`

> This templated constructor stores a copy of the argument of type `ValueType` passed to the constructor. The argument is a `const` reference, so it is legal to

pass a temporary object to be stored in `any`. Note that the constructor is not explicit, which would make typical uses of `any` awkward and would not impart additional safety.

```
~any();
```

The destructor destroys the contained value, but note that because the destruction of a raw pointer does not invoke operator `delete` or operator `delete[]` on the pointer, you should always wrap raw pointers in smart pointers such as `shared_ptr` (see "Library 1: Smart_ptr") when using pointers with `any`.

```
any& swap(any& other);
```

Exchanges the values stored by the two `any` objects.

```
any& operator=(const any& other);
```

Discards the stored value, if the instance of `any` is not empty, and stores a copy of the value in `other`.

```
template<typename ValueType>
  any& operator=(const ValueType& value);
```

Discards the stored value, if the instance of `any` is not empty, and stores a copy of `value`, which can be of an arbitrary type that fulfills `any`'s requirements.

```
bool empty() const;
```

Indicates whether an instance of `any` currently has a value, regardless of what that value is. Thus, when an `any` holds a pointer, `empty` returns `false` even if the pointer value is null.

```
const std::type_info& type() const;
```

Indicates the type of the stored value. If the `any` is empty, the type is `void`.

Free Functions

```
template<typename ValueType>
  ValueType any_cast(const any& operand);
```

any_cast gives you access to the value stored in an any. The argument is the any whose value is to be retrieved. If the type ValueType does not correspond to the type of the stored value, any throws a bad_any_cast exception. Note that the syntax is like that of dynamic_cast.

```
template<typename ValueType>
  const ValueType* any_cast(const any* operand);
```

This overloaded any_cast takes a pointer to any, and returns a pointer to the stored value. If the type in the any isn't ValueType, a null pointer is returned. Note, again, that the syntax is like that of dynamic_cast.

```
template<typename ValueType>
  ValueType* any_cast(any* operand);
```

This overloaded any_cast is similar to the preceding version, but whereas the previous version used const-qualified pointers for return type and argument type, this version doesn't.

Exceptions

bad_any_cast

This exception is thrown when trying to cast an any object to a type other than the type stored in the any. bad_any_cast is derived from std::bad_cast. Note that when calling any_cast with a pointer argument, no exception is thrown (similar to how dynamic_cast with pointer types return the null pointer), whereas dynamic_cast to reference types throws an exception on failure.

Usage

The Any library resides in namespace boost. You use the class any to store values, and the template function any_cast to subsequently retrieve the stored values. To use any, include the header "boost/any.hpp". The creation of an instance capable of storing any conceivable value is straightforward.

```
boost::any a;
```

To assign a value of some type is just as easy.

```
a=std::string("A string");
a=42;
a=3.1415;
```

Almost anything is acceptable to any! However, to actually *do* anything with the value contained in an any, we need to retrieve it, right? For that, we need to know the value's type.

```
std::string s=boost::any_cast<std::string>(a);
// throws boost::bad_any_cast.
```

This obviously doesn't work; because a currently contains a double, any_cast throws a bad_any_cast exception. The following, however, does work.

```
double d=boost::any_cast<double>(a);
```

any only allows access to the value if you know the type, which is perfectly sensible. These two elements are all you need to remember, typewise, for this library: the class any, for storing the values, and the template function any_cast, to retrieve them.

Anything Goes!

Consider three classes, A, B, and C, with no common base class, that we'd like to store in a std::vector. If there is no common base class, it would seem we would have to store them as void*, right? Well, not any more (pun intended), because the type of any does not change depending on the type of the value it contains. The following code shows how to solve the problem.

```
#include <iostream>
#include <string>
#include <utility>
#include <vector>
#include "boost/any.hpp"

class A {
public:
  void some_function() { std::cout << "A::some_function()\n"; }
};
```

```
class B {
public:
  void some_function() { std::cout << "B::some_function()\n"; }
};

class C {
public:
  void some_function() { std::cout << "C::some_function()\n"; }
};

int main() {
  std::cout << "Example of using any.\n\n";

  std::vector<boost::any> store_anything;

  store_anything.push_back(A());
  store_anything.push_back(B());
  store_anything.push_back(C());

  // While we're at it, let's add a few other things as well
  store_anything.push_back(std::string("This is fantastic! "));
  store_anything.push_back(3);
  store_anything.push_back(std::make_pair(true, 7.92));

  void print_any(boost::any& a);
  // Defined later; reports on the value in a

  std::for_each(
    store_anything.begin(),
    store_anything.end(),
    print_any);
}
```

Running the example produces the following output.

```
Example of using any.

A::some_function()
B::some_function()
C::some_function()
string: This is fantastic!
Oops!
Oops!
```

Great, we can store anything we want, but how do we go about retrieving the values that are stored inside the elements of the vector? In the previous example, we used for_each to call print_any() on each element of the vector.

```
void print_any(boost::any& a) {
  if (A* pA=boost::any_cast<A>(&a)) {
    pA->some_function();
  }
  else if (B* pB=boost::any_cast<B>(&a)) {
    pB->some_function();
  }
  else if (C* pC=boost::any_cast<C>(&a)) {
    pC->some_function();
  }
}
```

So far, print_any has tried to retrieve a pointer to an A, B, or C object. This is done with the free function any_cast, which is parameterized on the type to "cast" to. Look closely at the cast—we are trying to unlock the any a by saying that we believe that a contains a value with the type A. Also note that we pass our any as a pointer argument to the any_cast function. The return value, therefore, will be a pointer to A, B, or C, respectively. If the any doesn't contain the type that we used in the cast, the null pointer is returned. In the example, if the cast succeeds, we call the some_function member function using the returned pointer. But any_cast can also be used with a slight variation.

```
  else {
    try {
      std::cout << boost::any_cast<std::string>(a) << '\n';
    }
    catch(boost::bad_any_cast&) {
      std::cout << "Oops!\n";
    }
  }
}
```

Now, this is a bit different. We still perform an any_cast parameterized on the type that we are interested in retrieving, but rather than passing the instance of any as a pointer, it is passed by const reference. This changes the behavior of any_cast; in the case of a failure—that is, asking for the wrong type—an exception of type bad_any_cast is thrown. Thus, we have to make sure that we protect the code performing the `any_cast` with a `try`/`catch` block if we are not absolutely sure what type of value is contained in the `any` argument. This behavioral difference (which is analogous with that of `dynamic_cast`) provides you with a great degree of flexibility. In cases where a cast failure is not an error, pass a pointer to an `any`, but if a cast failure is an error, pass by `const` reference, which makes `any_cast` throw an exception on failure.

Using `any` enables you to use the Standard Library containers and algorithms in situations not heretofore possible, thus allowing you to write more maintainable and understandable code.

A Property Class

Let's say that we want to define a property class for use in containers. We'll store the names of the properties as strings, and the values can be of any type. Although we could add the requirement that all values be derived from a common base class, that is often not viable. For instance, we may not have access to the source code for all of the classes that we need to use as property values, and some values can be built-in types, which cannot be derived from. (Besides, it wouldn't make for a good `any` example.) By storing the type of the value in an instance of `any`, we can leave it to the clients to handle the property values they know about and are interested in.

```cpp
#include <iostream>
#include <string>
#include <vector>
#include <algorithm>
#include "boost/any.hpp"

class property {
  boost::any value_;
  std::string name_;

public:
  property(
    const std::string& name,
    const boost::any& value)
  : name_(name),value_(value) {}

  std::string name() const { return name_; }
  boost::any& value() { return value_; }
```

```
friend bool operator<
    (const property& lhs, const property& rhs) {
    return lhs.name_<rhs.name_;
    }
};
```

This simple `property` class has a name stored in a `std::string` for identification, and an `any` to hold the value. The flexibility that `any` brings the implementation is that we are able to use built-in types and user-defined types without changing the property class. Be it simple or complex, an instance of `any` can always store anything. Of course, using `any` also means that we cannot know in advance that there is some set of operations that can always be performed on the value stored in a `property`—we need to retrieve the value first. This implies that if there is a known set of types that are applicable for use with a property class, we may elect to use a different implementation than `any`. That's a rare situation when designing frameworks—if we don't require a certain base class, all we can safely say is that we have absolutely no idea what classes may be sent our way. When you can get any type and don't need to do anything with it but hold it for a while and give it back, you'll find that `any` is ideal. Notice that the property class provides `operator<` to allow the class to be stored in Standard Library associative containers; even without that operator, `property` would work fine with the sequence containers.

The following program uses our new and flexible—thanks to `any`!—property class. Instances of the `property` class are stored in a `std::map`, where the names of the properties are used as the keys.

```
void print_names(const property& p) {
  std::cout << p.name() << "\n";
}

int main() {
  std::cout << "Example of using any for storing properties.\n";

  std::vector<property> properties;
  properties.push_back(
    property("B", 30));
  properties.push_back(
    property("A", std::string("Thirty something")));
  properties.push_back(property("C", 3.1415));

  std::sort(properties.begin(),properties.end());
```

```
std::for_each(
  properties.begin(),
  properties.end(),
  print_names);

std::cout << "\n";

std::cout <<
  boost::any_cast<std::string>(properties[0].value()) << "\n";
std::cout <<
  boost::any_cast<int>(properties[1].value()) << "\n";
std::cout <<
  boost::any_cast<double>(properties[2].value()) << "\n";
}
```

Notice that we didn't have to explicitly create the anys needed for property's constructor. That's because any's converting constructor isn't explicit. Although constructors taking one argument should typically be declared explicit, any is an exception to the rule. Running the program gives us this output.

```
Example of using any for storing properties.
A
B
C

Thirty something
30
3.1415
```

In this example, because the container was sorted, we retrieved the properties by index, and as we knew their respective types beforehand, we didn't need a try/catch block for the retrieval. When retrieving the value of an instance of any, pass the any by const reference to any_cast if a failure indicates a real error.

```
std::string s=boost::any_cast<std::string>(a);
```

When a failure is not necessarily an error, pass the any by pointer.

```
std::string* ps=boost::any_cast<std::string>(&a);
```

The different styles of getting the stored value differ not only in semantics, but also how they return the stored value. If you pass a pointer argument, you get a pointer to the stored value; if you pass a const reference argument, you get a copy of the value.

If the value type is expensive to copy, pass the any by pointer to avoid copying the value.

There's More to *any*

There are a few more member functions provided by any, such as testing whether an instance of any is empty or not, and swapping the values of two instances of any. The following example shows how to use them.

```cpp
#include <iostream>
#include <string>
#include "boost/any.hpp"

int main() {
  std::cout << "Example of using any member functions\n\n";

  boost::any a1(100);
  boost::any a2(std::string("200"));
  boost::any a3;

  std::cout << "a3 is ";
  if (!a3.empty()) {
    std::cout << "not ";
  }
  std::cout << "empty\n";

  a1.swap(a2);

  try {
    std::string s=boost::any_cast<std::string>(a1);
    std::cout << "a1 contains a string: " << s << "\n";
  }
  catch(boost::bad_any_cast& e) {
    std::cout << "I guess a1 doesn't contain a string!\n";
  }

  if (int* p=boost::any_cast<int>(&a2)) {
    std::cout << "a2 seems to have swapped contents with a1: "
      << *p << "\n";
  }
```

```
    else {
      std::cout << "Nope, no int in a2\n";
    }

    if (typeid(int)==a2.type()) {
      std::cout << "a2's type_info equals the type_info of int\n";
    }

}
```

Here's the output from running the program.

```
Example of using any member functions

a3 is empty
a1 contains a string: 200
a2 seems to have swapped contents with a1: 100
a2's type_info equals the type_info of int
```

Let's examine that code more closely. To test whether an instance of `any` contains a value, we called the member function `empty`. We tested the `any` a3 like this.

```
std::cout << "a3 is ";
if (!a3.empty()) {
  std::cout << "not ";
}
std::cout << "empty\n";
```

Because we default constructed a3, `a3.empty()` returns `true`. The next thing is to swap the contents of a1 with a2. You may wonder why you'd want to swap their contents. One plausible scenario is when the identities of the `any` instances are important (`swap` only exchanges the contained values). Another reason is to avoid copying when you don't need to keep the original value.

```
a1.swap(a2);
```

Finally, we use the member function `type`, which returns a `const std::type_info&`, to test if the contained value is of the type `int`.

```
if (typeid(int)==a2.type()) {
```

Note that if an `any` stores a pointer type, that is reflected in the returned
`std::type_info`.

Storing Pointers in *any*

Often, the test for `empty` is enough to know whether the object really contains
something valid. However, if an `any` might hold a pointer, be extra careful to test
the pointer before trying to dereference it. Simply testing whether the `any` is
empty is not enough, because an `any` is not considered to be empty when it holds
a pointer, even if that pointer is null.

```
boost::any a(static_cast<std::string*>(0));

if (!a.empty()) {
   try {
      std::string* p=boost::any_cast<std::string*>(a);
      if (p) {
            std::cout << *p;
      }
      else {
         std::cout << "The any contained a null pointer!\n";
      }
   }
   catch(boost::bad_any_cast&) {}
}
```

A Better Way—Using *shared_ptr*

Another complication when storing raw pointers in `any` is the destruction semantics. The `any` class accepts ownership of the value it stores, because it keeps an
internal copy of the value, which is destroyed together with the `any`. However,
destroying a raw pointer doesn't invoke `delete` or `delete[]` on it! It only
reclaims the memory occupied by the pointer. This makes storing a raw pointer
in `any` problematic, so it's a good idea to use smart pointers instead. Indeed,
using smart pointers (see "Library 1: Smart_ptr") is an ideal way to store a pointer to data in an `any`. This solves the problem of making sure that the memory
associated with a contained pointer is properly deleted. When the smart pointer
is destroyed, it takes appropriate action to ensure the memory and any data in it
are properly destroyed. By contrast, note that `std::auto_ptr` is not appropriate.

This is because `auto_ptr` doesn't have normal copy semantics; accessing the value in an `any` would transfer ownership of the memory and any data in it from the `any` to the returned `auto_ptr`.

Consider the following code.

```
#include <iostream>
#include <string>
#include <algorithm>
#include <vector>
#include "boost/any.hpp"
#include "boost/shared_ptr.hpp"
```

First, we'll define two classes, A and B, each with operations `is_virtual`, which is virtual, and `not_virtual`, which is not virtual (had it been virtual, the name would be an extremely bad choice). We want to store objects of these types in `any`s.

```
class A {
public:
  virtual ~A() {
    std::cout << "A::~A()\n";
  }

  void not_virtual() {
    std::cout << "A::not_virtual()\n";
  }

  virtual void is_virtual () {
    std::cout << "A:: is_virtual ()\n";
  }
};

class B : public A {
public:

  void not_virtual() {
    std::cout << "B::not_virtual()\n";
  }

  virtual void is_virtual () {
    std::cout << "B:: is_virtual ()\n";
  }
};
```

Let's now define a free function, foo, which accepts an argument that is a reference to any and that examines the any using any_casts to the types that the function knows how to handle. If there's no match, the function simply ignores the any and returns. It tests for the types shared_ptr<A> and shared_ptr<B>, respectively, and calls is_virtual (the virtual function) and not_virtual on them.

```cpp
void foo(boost::any& a) {

  std::cout << "\n";

  // Try boost::shared_ptr<A>
  try {
    boost::shared_ptr<A> ptr=
      boost::any_cast<boost::shared_ptr<A> >(a);

    std::cout << "This any contained a boost::shared_ptr<A>\n";
    ptr-> is_virtual ();
    ptr->not_virtual();
    return;
  }
  catch(boost::bad_any_cast& e) {}

  // Try boost::shared_ptr<B>
  try {
    boost::shared_ptr<B> ptr=
      boost::any_cast<boost::shared_ptr<B> >(a);

    std::cout << "This any contained a boost::shared_ptr<B>\n";
    ptr-> is_virtual ();
    ptr->not_virtual();
    return;
  }
  catch(boost::bad_any_cast& e) {}

  // If anything else (like just a string), ignore it
  std::cout <<
    "The any didn't contain anything that \
    concerns this function!\n";
}
```

In main, we create two anys at function scope. We then introduce a new scope, and create two new anys. Next, we store all of the anys in the vector and send every element in it to the function foo, which examines their contents and exercises them. It should be duly noted that we are actually violating the advice that was given earlier, to use the pointer form of `any_cast` when a failure does not designate an error. However, because we are dealing with smart pointers here, the syntactic advantage of using the exception-throwing form of `any_cast` is reason enough to ignore the advice this time.

```cpp
int main() {
  std::cout << "Example of any and shared_ptr\n";

  boost::any a1(boost::shared_ptr<A>(new A));
  boost::any a2(std::string("Just a string"));

  {
    boost::any b1(boost::shared_ptr<A>(new B));
    boost::any b2(boost::shared_ptr<B>(new B));
    std::vector<boost::any> vec;
    vec.push_back(a1);
    vec.push_back(a2);
    vec.push_back(b1);
    vec.push_back(b2);

    std::for_each(vec.begin(),vec.end(),foo);
    std::cout << "\n";
  }

  std::cout <<
    "any's b1 and b2 have been destroyed which means\n"
    "that the shared_ptrs' reference counts became zero\n";

}
```

When this program is run, it produces the following output.

```
Example of any and shared_ptr

This any contained a boost::shared_ptr<A>
A:: is_virtual ()
A::not_virtual()

The any didn't contain anything that concerns this function!

This any contained a boost::shared_ptr<A>
B:: is_virtual ()
A::not_virtual()
```

```
This any contained a boost::shared_ptr<B>
B:: is_virtual ()
B::not_virtual()

A::~A()

A::~A()
```

First, we see that the `any` passed to `foo` contains a `shared_ptr<A>`, which also happens to own an instance of `A`. The output is what one would expect.

Next, the `any` contains the `string` that we added to our `vector`. This shows that it is quite possible, and often reasonable, to store types that are unknown to some of the functions that will be called with an `any` argument; the functions only need to handle the types they are required to operate on!

Then things get really interesting—the third element contains a `shared_ptr<A>` that is pointing to an instance of `B`. This is an example of how polymorphism works just the same for `any` as for other types. Of course, if we were using raw pointers, we could have used `static_cast` to store the pointer as the type that we want to be the identification tag that unlocks the `any`. Note that the function `A::not_virtual` is called instead of `B::not_virtual`. The reason is that the static type of the pointer is `A*`, not `B*`.

The final element contains a `shared_ptr<B>` that also points to an instance of `B`. Again, we are controlling the type stored in `any`, which sets the preferences for those who later try to unlock it.

At the end of the inner scope, the `vector` is destroyed, which destroys the contained instances of `any`, which in turn destroys the `shared_ptrs`, effectively setting the reference counts to zero. Consequently, this means that our pointers are safely and effortlessly destroyed as well!

This example shows something that's more important than how to use smart pointers together with `any`; it (again) shows that it doesn't really matter how simple or complex the type that we store in `any` is. If the cost of copying the stored values is prohibitive, or if shared usage and lifetime control is an issue, consider using smart pointers, just as when using the Standard Library containers to store the values. The exact same reasoning applies equally well to using `any`, and often the two principles coincide, as it is common to use `any` as a means to store heterogeneous types in containers.

What About Input and Output Operators?

A common question from users of any is "why aren't there input and output operators?" There are indeed good reasons for that. Let's start with the input operator. What would be the semantics for input? Would it default to a string type? Would the current type held by the any be used for extraction from the stream? If so, why would an any be used in the first place? These questions come without good answers, and that's the reason why there's no input operator for any. Answering the second question is not as easy, but almost. Supplying a forwarding output operator for any would mean that any is no longer capable of storing arbitrary types as that operator would impose the same requirement on the types stored by any. It wouldn't even matter if we never intended to use operator<<; an instantiation of an any containing a type that doesn't have an output operator is still illegal, and results in an error when compiling. Of course, were we to provide a template version of operator<<, we would be able to use any without requiring that the contained types support streaming, but as soon as that operator is instantiated, the requirement is on.

There seems to be a cure for missing operators, right? What if we were to supply a valid output operator for any that matches anything, and introduce that operator<< in a scope that is only accessible from the implementation details of the any class? That way, we could elect to throw an exception or return an error code when an output to a stream was performed (the function would only match for arguments without support for operator<<), and we could do this at runtime, without affecting the legality of any other code. This idea struck me as so appealing that I gave it a try on a few of the compilers I have at hand. The results were not good. I won't go into detail, but in short, the solution requires techniques that many compilers can't currently handle. However, we don't necessarily need to change the any class—we could create a new class that takes advantage of any to store arbitrary types, and have that class support operator<<. Basically, we need to do whatever it is any does to keep track of the contained type to know how to write the output, and then add the output streaming.

Adding Support for Output—*any_out*

We will define a class that is capable of output through operator<<. This adds to the requirements of the types that are to be stored; to be a valid type for storage in the class any_out, the type must support operator<<.

```
#include <iostream>
#include <vector>
#include <string>
#include <ostream>

#include "boost/any.hpp"

class any_out {
```

The `any_out` class stores the (arbitrary) value in a datum of type `boost::any`. Always select reuse over reinvention!

```
boost::any o_;
```

Next, we declare an abstract class `streamer`, which uses the same design as `any`. We cannot use a parameterized type directly, because we would then need to parameterize `any_out` as well, which in turns makes the type of `any_out` dependent on the type of its contained value, effectively rendering the class useless in the context of heterogeneous storage. The type of the contained value must not be a part of the signature for the `any_out` class.

```
struct streamer {
  virtual void print(std::ostream& o,boost::any& a)=0;
  virtual streamer* clone()=0;
  virtual ~streamer() {}
};
```

Here's the trick: We add a parameterized class, `streamer_imp`, parameterized on the contained type and inheriting from `streamer`. Thus, we are able to store a pointer to `streamer` in `any_out`, and rely on polymorphism to do the rest of the work (next, we'll add a virtual member function for that purpose).

```
template <typename T> struct streamer_imp : public streamer {
```

Now, let's implement a virtual function `print` to output the value contained in the `any` by performing an `any_cast` on the type that `streamer_imp` is parameterized with. Because we're going to instantiate a `streamer_imp` on the same type as the value put in the `any`, the cast doesn't fail.

```
virtual void print(std::ostream& o,boost::any& a) {
  o << *boost::any_cast<T>(&a);
}
```

A cloning function is needed when an `any_out` is being copied—we are going to store a pointer to `streamer`, so the virtual function `clone` takes care of copying the correct type of `streamer`.

```
    virtual streamer* clone() {
       return new streamer_imp<T>();
    }
};

class any_out {
   streamer* streamer_;
   boost::any o_;public:
```

The default constructor creates an empty `any_out`, and sets the `streamer` pointer to zero.

```
any_out() : streamer_(0) {}
```

The most interesting function for `any_out` is the parameterized constructor. The type `T`, deduced from the type of the value to store, is used when creating the `streamer`. The value is stored in the `any o_`.

```
template <typename T> any_out(const T& value) :
    streamer_(new streamer_imp<T>),o_(value) {}
```

Copy construction is straightforward; all we need is to make sure that the `streamer` in the source `any_out a` is not zero.

```
any_out(const any_out& a)
   : streamer_(a.streamer_?a.streamer_->clone():0),o_(a.o_) {}[1]

template<typename T> any_out& operator=(const T& r) {
   any_out(r).swap(*this);
   return *this;
}

any_out& operator=(const any_out& r) {
   any_out(r).swap(*this);
   return *this;
```

---

[1]. Rob Stewart asked me whether I wrote this line to go for first prize in an obfuscation contest or if I just wanted to be able to write the ():0) emoticon. I'm not really sure, but decided to keep the line for your reading pleasure....

```
  }

  ~any_out() {
    delete streamer_;
  }
```

The `swap` function is supplied to facilitate exception-safe assignment.

```
  any_out& swap(any_out& r) {
    std::swap(streamer_, r.streamer_);
    std::swap(o_,r.o_);
    return *this;
  }
```

And now, let's add what we came here for: the output operator. It should accept a reference to an `ostream` and an `any_out`. The `any` stored in the `any_out` should be passed on to the virtual function `print` of the streamer.

```
  friend std::ostream& operator<<(std::ostream& o,any_out& a) {
    if (a.streamer_) {
      a.streamer_->print(o,a.o_);
    }
    return o;
  }
};
```

This class not only offers a way to perform stream output of arbitrary (unknown) types contained in a general class, it is also a display of how `any` is designed. This design, and the techniques used to safely wrap the type behind a polymorphic facade are general, and applicable in more cases than this. For instance, it would be possible to create a generic function adaptor.

Let's take our `any_out` class for a test drive.

```
int main() {
  std::vector<any_out> vec;

  any_out a(std::string("I do have operator<<"));

  vec.push_back(a);
  vec.push_back(112);
  vec.push_back(65.535);
```

```
// Print everything in vector vec
std::cout << vec[0] << "\n";
std::cout << vec[1] << "\n";
std::cout << vec[2] << "\n";

a=std::string("This is great!");
std::cout << a;
}
```

If the class X does not support `operator<<`, the code does not compile. Unfortunately, it doesn't matter whether we are actually going to use `operator<<` or not, it just doesn't work. `any_out` always requires that the output operator be available.

```
any_out nope(X());
std::cout << nope;
```

}

Convenient, don't you think? If a certain operation is available for all types that you plan to use in a certain context, adding those can be done in the same way we did to supply `operator<<` for our `any_out` class. It is not much harder to generalize the solution and parameterize on the operations, which makes this solution for extending the interface of `any` reusable.

Predicates

Before we end this section on the usage of `any`, let's examine how to build functionality around `any` to simplify usage and to add expressive power. When `any` is used to enable storage of different types in container classes, it turns out that it's easy to *store* those values but quite hard to *operate* on them.

First, we will create two predicates, `is_int` and `is_string`, which can be used to determine if an `any` contains an `int` or a `string`, respectively. These can be useful when we want to search for a particular type in a container of heterogeneous objects, or want to test the type of an `any` to determine further actions. The implementation uses the `any` member function `type` for the test.

```
bool is_int(const boost::any& a) {
  return typeid(int)==a.type();
}
```

```
bool is_string(const boost::any& a) {
  return typeid(std::string)==a.type();
}
```

The preceding solution works, but it is tedious to write predicates for every type we are interested in testing for. The implementation is repeated, so this would be the perfect fit for a template solution like the following.

```
template <typename T> bool contains (const boost::any& a) {
  return typeid(T)==a.type();
}
```

The function `contains` saves us from having to manually create new predicates. This is a canonical example of how templates are used to minimize redundant coding.

Counting Non-Empty Values

For certain applications, it is useful to iterate over the elements of a container and test whether the `any`s contain a value or not. An empty `any` might imply that it should be removed, or perhaps we need to extract all non-empty elements of `any` for some further processing. To make this useful in an algorithm, we create a function object with a function call operator taking an `any` argument. The operator just tests whether the `any` is empty and, if it is not, increments the counter.

```
class any_counter {
  int count_;
public:
  any_counter() : count_(0) {}

  int operator()(const boost::any& a) {
    return a.empty() ? count_ : ++count_;
  }

  int count() const { return count_; }
};
```

For a container `c` storing values of `any`, counting the non-empty values is accomplished like this.

```
int i=std::for_each(C.begin(),C.end(),any_counter()).count();
```

Note that the `for_each` algorithm returns the function object, so we can easily access the count. Because `for_each` accepts its arguments by value, the following code does not accomplish the same thing.

```
any_counter counter;
std::for_each(C.begin(),C.end(),counter);
int i=counter.count();
```

The second version always yields 0, because the function object counter simply is copied when calling the `for_each`. The first version works, because the returned function object (the copy of `counter`) is used for retrieving the count.

Extracting Elements of Certain Types from a Container

Here's an extra treat: An extractor for retrieving certain types from a container. This can be a useful utility when parts of a heterogeneous container are to be transferred to a homogeneous container. Manually, this is a tedious and error-prone task, but one simple function object takes care of everything for us. We will parameterize the function object on the type of output iterator for the retrieved elements, and the type to extract from the `any` arguments that are passed to it.

```
template <typename OutIt,typename Type> class extractor {
  OutIt it_;
public:
  extractor(OutIt it) : it_(it) {}

  void operator()(boost::any& a) {
    Type* t(boost::any_cast<Type>(&a));
    if (t) {
      *it_++ = *t;
    }
  }
};
```

As a convenience for creating an extractor, here's a function that deduces the type of the output iterator and returns an appropriate extractor.

```
template <typename Type, typename OutIt>
  extractor<OutIt,Type>   make_extractor(OutIt it) {
    return extractor<OutIt,Type>(it);
  }
```

Using the Predicates and the Extractor

It's high time to test our new any companions with a sample program.

```
int main() {
    std::cout << "Example of using predicates and the "
     "function object any_counter\n";

  std::vector<boost::any> vec;
  vec.push_back(boost::any());
  for(int i=0;i<10;++i) {
    vec.push_back(i);
  }
  vec.push_back(boost::any());
```

We have added 12 any objects to the vec, and now we're interested in finding out how many of the elements contain a value. To count elements with values, we use the function object any_counter that we've created.

```
// Count the instances of any that contain a value
int i=std::for_each(
  vec.begin(),
  vec.end(),
  any_counter()).count();
std::cout
  << "There are " << i << " non-empty any's in vec\n\n";
```

Here is how the extractor function object that operates on a container of anys works, populating a new container with a certain type collected from the source container.

```
  // Get all ints in vec
std::list<int> lst;
std::for_each(vec.begin(),vec.end(),
  make_extractor<int>(std::back_inserter(lst)));
std::cout << "Found " << lst.size() << " ints in vec\n\n";
```

Let's clear the contents of the container vec and add some new values.

```
vec.clear();

vec.push_back(std::string("This is a string"));
```

```
vec.push_back(42);
vec.push_back(3.14);
```

Now, let's try the predicates that we created. First, we use the two predicates that indicate whether an `any` contains a `string` or an `int`, respectively.

```
if (is_string(vec[0])) {
  std::cout << "Found me a string!\n";
}

if (is_int(vec[1])) {
  std::cout << "Found me an int!\n";
}
```

As we concluded earlier, defining predicates for every type we are ever interested in is tedious and utterly unnecessary, when we can use the language to our advantage in a straightforward manner.

```
  if (contains<double>(vec[2])) {
    std::cout <<
      "The generic tool is sweeter, found me a double!\n";
  }
}
```

Running this example gives you this output.

```
Example of using predicates and the function object any_counter
There are 10 non-empty any's in vec

Found 10 ints in vec

Found me a string!
Found me an int!
The generic tool is sweeter, found me a double!
```

Small and simple tools like these have proven to be very useful. Of course, this is not only true for `any`; it's a property of the design of the Standard Library containers and algorithms. The examples show how to take advantage of function composition together with `any`. Providing filtering, counting, operations on certain types, and so forth are powerful ways of hiding implementation details, and simplifying the usage of `any`.

Complying with the Requirements of Standard Library Adapters

If you found the predicate `contains` useful, you may have noticed that it is not quite all it can be. There is no way to use it together with the Standard Library adapters. The following example is slightly outside the scope of this chapter, but because `any` fits so well with the container classes, it would be a shame to leave a somewhat flawed predicate of `contains` as is. The problem is that the Standard Library adapters (`bind1st`, `bind2nd`, `not1`, and `not2`) impose requirements on the predicates they adapt. The type of the argument and the result type must be exposed through provided `typedefs`, and that means that we need a function object rather than a function.

First comes the definition of our new function object, `contains_t`. It could have inherited from the helper class `std::unary_function` (part of the C++ Standard Library, intended to facilitate the creation of the correct `typedefs`) and have the argument and result types defined automatically, but to make things clear, the required `typedefs` are provided explicitly. The argument type has changed from `const boost::any&` to `boost::any`, to avoid a potential reference-to-reference, which is illegal. The implementation is just as before, only here it is placed in the function call operator.

```
template <typename T> struct contains_t {
  typedef boost::any argument_type;
  typedef bool result_type;
  bool operator()(boost::any a) const {
    return typeid(T)==a.type();
  }
};
```

To save the name `contains` for subsequent use in the helper function that's soon to come, the name of the function object is `contains_t`. Here is a helper function that creates and returns an instance of `contains_t` with the appropriate type set automatically. The reason is that we want to overload `contains` so that we are still able to provide the original predicate that we created.

```
template <typename T> contains_t<T> contains() {
  return contains_t<T>();
}
```

Finally, the good old predicate is changed to take advantage of the `contains_t` implementation. Now, if we need to change the implementation of `contains_t` for some reason, `contains` will reflect those changes without any further effort.

```
template <typename T> bool contains(const boost::any& a) {
  return contains_t<T>()(a);
}
```

Here's a sample program that demonstrates what we have gained, using both the new function object and the predicate from the previous example.

```
int main() {
  std::cout << "Example of using the improved is_type\n";

  std::vector<boost::any> vec;

  vec.push_back(std::string("This is a string"));
  vec.push_back(42);
  vec.push_back(3.14);
```

Using the predicate is no different than before. Testing an any for a certain type is still easy.

```
if (contains<double>(vec[2])) {
  std::cout << "The generic tool has become sweeter! \n";
}

vec.push_back(2.52f);
vec.push_back(std::string("Another string"));
```

Another example of the use of contains is to search a container for occurrences of a certain type. This example finds the first float.

```
std::vector<boost::any>::iterator
  it=std::find_if(vec.begin(),vec.end(),contains<float>());
```

As yet another reminder, the two ways of retrieving the contained value of an any are demonstrated. Pass the any to any_cast by const reference for the exception-throwing version. Pass the address of the any to return a pointer to the stored value.

```
if (it!=vec.end()) {
  std::cout << "\nPrint the float twice!\n";
  std::cout << boost::any_cast<float>(*it) << "\n";
  std::cout << *boost::any_cast<float>(&*it) << "\n";
}
```

```
std::cout <<
    "There are " << vec.size() << " elements in vec\n";
```

I still haven't given a good example of why `contains` should be a full-fledged function object. In many cases, the reasons why may not be known beforehand, because we cannot anticipate every situation that our implementations will face. That's a strong reason to comply with the requirements of the Standard Library facilities, preferably in more than just the use cases that we are currently aware of. Nevertheless, I do have an example for you: The task is to remove all elements from a container `vec` that do not contain `string`s. Of course, writing another predicate that does the exact opposite of `contains` is one alternative, but that's an alternative that quickly can lead to maintenance nightmares, because of proliferation of function objects with similar work descriptions. The Standard Library provides us with an adapter called `not1`, which negates the result of an invocation of a function object, and this makes it trivial to clean out all non-`string` elements from our `vector vec`.

```
vec.erase(std::remove_if(vec.begin(),vec.end(),
std::not1(contains<std::string>())),vec.end());

std::cout << "Now, there are only " << vec.size()
    << " elements left in vec!\n";
}
```

The examples in this section have demonstrated how to make effective use of `any`. Because the type of the stored value is not part of `any`'s type, `any` is an essential tool when providing storage without imposing requirements on the stored types, including inheriting from a certain base class. We have seen that there is a price for this type hiding. `any` disallows access to the stored value without knowledge of the value's type, restricting opportunities to operate on the stored values. To a large extent, this can be amended by creating helper classes—predicates and function objects—that provide the necessary logic to access the values.

Any Summary

Discriminated types can contain values of different types and are quite different from indiscriminate (read `void*`) types. We always depend heavily on type safety in C++, and there are few situations in which we are willing to do without it.

This is for good reasons: Type safety keeps us from making mistakes and improves the performance of our code. So, we avoid indiscriminate types. Still, it is not uncommon to find oneself in need of heterogeneous storage, or to insulate clients from the details of types, or to gain the utmost flexibility at lower levels of a hierarchy. `any` provides this functionality while maintaining full type safety, and that makes it an excellent addition to our toolbox!

Use the Any library when

- You need to store values of heterogeneous types in containers

- Storage for unknown types is required

- Types are being passed through layers that need not know anything about the types

The design of Any also serves as a valuable lesson on how to encapsulate a type without effect on the type of the enclosing class. This design can be used to create generic function objects, generic iterators, and much more. It is an example of the power of encapsulation and polymorphism in conjunction with templates.

In the Standard Library, there are excellent tools for storing collections of elements. When the need for storage of heterogeneous types arises, we want to avoid having to use new collection types. `any` offers a solution that works in many cases with existing containers. In a way, the template class `any` extends the capabilities of the Standard Library containers by packaging disparate types in a homogeneous wrapper that allows them to be made elements of those aforementioned containers.

Adding Boost.Any to an existing code base is straightforward. It doesn't require changes to the design, and immediately increases flexibility where it's applied. The interface is small, making it a tool that is easily understood.

The Any library was created by Kevlin Henney, and like all Boost libraries, has been reviewed, influenced, and refined by the Boost community.

Library 7
Variant

How Does the Variant Library Improve Your Programs?

- Typesafe storage and retrieval of a user-specified set of types

- A means to store heterogeneous types in Standard Library containers

- Compile-time checked visitation of variants

- Efficient, stack-based storage for variants

The Variant library focuses on typesafe storage and retrieval of a bounded set of types—that is, on discriminated unions. The Boost.Variant library has many features in common with Boost.Any, but there are different tradeoffs as well as differences in functionality. The need for discriminated unions (variant types) is very common in everyday programming. One typical solution while retaining type safety is to use abstract base classes, but that's not always possible; even when it is, the cost of heap allocation and virtual functions[1] may be too high. One might also try using unsafe indiscriminate types such as void* (which leads to disaster), or typesafe but unbounded variant types, such as Boost.Any. The library we look at here—Boost.Variant—supports *bounded* variant types—that is, variants where the elements come from a set of supported types.

---

1. Although virtual functions do come with a very reasonable price with regard to performance.

Variant types are available in many other programming languages, and they have proven their worth time and again. There is very limited built-in support in C++ for variant types, only in the form of unions, that exist mainly for C compatibility. Boost.Variant remedies the situation through a class template `variant`, and accompanying tools for safely storing and retrieving values. A variant data type exposes an interface independent of the current value's type. If you've used some proprietary variant types before, you may have been exposed to types that only support a fixed set of types. That is not the case with this library; *you* define the set of types that are allowed in a `variant` when you use it, and a program can contain any number of disparate `variant` instantiations. To retrieve the value that is held in a `variant`, you either need to know the exact type of the current value, or use the provided typesafe visitor mechanism. The visitor mechanism makes Variant quite different from most other variant libraries, including Boost.Any (which on the other hand can hold a value of any conceivable type), and thereby enables a safe and robust environment for handling such types. C++ unions are only useful for built-in types and POD types, but this library offers discriminated union support for all types. Finally, efficiency aspects are covered, too, as the library stores its values in stack-based storage, thus avoiding more expensive heap allocations.

How Does Variant Fit with the Standard Library?

Boost.Variant permits storing heterogeneous types in the Standard Library containers. As there is no real support for variant types in C++, or in the C++ Standard Library, this makes Variant an excellent and useful extension to the Standard Library.

Variant

Header: `"boost/variant.hpp"`

This contains all of the Variant library through a single header file.

`"boost/variant/variant_fwd.hpp"`

contains forward declarations of the `variant` class templates.

"boost/variant/variant.hpp"

> contains the definitions for the variant class templates.

"boost/variant/apply_visitor.hpp"

> contains the functionality for applying visitors to variants.

"boost/variant/get.hpp"

> contains the template function get.

"boost/variant/bad_visit.hpp"

> contains the definition for the exception class bad_visit.

"boost/variant/static_visitor.hpp"

> contains the definition for the visitor class template.

The following partial synopsis covers the most important members of the variant class template. Other functionality, such as the visitation mechanism, direct typesafe value retrieval, and advanced features such as creating the set of types through type sequences, are described in the "Usage" section.

```cpp
namespace boost {
  template <typename T1,typename T2=unspecified, ...,
    typename TN=unspecified>
  class variant {
  public:

    variant();

    variant(const variant& other);

    template <typename T> variant(const T& operand);

    template <typename U1, typename U2, ..., typename UN>
      variant(const variant<U1, U2, ..., UN>& operand);

    ~variant();

    template <typename T> variant& operator=(const T& rhs);

    int which() const;
```

```
    bool empty() const;
    const std::type_info& type() const;

    bool operator==(const variant& rhs) const;
    bool operator<(const variant& rhs) const;
};
}
```

Members

```
variant();
```

> This constructor default constructs the first type of the set of types for the variant. This means that the first type used when declaring the variant type must be default constructible, or else the variant type itself cannot be default constructed. This constructor propagates any exceptions thrown from the first type's constructor.

```
variant(const variant& other);
```

> The copy constructor copies the current value of other, propagating any exceptions thrown from other's current type's copy constructor.

```
template <typename T> variant(const T& operand);
```

> This constructor creates a new variant from operand. The operand, of type T, must be unambiguously convertible to one of the set of bound types. Exceptions thrown when copying or converting the operand are propagated.

```
template <typename U1,typename U2,...,typename UN>
  variant(const variant<U1,U2,...,UN>& operand);
```

> This constructor allows construction from another variant type, where for each of the types U1, U2...UN, there exists an unambiguous conversion to T1,T2...TN (the set of types of the variant being constructed). Exceptions thrown when copying or converting the operand are propagated.

```
~variant();
```

Destroys the variant, and calls the destructor for the active value. Note that for pointer types, the destructor is not called (destroying the pointer is a no-op). This destructor never throws.

```
template <typename T> variant& operator=(const T& rhs);
```

This operator discards the current value and assigns the value `rhs`. The type `T` must be unambiguously convertible to one of the bound types in the `variant`. If `T` is the type of the current value in the `variant`, `rhs` is copy assigned to the current value; any exceptions thrown by `T`'s copy assignment operator, if any, will propagate. If the `variant`'s current value's type is not `T`, the current value is replaced by one created by the (copy) constructor of the type, corresponding to `T`, selected from the set of bound types. Any exceptions thrown by that constructor will propagate. This function may also throw `bad_alloc`.

```
int which() const;
```

Returns the zero-based index, in the set of bounded types, of the current value's type. This function never throws.

```
bool empty() const;
```

This function always returns `false`, because a `variant` is never empty. This function exists to allow generic code to treat `variant`s and `boost::any`s uniformly. This function never throws.

```
const std::type_info& type() const;
```

Returns the `type_info` for the current value. This function never throws.

```
bool operator==(const variant& rhs) const;
```

Returns `true` if `*this` and `rhs` are equal, which means that `which()==rhs.which()` and the current value of `*this` and `rhs` are equal according to the equality operator of the current value's type. This necessitates that all of the bounded types be *EqualityComparable*. Any exceptions thrown by `operator==` of the current value's type are propagated.

```
bool operator<(const variant& rhs) const;
```

The less than comparison returns `which()<rhs.which()` or if the indices are equal, it returns the result of calling `operator<` on the current value of `*this` and `rhs`. Any exceptions thrown by `operator<` of the current value's type are propagated.

Usage

To start using `variant`s in your programs, include the header `"boost/variant.hpp"`. This header includes the entire library, so you don't need to know which individual features to use; later, you may want to reduce the dependencies by only including the relevant files for the problem at hand. When declaring a `variant` type, we must define the set of types that it will be capable of storing. The most common way to accomplish this is using template arguments. A `variant` that is capable of holding a value of type `int`, `std::string`, or `double` is declared like this.

```
boost::variant<int,std::string,double> my_first_variant;
```

When the variable `my_first_variant` is created, it ends up containing a default-constructed `int`, because `int` is first among the types that the `variant` can contain. We can also pass a value that is convertible to one of those types to initialize the `variant`.

```
boost::variant<int,std::string,double>
    my_first_variant("Hello world");
```

At any give time, we can assign a new value, and as long as the new value is unambiguously and implicitly convertible to one of the types that the `variant` can contain, it works perfectly.

```
my_first_variant=24;
my_first_variant=2.52;
my_first_variant="Fabulous!";
my_first_variant=0;
```

After the first assignment, the contained value is of type `int`; after the second, it's a `double`; after the third, it's a `std::string`; and then finally, it's back to an `int`. If we want to see that this is the case, we can retrieve the value using the function `boost::get`, like so:

```
assert(boost::get<int>(my_first_variant)==0);
```

Note that if the call to `get` fails (which would happen if `my_first_variant` didn't contain a value of type `int`), an exception of type `boost::bad_get` is thrown. To avoid getting an exception upon failure, we can pass a pointer to a `variant` to `get`, in which case `get` returns a pointer to the value or, if the requested type doesn't match the type of the value in the `variant`, it returns the null pointer. Here's how it is used:

```
int* val=boost::get<int>(&my_first_variant);
assert(val && (*val)==0);
```

The function `get` is a very direct way of accessing the contained value—in fact, it works just like `any_cast` does for `boost::any`. Note that the type must match exactly, including at least the same cv-qualification (`const` and `volatile`). However, a more restrictive cv-qualification will succeed. If the type doesn't match and a `variant` pointer is passed to `get`, the null pointer is returned. Otherwise, an exception of type `bad_get` is thrown.

```
const int& i=boost::get<const int>(my_first_variant);
```

Code that relies too heavily on `get` can quickly become fragile; if we don't know the type of the contained value, we might be tempted to test for all possible combinations, like the following example does.

```cpp
#include <iostream>
#include <string>
#include "boost/variant.hpp"

template <typename V> void print(V& v) {
  if (int* pi=boost::get<int>(&v))
    std::cout << "It's an int: " << *pi << '\n';
  else if (std::string* ps=boost::get<std::string>(&v))
    std::cout << "It's a std::string: " << *ps << '\n';
  else if (double* pd=boost::get<double>(&v))
    std::cout << "It's a double: " << *pd << '\n';

  std::cout << "My work here is done!\n";
}
```

```
int main() {
  boost::variant<int,std::string,double>
    my_first_variant("Hello there!");
  print(my_first_variant);
  my_first_variant=12;
  print(my_first_variant);
  my_first_variant=1.1;
  print(my_first_variant);
}
```

The function `print` does its job correctly now, but what if we decide to change the set of types for the `variant`? Then we will have introduced a subtle bug that won't be caught at compile time; the function `print` will not print the value of any other types than the ones we've originally anticipated. If we hadn't used a template function, but required an exact signature of a `variant`, we would risk proliferation of overloads to accommodate the same functionality for different types of `variant`s. The next section discusses the concept of visiting `variant`s, and the problem that (typesafe) visitation solves.

Visiting Variants

Let's start with an example that explains why using `get` isn't as robust as one would like. Starting with the code from the previous example, let's alter the types that the `variant` can contain, and call `print` with the `char` value for the `variant`, too.

```
int main() {
  boost::variant<int,std::string,double,char>
    my_first_variant("Hello there!");

  print(my_first_variant);
  my_first_variant=12;
  print(my_first_variant);
  my_first_variant=1.1;
  print(my_first_variant);
  my_first_variant='a';
  print(my_first_variant);
}
```

This compiles cleanly even though we have added `char` to the set of types that the `variant` can contain and the last two lines of the program set a `char` value and call `print`. (Note that `print` is parameterized on the `variant` type, so it adapts to the new `variant` definition easily.) Here's the output of running the program:

```
It's a std::string: Hello there!
My work here is done!
It's an int: 12
My work here is done!
It's a double: 1.1
My work here is done!
My work here is done!
```

There's a problem showing in that output. Notice that there is no value reported before the final, "My work here is done!" The reason is that as it stands, `print` doesn't output the value for any types other than those it was originally designed for (`std::string`, `int`, and `double`), yet it compiles and runs cleanly. The value of the `variant` is simply ignored if its current type isn't among those supported by `print`. There are more potential problems with using `get`, such as getting the order of the if-statements right for class hierarchies. Note that this doesn't mean you should avoid using `get` altogether; it just emphasizes that it's sometimes not the best solution. What would be better here is a mechanism that somehow allows us to state which types of values are acceptable, and have that statement be validated at compile time. This is exactly what the `variant` visitation mechanism does. By applying a visitor to a `variant` the compiler ensures that they are fully compatible. Such visitors in Boost.Variant are function objects with function call operators that accept arguments corresponding to the set of types that the `variants` they visit can contain.

Rewriting the now infamous function `print` as a visitor looks like this:

```
class print_visitor : public boost::static_visitor<void> {
public:
  void operator()(int i) const {
    std::cout << "It's an int: " << i << '\n';
  }

  void operator()(std::string s) const {
    std::cout << "It's a std::string: " << s << '\n';
  }
```

```
    void operator()(double d) const {
      std::cout << "It's a double: " << d << '\n';
    }

};
```

To make `print_visitor` a visitor for `variant`s, we have it inherit publicly from `boost::static_visitor` to get the correct `typedef` (`result_type`), and to explicitly state that this class is a visitor type. The class implements three overloaded versions of the function call operator, which accept an `int`, a `std::string`, and a `double`, respectively. To visit a `variant`, one uses the function `boost::apply_visitor`(*visitor*, *variant*). If we replace the existing calls to `print` with calls to `apply_visitor`, we end up with something like this:

```
int main() {
  boost::variant<int,std::string,double,char>
    my_first_variant("Hello there!");

  print_visitor v;

  boost::apply_visitor(v,my_first_variant);
  my_first_variant=12;
  boost::apply_visitor(v,my_first_variant);
  my_first_variant=1.1;
  boost::apply_visitor(v,my_first_variant);
  my_first_variant='a';
  boost::apply_visitor(v,my_first_variant);
}
```

Here, we create a `print_visitor`, named `v`, and apply it to `my_first_variant` after putting each value in it. Because we don't have a function call operator accepting `char`, this code fails to compile, right? Wrong! A `char` can be unambiguously converted to an `int`, so the visitor is compatible with our `variant` type. This is what we get when running the program.

```
It's a std::string: Hello there!
It's an int: 12
It's a double: 1.1
It's an int: 97
```

We learn two things from this—the first is that the character `a` has the ASCII value 97, and the second, more important, lesson is that if a visitor accepts its arguments by value, any implicit conversions will be applied to the values being passed. If we want only the exact types to be compatible with the visitor (and also avoid copying the value from the `variant`), we must change how the visitor function call operators accept their arguments. The following version of `print_visitor` only works for the types `int`, `std::string`, and `double`; and any other types that provide an implicit conversion to a *reference* of one of those types.

```
class print_visitor : public boost::static_visitor<void> {
public:
  void operator()(int& i) const {
    std::cout << "It's an int: " << i << '\n';
  }

  void operator()(std::string& s) const {
    std::cout << "It's a std::string: " << s << '\n';
  }

  void operator()(double& d) const {
    std::cout << "It's a double: " << d << '\n';
  }
};
```

If we compile the example again, the compiler will be really upset, saying something like this:

```
c:/boost_cvs/boost/boost/variant/variant.hpp:
In member function `typename Visitor::result_type boost::detail::
variant::
invoke_visitor<Visitor>::internal_visit(T&, int)
[with T = char, Visitor = print_visitor]':

[Snipped lines of irrelevant information here]

c:/boost_cvs/boost/boost/variant/variant.hpp:807:
error: no match for call to `(print_visitor) (char&)'
variant_sample1.cpp:40: error: candidates are:
  void print_visitor::operator()(int&) const
variant_sample1.cpp:44: error:
  void print_visitor::operator()(std::string&) const
variant_sample1.cpp:48: error:
  void print_visitor::operator()(double&) const
```

This error pinpoints the problem: There is no candidate function for `char` arguments! That's one important reason why typesafe compile time visitation is such a powerful mechanism. It makes the visitation robust with regard to types, and avoids the tedium of type-switching. Creating visitors is just as easy as creating other function objects, so the learning curve here isn't very steep. When the set of types in the `variant`s may change (they tend to do that!), creating visitor classes is much more robust than relying solely on `get`. There is a higher initial cost, but it's typically worth it for non-trivial uses.

Generic Visitors

By using the visitor mechanism and a parameterized function call operator, it's possible to create generic visitors that are capable of accepting values of any type (that can syntactically and semantically handle whatever the generic function call operator implementation requires). This is very useful for treating disparate types uniformly. Typical examples of "universal" features are the C++ operators, such as arithmetic and IOStreams shift operators. The following example uses `operator<<` to print the `variant` values to a stream.

```cpp
#include <iostream>
#include <sstream>
#include <string>
#include <sstream>
#include "boost/variant.hpp"

class stream_output_visitor :
  public boost::static_visitor<void> {
  std::ostream& os_;
public:
  stream_output_visitor(std::ostream& os) : os_(os) {}

  template <typename T> void operator()(T& t) const {
    os_ << t << '\n';
  }
};

int main() {
  boost::variant<int,std::string> var;
  var=100;
```

```
    boost::apply_visitor(stream_output_visitor(std::cout),var);
    var="One hundred";
    boost::apply_visitor(stream_output_visitor(std::cout),var);
}
```

The idea is that the member function template for the function call operator in `stream_output_visitor` will be instantiated once for each type visited (`int` and `std::string`, in this case). Because `std::cout << 100` and `std::cout << std::string("One hundred")` are both well defined, the code compiles and works flawlessly.

Of course, operators are just one example of what could be used in a generic visitor; they simply happen to apply to a great many types. When calling functions on the values, or passing them as arguments to other functions, the requirements are that the member function exists for all types being passed to the operator, and that there are suitable overloads for the functions being called. Another interesting aspect of this parameterized function call operator is specializing the behavior for some types, but still allowing a generic implementation to be available for the rest of the types. In other words, you create overloaded function call operators for some types and rely on the member function template for the rest. This is, in a sense, related to template specialization, where behavior is specialized based on type information.

Binary Visitors

The visitors that we've seen so far have all been unary—that is, they accept one `variant` as their sole argument. Binary visitors accept two (possibly different) `variant`s. This concept is, among other things, useful for implementing relations between `variant`s. As an example, we shall create a lexicographic sort order for `variant` types. To do so, we'll use an enormously useful component from the Standard Library: `std::ostringstream`. It will take anything *OutputStreamable* and, on demand, produce a `std::string` out of it. We can thus lexically compare fundamentally different `variant` types, assuming that all of the bound types support streaming. Just as with regular visitors, binary visitors should derive publicly from `boost::static_visitor`, and the template parameter denotes the return type of the function call operator(s). Because we are creating a predicate, the return type is `bool`. Here, then, is the binary predicate, which we shall put to use shortly.

```
class lexicographical_visitor :
  public boost::static_visitor<bool> {
public:
  template <typename LHS,typename RHS>
    bool operator()(const LHS& lhs,const RHS& rhs) const {
      return get_string(lhs)<get_string(rhs);
    }
private:
  template <typename T> static std::string
    get_string(const T& t) {
    std::ostringstream s;
    s << t;
    return s.str();
  }

  static const std::string& get_string(const std::string& s) {
    return s;
  }
};
```

The function call operator is parameterized on both of its arguments, which means that it accepts any combination of two types. The requirements for the set of possible types in the `variants` is that they be *OutputStreamable*. The member function template `get_string` uses a `std::ostringstream` to convert its argument to its string representation—hence the *OutputStreamable* requirement. (To use `std::ostringstream`, remember to include the header `<sstream>`.) The member function `get_string` simply accounts for the fact that a value of type `std::string` is already of the required type and so it skips the trip through `std::ostringstream` and just returns its argument. After the two arguments have been converted to `std::string`, all that remains is to compare them, which we do using `operator<`. Now let's put this visitor to the test by sorting the elements of a container using its services (we'll also reuse the `stream_output_visitor` that we created earlier in this chapter).

```
#include <iostream>
#include <string>
#include <vector>
#include <algorithm>
#include "boost/variant.hpp"

int main() {
  boost::variant<int,std::string> var1="100";
  boost::variant<double> var2=99.99;
```

```
    std::cout << "var1<var2: " <<
      boost::apply_visitor(
        lexicographical_visitor(),var1,var2) << '\n';

    typedef std::vector<
      boost::variant<int,std::string,double> > vec_type;

    vec_type vec;
    vec.push_back("Hello");
    vec.push_back(12);
    vec.push_back(1.12);
    vec.push_back("0");

    stream_output_visitor sv(std::cout);
    std::for_each(vec.begin(),vec.end(),sv);

    lexicographical_visitor lv;
    std::sort(vec.begin(),vec.end(),boost::apply_visitor(lv));

    std::cout << '\n';
    std::for_each(vec.begin(),vec.end(),sv);
};
```

First of all, we apply the visitor to two `variants`, `var1` and `var2`, like so:

```
boost::apply_visitor(lexicographical_visitor(),var1,var2)
```

As you can see, the difference from the unary visitors is that two `variants` are passed to the function `apply_visitor`. A more common example of usage is to use the predicate for sorting the elements, which we do like this:

```
lexicographical_visitor lv;
std::sort(vec.begin(),vec.end(),boost::apply_visitor(lv));
```

When the `sort` algorithm is invoked, it compares its elements using the predicate that we pass to it, which is an instance of `lexicographical_visitor`. Note that `boost::variant` already defines `operator<`, so it's possible to simply sort the container without our predicate.

```
std::sort(vec.begin(),vec.end());
```

But the default sort order, which first checks the current value index via `which`, arranges the elements in the order *12, 0, Hello, 1.12,* and we wanted a lexicographical order. Because both `operator<` and `operator==` is provided for the `variant` class, `variants` can be used as the element type of all Standard Library containers. When these default relations aren't enough, implement the ones you need with binary visitors.

There Is More to Know

We haven't covered all of the functionality of the Boost.Variant library. The remaining advanced features are not needed as often as those we have explored. However, I'll mention them briefly, so you will at least know what's available should you find that you need them. The macro, `BOOST_VARIANT_ENUM_PARAMS`, is useful when overloading/specializing functions and class templates for `variant` types. The macro helps by enumerating the set of types that the `variant` can contain. There is support for creating `variant` types using type sequences—that is, compile-time lists that denote the set of types for the `variant`, through `make_variant_over`. Recursive `variant` types, which are useful for creating expressions that are themselves `variant` types, are available using `recursive_wrapper`, `make_recursive_variant`, and `make_recursive_variant_over`. If you need these additional features, the online documentation does an excellent job of explaining them.

Variant Summary

The fact that discriminated unions are useful in everyday programming should come as no surprise, and the Boost.Variant library does an excellent job of providing efficient and easy-to-use `variant` types based upon discriminated unions. Because C++ unions aren't terribly useful for many types (they support only built-in types and POD types), the need for something else has been prevalent for a long time. Many attempts at creating discriminated unions have suffered from significant drawbacks. For example, previous attempts usually come with a fixed set of supported types, which seriously impedes maintainability and flexibility. Boost.Variant avoids this limitation through templates, which theoretically allows creating any `variant` type. Type-switching code has always been a problem when dealing with discriminated unions; it was necessary to test for the type of the current value before acting, creating maintenance headaches. Boost.Variant offers straightforward value extraction and typesafe visitation, which is a novel approach that elegantly solves that problem. Finally, efficiency has often been a concern with previous attempts, but this library addresses that too, by using stack-based storage rather than the heap.

Boost.Variant is a mature library, with a rich set of features that makes it easy and efficient to work with `variant` types. It nicely complements the Boost.Any library, and it should definitely be part of your professional C++ toolbox.

The authors of Boost.Variant are Eric Friedman and Itay Maman.

Library 8
Tuple

How Does the Tuple Library Improve Your Programs?

- Multiple return values from functions

- Grouping of related types

- Ties values together

C++, like many other programming languages, allows a function to return one value. However, that one value can be of arbitrary type, which allows grouping multiple values as the result, with a `struct` or `class`. Although possible, it is often inconvenient to group related return values in such constructs, because it means defining types for every distinct return type needed. To avoid copying large objects in a return value, and to avoid creating a special type to return multiple values from a function, we often resort to using non-`const` reference arguments or pointers, thereby allowing a function to set the caller's variables through those arguments. This works well in many cases, but some find the output parameters disconcerting in use. Also, output parameters don't emphasize that the return value is in fact return values. Sometimes, `std::pair` is sufficient, but even that proves insufficient when returning more than two values.

To provide for multiple return values, we need a tuple construct. A tuple is a fixed-size collection of values of specified types. Examples include pairs, triples, quadruples, and so on. Some languages come with such tuple types built in, but C++ doesn't. Given the power inherent in C++, this shortcoming can be amended by a library, which as you no doubt guessed, is just what Boost.Tuple does.

The Tuple library provides tuple constructs that are convenient to use for returning multiple values but also to group any types and operate on them with generic code.

How Does the Tuple Library Fit with the Standard Library?

The Standard Library provides a special case of tuple, a 2-tuple, called `std::pair`. This construct is used by Standard Library containers, which you have probably noted when operating on elements of `std::map`. You can store `pairs` in container classes, too. Of course, `std::pair` is not just a tool for container classes, it's useful on its own, and it comes with the convenience function `std::make_pair`, which automates type deduction, plus a set of operators for comparing `pairs`. A general solution for tuples, not just 2-tuples, is definitely even more useful. The offering from the Tuple library is not fully general, but it allows tuples up to 10 elements. (If more are needed, which seems unlikely but certainly not impossible, this limit can be extended.) What's more, these tuples are as efficient as a handcrafted solution using `structs`!

Tuple

Header: `"boost/tuple/tuple.hpp"`

This includes the `tuple` class template and the core of the library.

Header: `"boost/tuple/tuple_io.hpp"`

includes input and output operations for `tuples`.

Header: `"boost/tuple/tuple_comparison.hpp"`

includes relational operators for `tuples`.

The Tuple library resides in a nested namespace within `boost` called `boost::tuples`. To use tuples, include "`boost/tuple/tuple.hpp`", which contains the core library. For input and output operations, include "`boost/tuple/tuple_io.hpp`", and to include support for `tuple` comparisons, include "`boost/tuple/tuple_comparison.hpp`". Some Boost libraries have a convenience header that includes all of the library; Boost.Tuple doesn't. The reason for separating the library into different headers is to reduce compile times; if you won't be using relational operators, you shouldn't need to pay for them in terms of time and dependencies. For convenience, some of the names from the Tuple library are present in namespace boost: tuple, make_tuple, tie, and get. The following is a partial synopsis for Boost.Tuple, showing and briefly discussing the most important functions.

```
namespace boost {

  template <class T1,class T2,...,class TM> class tuple {
  public:
    tuple();

    template <class P1,class P2...,class PM>
      tuple(class P1,class P2,...,PN);

    template <class U1,class U2,...,class UN>
    tuple(const tuple<U1,U2,...,UN>&);

    tuple& operator=(const tuple&);
  };

  template<class T1,class T2,...,class TN> tuple<V1,V2,...,VN>
    make_tuple(const T1& t1,const T2& t2,...,const TN& tn);

  template<class T1,class T2,...,class TN> tuple<T1&,T2&,...,TN>
    tie(T1& t1,T2& t2,...,TN& tn);

  template <int I,class T1,class T2,...,class TN>
    RI get(tuple<T1,T2,...,TN>& t);

  template <int I,class T1,class T2,...,class TN>
    PI get(const tuple<T1,T2,...,TN>& t);

  template <class T1,class T2,...,class TM,
            class U1,class U2,...,class UM>
    bool operator==(const tuple<T1,T2,...,TM>& t,
                    const tuple<U1,U2,...,UM>& u);

  template <class T1,class T2,...,class TM,
            class U1,class U2,...,class UM>
    bool operator!=(const tuple<T1,T2,...,TM>& t,
                    const tuple<U1,U2,...,UM>& u);
```

```
template <class T1,class T2,...,class TN,
          class U1,class U2,...,class UN>
  bool operator<(const tuple<T1,T2,...,TN>&,
                 const tuple<U1,U2,...,UN>&);
}
```

Members

```
tuple();
```

The default constructor of `tuple` initializes all elements, which implies that they must also be default constructible—they must have a public default constructor. Any exceptions from the constructors of the contained elements are propagated.

```
template <class P1,class P2...,class PM>
  tuple(class P1,class P2,...,PN);
```

This constructor accepts arguments that are used to initialize the corresponding elements of the `tuple`. For some `tuple` types, with non-default constructible types, this form of construction is a requirement; there's no way to default-construct a `tuple` without also constructing its elements. For example, reference type elements must be initialized at construction. Note that the number of arguments doesn't need to be the same as the number of elements of the tuple type. It is possible to supply values for some of the elements, leaving the remaining elements to be default initialized. Any exceptions from the elements' constructors are propagated.

```
template <class U1,class U2,...,class UN>
  tuple(const tuple<U1,U2,...,UN>&);
```

This constructor initializes the elements using the elements from another tuple, where each of the elements from the other tuple (T1, T2,...,TM) must be constructible from (U1,U2,...,UN). Any exceptions from constructing the elements are propagated.

```
T_Index & get<int Index>();
const T_Index & get<int Index>() const;
```

Returns a reference to the element at the indicated `Index`. `Index` must be a constant integral expression; a compile-time error is produced if the index is greater than or equal to the number of elements in the `tuple`. The result has the type given by the corresponding template argument, indicated above by T_{Index}.

```
tuple& operator=(const tuple& other);
```

Copy assignment of tuples requires that the two tuples have the same length and element types. Each element in `*this` is assigned the corresponding element in `other`. Any exceptions from assigning the elements are propagated.

Free Functions

```
template<class T1,class T2,...,class TN> tuple<V1,V2,...,VN>
    make_tuple(const T1& t1,const T2& t2,...,const TN& tn);
```

The function template `make_tuple` is the `tuple` analogue of `std::make_pair`. It uses function template argument deduction to determine the element types for a `tuple` containing the arguments. The top-level cv-qualifications of the arguments are not used in creating the `tuple` element types. To control the type deduction for reference types, the Boost.Ref utilities `ref` and `cref` can be used to wrap the arguments and thus affect the resulting type in the returned tuple. (We'll see more about `ref` and `cref` shortly.)

```
template<class T1,class T2,...,class TN> tuple<T1&,T2&,...,TN>
    tie(T1& t1,T2& t2,...,TN& tn);
```

The function template `tie` is similar to `make_tuple`. The function call `tie(t1,t2,...,tn)` is equivalent to `make_tuple(ref(t1),ref(t2)... ref(tn))`—that is, it creates a `tuple` of references to the function arguments. The net effect is that assigning a `tuple` to one created by `tie` copies the source `tuple`'s elements to `tie`'s arguments. Thus, `tie` makes it easy to copy the values from a `tuple` returned from a function to existing variables. You can also assign to a 2-tuple created by `tie` from a `std::pair`.

```
template <int I,class T1,class T2,...,class TN>
    RI get(tuple<T1,T2,...,TN>& t);
```

This overload of the function `get` is used to retrieve one of the elements of the tuple t. Index I must be in the range *[0..N)*, where *N* is the number of elements in the tuple. If `TI` is a reference type, `RI` is `TI`; otherwise, `RI` is `TI&`.

```
template <int I,class T1,class T2,...,class TN>
  PI get(const tuple<T1,T2,...,TN>& t);
```

This function `get` is used to retrieve one of the elements of the tuple t. Index I must be in the range *[0..N)*, where *N* is the number of elements in the tuple. If `TI` is a reference type, `RI` is `TI`; otherwise, `RI` is `const TI&`.

Relational Operators

```
bool operator==(
   const tuple<T1,T2,...,TN>& lhs,
   const tuple<U1,U2,...,UN>& rhs);
```

The equality operator returns `true` if `get<i>(lhs)==get<i>(rhs)` for all i in the range *[0..N)*, where *N* is the number of elements. The two tuples must have the same number of elements. Always returns `true` for empty tuples, where *N=0*.

```
bool operator!=(
   const tuple<T1,T2,...,TN>& lhs,
   const tuple<U1,U2…,...,>& rhs);
```

The inequality operator returns `true` if `get<i>(lhs)!=get<i>(rhs)` for any i in the range *[0..N)*, where *N* is the number of elements. The two tuples must have the same number of elements. Always returns `false` for empty tuples, where *N=0*.

```
bool operator<(
   const tuple<T1,T2,...,TN>& lhs,
   const tuple<U1,U2,...,UN>& rhs);
```

The less than operator returns `true` if `get<i>(lhs)<get<i>(rhs)` for any i in the range *[0..N)*, where *N* is the number of elements, assuming that for each such comparison returning `false`, the expression `!(get<i>(rhs)<get<i>(lhs))` is `true`; otherwise, it returns `false`. The two tuples must have the same number of elements. Always returns `true` for empty `tuples`—that is, where *N=0*.

It's worth noting that for all of the supported relational operators (operators `==`, `!=`, `<`, `>`, `<=`, and `>=`), the two `tuples` must meet a couple of constraints. First, they both must be of the same length. Second, each element pair (first with first, second with second, and so on) between the two `tuples` must support the same relational operator. When these constraints are met, the `tuple` operator is implemented such that it compares each element pair, in turn—that is, the operators are short-circuited, returning as soon as the answer is obvious. The `<`, `>`, `<=`, and `>=` operators perform lexicographical comparisons, and expect the same of the element pair operators they invoke. Any exceptions emitted by the element pair operators are propagated, but the `tuple` operators do not throw any exceptions of their own.

Usage

Tuples live in namespace `tuples`, which in turn is inside namespace `boost`. Include `"boost/tuple/tuple.hpp"` to use the library. The relational operators are defined in the header `"boost/tuple/tuple_comparison.hpp"`. Input and output of tuples are defined in `"boost/tuple/tuple_io.hpp"`. A few of the key `tuple` components (`tie` and `make_tuple`) are also available directly in namespace `boost`. In this section, we'll cover how tuples are used in some typical scenarios, and how it is possible to extend the functionality of the library to best fit our purposes. We'll start with the *construction* of tuples, and gradually move on to topics that include the details of how tuples can be utilized.

Constructing Tuples

The construction of a `tuple` involves declaring the types and, optionally, providing a list of initial values of compatible types.[1]

```
boost::tuple<int,double,std::string>
   triple(42,3.14,"My first tuple!");
```

---

1. The constructor arguments do not have to be of the exact type specified for the elements when specializing the `tuple` so long as they are implicitly convertible to those types.

The template parameters to the class template `tuple` specify the element types. The preceding example shows the creation of a `tuple` with three types: an `int`, a `double`, and a `std::string`. Providing three parameters to the constructor initializes the values of all three elements. It's also possible to pass fewer arguments than there are elements, which results in the remaining elements being default initialized.

```
boost::tuple<short,int,long> another;
```

In this example, `another` has elements of types `short`, `int`, and `long`, and they are all initialized to 0.[2] Regardless of the set of types for your `tuples`, this is how they are defined and constructed. So, if one of your `tuple`'s element types is not default constructible, you need to initialize it yourself. Compared to defining `struct`s, `tuples` are much simpler to declare, define, and use. There's also the convenience function, `make_tuple`, which makes creating `tuples` easier still. It deduces the types, relieving you from the monotony (and chance of error!) of specifying them explicitly.

```
boost::tuples::tuple<int,double> get_values() {
   return boost::make_tuple(6,12.0);
}
```

The function `make_tuple` is analogous to `std::make_pair`. By default, `make_tuple` sets the types of the elements to non-`const`, non-reference—that is, the plain, underlying types of the arguments. For example, consider the following variables:

```
int plain=42;
int& ref=plain;
const int& cref=ref;
```

These three variables are named after their cv-qualification (constness) and whether they are references. The `tuples` created by the following invocations of `make_tuple` all have one `int` element.

```
boost::make_tuple(plain);
boost::make_tuple(ref);
boost::make_tuple(cref);
```

---

2. Within the context of a template, `T()` for a built-in type means initialization with zero.

This isn't always the right behavior, but on most occasions it is, which is the reason why it's the default. To make an element of a `tuple` to be of reference type, use the function `boost::ref`, which is part of another Boost library called Boost.Ref. The following three lines use the variables that we declared earlier, but this time the `tuples` have an `int&` element, except for the last, which has a `const int&` element (we can't remove the constness of `cref`):

```
boost::make_tuple(boost::ref(plain));
boost::make_tuple(boost::ref(ref));
boost::make_tuple(boost::ref(cref));
```

If the elements should be `const` references, use `boost::cref` from Boost.Ref. Here, the three tuples have one `const int&` element:

```
boost::make_tuple(boost::cref(plain));
boost::make_tuple(boost::cref(ref));
boost::make_tuple(boost::cref(cref));
```

It's probably obvious, but `ref` and `cref` have plenty of uses in other contexts too. In fact, they were created as a part of the Boost.Tuple library, but were later moved to a separate library because of their general utility.

Accessing *tuple* Elements

The elements of a `tuple` are accessed either through the `tuple` member function `get` or the free function `get`. They both require a constant integral expression designating the index of the element to retrieve.

```
#include <iostream>
#include <string>

#include "boost/tuple/tuple.hpp"

int main() {
  boost::tuple<int,double,std::string>
  triple(42,3.14,"The amazing tuple!");

  int i=boost::tuples::get<0>(triple);
  double d=triple.get<1>();
  std::string s=boost::get<2>(triple);
}
```

In the example, a `tuple` with three elements with the innovative name `triple` was created. `triple` contained an `int`, a `double`, and a `string`, which were retrieved through the `get` functions.

```
int i=boost::tuples::get<0>(triple);
```

Here, you see the free function `get` at work. It takes a `tuple` as its one argument. Note that supplying an invalid index causes an error at compilation time. The precondition is that the index be a valid index for the `tuple` type.

```
double d=triple.get<1>();
```

This code shows using the member function `get`. The preceding line could also have been written like this:

```
double& d=triple.get<1>();
```

The preceding binding to a reference works because `get` always returns a *reference* to the element. If the `tuple`, or the type, is `const`, a `const` reference is returned. The two functions are equivalent, but on some compilers only the free function works correctly. The free function has the advantage of providing a consistent extraction style for types other than `tuple`. One advantage of accessing the elements of `tuples` by index rather than by name is that it enables generic solutions, because there are no dependencies on a certain name, but only to an index. More on this later.

Tuple Assignment and Copy Construction

`tuples` can be assigned and copy constructed, providing that there are suitable conversions between the types of the elements in the two `tuples`. To assign or copy `tuples`, member-wise assignment or copying is performed, so the two `tuples` must have the same number of elements. The elements in the source `tuple` must be convertible to those of the destination `tuple`. The following example shows how this works.

```
#include <iostream>
#include <string>

#include "boost/tuple/tuple.hpp"

class base {
```

```
public:
  virtual ~base() {};
  virtual void test() {
    std::cout << "base::test()\n";
  }
};

class derived : public base {
public:
  virtual void test() {
    std::cout << "derived::test()\n";
  }
};

int main() {
  boost::tuple<int,std::string,derived> tup1(-5,"Tuples");
  boost::tuple<unsigned int,std::string,base> tup2;
  tup2=tup1;

  tup2.get<2>().test();
  std::cout << "Interesting value: "
            << tup2.get<0>() << '\n';

  const boost::tuple<double,std::string,base> tup3(tup2);
  tup3.get<0>()=3.14;
}
```

The example begins by defining two classes, base and derived, which are used as elements of two tuple types. The first tuple contains three elements of types, int, std::string, and derived. The second tuple consists of three elements of the compatible types unsigned int, std::string, and base. Consequently, the two tuples meet the requirements for assignment, which is why tup2=tup1 is valid. In that assignment, the third element of tup1, which is of type derived, is assigned to the third element of tup2, which is of type base. The assignment succeeds, but the derived object is sliced, so this defeats polymorphism.

```
tup2.get<2>().test();
```

That line extracts a base&, but the object in tup2 is of type base, so it winds up calling base::test. We could have made the behavior truly polymorphic by changing the tuples to contain references or pointers to base and derived, respectively. Note that numeric conversion dangers (loss of precision, positive and negative overflow) apply when converting between `tuples` as well. These dangerous conversions can be made safe with the help of the Boost.Conversion library, covered in "Library 2: Conversion."

The next line in the example copy-constructs a new `tuple`, `tup3`, with different, but still compatible types, from `tup2`.

```
const boost::tuple<double,std::string,base> tup3(tup2);
```

Note that `tup3` is declared `const`. This implies that there is an error in the example. See if you can you spot it. I'll wait.... Did you see it? Here it is:

```
tup3.get<0>()=3.14;
```

Because `tup3` is const, `get` returns a `const double&`. This means that the assignment statement is ill-formed, and the example doesn't compile. Assignment and copy construction between `tuples` are intuitive, because the semantics are exactly the same for the `tuples` as for the individual elements. By way of example, let's see how to give polymorphic behavior to the derived-to-base assignment between `tuples`.

```
derived d;
boost::tuple<int,std::string,derived*>
  tup4(-5,"Tuples",&d);
boost::tuple<unsigned int,std::string,base*> tup5;
tup5=tup4;

tup5.get<2>()->test();

boost::tuple<int,std::string,derived&>
  tup6(12,"Example",d);

boost::tuple<unsigned int,std::string,base&> tup7(tup6);

tup7.get<2>()->test();
```

In both cases, `derived::test` is called, which is exactly what we want. `tup6` and `tup7` are not assignable because you can't assign to a reference, which is why `tup7` is copy constructed from `tup6` and `tup6` is initialized with `d`. Because `tup4` and `tup5` use pointers for their third element, they do support assignment. Note that typically smart pointers are best in tuples (as opposed to raw pointers), because they alleviate the need to manage the lifetime of the resources to which the pointers refer. However, as `tup4` and `tup5` show, pointers don't always refer to something requiring memory management in the `tuples`. (Refer to "Library 1: Smart_ptr" for the details on the powerful smart pointers in Boost.)

Comparing Tuples

To compare `tuples`, you must include `"boost/tuple/tuple_comparison.hpp"`. The relational `tuple` operators are `==`, `!=`, `<`, `>`, `<=` and `>=`, and they invoke the same operator for each element pair, in order, in the `tuples` being compared. These pair-wise comparisons short circuit, meaning that they only compare as many pairs as needed to arrive at the correct result. Only `tuples` with the same number of elements can be compared and, as should be obvious, the corresponding element types in the two `tuples` must be comparable. The test for equality returns `true` if all of the element pairs of the two `tuples` are also equal. If any one equality comparison between element pairs returns `false`, so does `operator==`. The inequality test is analogous, but returns the inverse result. The rest of the relational operators perform lexicographical comparisons.

Here's a sample program showing the comparison operators in action.

```
#include <iostream>
#include <string>

#include "boost/tuple/tuple.hpp"
#include "boost/tuple/tuple_comparison.hpp"

int main() {
  boost::tuple<int,std::string> tup1(11,"Match?");
  boost::tuple<short,std::string> tup2(12,"Match?");

  std::cout << std::boolalpha;

  std::cout << "Comparison: tup1 is less than tup2\n";

  std::cout << "tup1==tup2: " << (tup1==tup2) << '\n';
  std::cout << "tup1!=tup2: " << (tup1!=tup2) << '\n';
  std::cout << "tup1<tup2:  " << (tup1<tup2) << '\n';
  std::cout << "tup1>tup2:  " << (tup1>tup2) << '\n';
  std::cout << "tup1<=tup2: " << (tup1<=tup2) << '\n';
  std::cout << "tup1>=tup2: " << (tup1>=tup2) << '\n';

  tup2.get<0>()=boost::get<0>(tup1); // tup2=tup1 also works
```

```
std::cout << "\nComparison: tup1 equals tup2\n";

std::cout << "tup1==tup2: " << (tup1==tup2) << '\n';
std::cout << "tup1!=tup2: " << (tup1!=tup2) << '\n';
std::cout << "tup1<tup2:  " << (tup1<tup2) << '\n';
std::cout << "tup1>tup2:  " << (tup1>tup2) << '\n';
std::cout << "tup1<=tup2: " << (tup1<=tup2) << '\n';
std::cout << "tup1>=tup2: " << (tup1>=tup2) << '\n';
}
```

As you can see, the two `tuples`, `tup1` and `tup2`, don't have exactly the same type, but the types are still comparable. For the first set of comparisons, the `tuples` have different values for the first element, but for the second set, the `tuples` are equal. This is the output from running the program.

```
Comparison: tup1 is less than tup2
tup1==tup2: false
tup1!=tup2: true
tup1<tup2:  true
tup1>tup2:  false
tup1<=tup2: true
tup1>=tup2: false

Comparison: tup1 equals tup2
tup1==tup2: true
tup1!=tup2: false
tup1<tup2:  false
tup1>tup2:  false
tup1<=tup2: true
tup1>=tup2: true
```

One important aspect of the support for comparisons is that `tuples` can be sorted, which means they can be stored in associative containers. It is sometimes desirable to sort based on one of the elements of a `tuple` (creating a strict weak ordering), which we can accomplish with a simple, generic solution.

```
template <int Index> class element_less {
public:
  template <typename Tuple>
  bool operator()(const Tuple& lhs,const Tuple& rhs) const {
    return boost::get<Index>(lhs)<boost::get<Index>(rhs);
  }
};
```

This shows one of the advantages of accessing elements by index rather than by name; it is very easy to create generic constructs that perform powerful operations. The sorting performed by our element_less can be used like this:

```cpp
#include <iostream>
#include <vector>
#include "boost/tuple/tuple.hpp"
#include "boost/tuple/tuple_comparison.hpp"

template <int Index> class element_less {
public:
  template <typename Tuple>
  bool operator()(const Tuple& lhs,const Tuple& rhs) const {
    return boost::get<Index>(lhs)<boost::get<Index>(rhs);
  }
};


int main() {
  typedef boost::tuple<short,int,long,float,double,long double>
    num_tuple;

  std::vector<num_tuple> vec;

  vec.push_back(num_tuple(6,2));
  vec.push_back(num_tuple(7,1));
  vec.push_back(num_tuple(5));

  std::sort(vec.begin(),vec.end(),element_less<1>());

  std::cout << "After sorting: " <<
    vec[0].get<0>() << '\n' <<
    vec[1].get<0>() << '\n' <<
    vec[2].get<0>() << '\n';
}
```

vec is populated with three elements. The sorting is performed on the second element of the tuples using the element_less<1> function object from the template that we created earlier. There are more applications for this kind of function object, such as when searching for certain tuple elements.

Tying Tuple Elements to Variables

A handy feature of the Boost.Tuple library is "tying" tuples to variables. Tiers are tuples created by the overloaded function template boost::tie, such that all of the elements are non-const reference types. As a result, ties must be initialized with lvalues, and thus tie's arguments are non-const reference types, too. Because the resulting tuples have non-const reference elements, any assignment to the elements of such a tuple are assignments through non-const references to the lvalues with which tie was called. This ties existing variables to a tuple, hence the name!

The following example first shows the obvious way of getting values out of a returned tuple. Then, it shows the same operation using a tied tuple to assign values directly to variables. To make the example more interesting, we'll begin by defining a function that returns the greatest common divisor and the least common multiple of two values. The values are, of course, grouped together as a tuple return type. You'll notice that the functions for calculating the greatest common divisor and least common multiple come from another Boost library—Boost.Math.

```
#include <iostream>
#include "boost/tuple/tuple.hpp"
#include "boost/math/common_factor.hpp"

boost::tuple<int,int> gcd_lcm(int val1,int val2) {
  return boost::make_tuple(
    boost::math::gcd(val1,val2),
    boost::math::lcm(val1,val2));
}

int main() {
  // The "old" way
  boost::tuple<int,int> tup;
  tup=gcd_lcm(12,18);
  int gcd=tup.get<0>());
  int lcm=tup.get<1>());

  std::cout << "Greatest common divisor: " << gcd << '\n';
  std::cout << "Least common multiple:   " << lcm << '\n';

  // The "new" way
  boost::tie(gcd,lcm)=gcd_lcm(15,20);
```

```
    std::cout << "Greatest common divisor:  " << gcd << '\n';
    std::cout << "Least common multiple:    " << lcm << '\n';
}
```

In some cases, we may not be interested in all of the elements of the returned tuple, and this too is supported by `tie`. There is a special object—`boost::tuples::ignore`—that discards a `tuple` element's value. If in the preceding example we were only interested in the greatest common divisor, we could have expressed it as follows:

```
boost::tie(gcd,boost::tuples::ignore)=gcd_lcm(15,20);
```

The alternative is to create a variable, pass it to `tie`, and then ignore it in the rest of the current scope. That leaves maintainers to question the variable's existence. Using `ignore` clearly proclaims that the code doesn't use that value from the `tuple`.

Note that `tie` also supports `std::pair`. The usage is just like tying values from `boost::tuples`.

```
std::pair<short,double> p(3,0.141592);
short s;
double d;

boost::tie(s,d)=p;
```

Tying `tuples` is more than a mere convenience; it helps make the code clearer.

Streaming Tuples

Each of the examples in this chapter extracted the elements of `tuples` just to be able to stream them to `std::cout`. This works, but there's actually an easier way. The `tuple` library supports both input and output streaming; `operator>>` and `operator<<` are overloaded for `tuples`. There are also manipulators to change the default delimiters used for input and output streaming. Changing the delimiters for input changes what `operator>>` looks for to recognize element values. Let's examine these things in a simple program that reads and writes `tuples`. Note that to use `tuple` streaming, you need to include the header `"boost/tuple/tuple_io.hpp"`.

```
#include <iostream>
#include "boost/tuple/tuple.hpp"
#include "boost/tuple/tuple_io.hpp"

int main() {
  boost::tuple<int,double> tup1;
  boost::tuple<long,long,long> tup2;

  std::cout << "Enter an int and a double as (1 2.3):\n";
  std::cin >> tup1;

  std::cout << "Enter three ints as |1.2.3|:\n";
  std::cin >> boost::tuples::set_open('|') >>
    boost::tuples::set_close('|') >>
    boost::tuples::set_delimiter('.') >> tup2;

  std::cout << "Here they are:\n"
            << tup1 << '\n'
            << boost::tuples::set_open('\"') <<
    boost::tuples::set_close('\"') <<
    boost::tuples::set_delimiter('-');

  std::cout << tup2 << '\n';
}
```

The previous example shows how to use the streaming operators together with tuples. The default delimiters for tuples are ((left parenthesis) as opening delimiter,) (right parenthesis) for the closing delimiter, and a space for delimiting tuple element values. This implies that to get our program working correctly, we need to give the program input like (12 54.1) and |4.5.3|. Here's a sample run.

```
Enter an int and a double as (1 2.3):
(12 54.1)
Enter three ints as |1.2.3|:
|4.5.3|
Here they are:
(12 54.1)
"4-5-3"
```

The support for streaming is convenient and, with the support of the delimiter manipulators, it's easy to make streaming compatible even with legacy code that has been updated to use tuples.

Finding Out More About Tuples

There are more facilities for tuples than those we've already seen. These more advanced features are vital for creating generic constructs that work with tuples. For example, you can get the length of a tuple (the number of elements), retrieve the type of an element, and use the null_type tuple sentinel to terminate recursive template instantiations.

It's not possible to iterate over the elements of a tuple with a for loop, because get requires a constant integral expression. However, using a template metaprogram, we can print all the elements of a tuple.

```cpp
#include <iostream>
#include <string>
#include "boost/tuple/tuple.hpp"

template <typename Tuple,int Index> struct print_helper {
  static void print(const Tuple& t) {
    std::cout << boost::tuples::get<Index>(t) << '\n';
    print_helper<Tuple,Index-1>::print(t);
  }
};

template<typename Tuple> struct print_helper<Tuple,0> {
  static void print(const Tuple& t) {
    std::cout << boost::tuples::get<0>(t) << '\n';
  }
};

template <typename Tuple> void print_all(const Tuple& t) {
  print_helper<
    Tuple,boost::tuples::length<Tuple>::value-1>::print(t);
}

int main() {
  boost::tuple<int,std::string,double>
    tup(42,"A four and a two",42.424242);

  print_all(tup);
}
```

In the example, a helper class template, print_helper, is a metaprogram that visits all indices of a tuple, printing the element for each index. The partial specialization terminates the template recursion. The function print_all supplies the length of its `tuple` parameter, plus the `tuple` to a `print_helper` constructor. The length of the tuple is retrieved like this:

```
boost::tuples::length<Tuple>::value
```

This is a constant integral expression, which means it can be passed as the second template argument for `print_helper`. However, there's a caveat to our solution, which becomes clear when we see the output from running the program.

```
42.4242
A four and a two
42
```

We're printing the elements in reverse order! Although this could be considered a feature in some situations (he says slyly), it's certainly not the intention here. The problem is that `print_helper` prints the value of the `boost::tuples::length<Tuple>::value-1` element first, then the value of the previous element, and so on, until the specialization prints the first element's value. Rather than using the first element as the special case and starting with the last element, we need to start with the first element and use the *last* element as the special case. How is that possible? The solution becomes apparent after you know that `tuples` are terminated with a special type, `boost::tuples::null_type`. We can always be certain that the last type in a `tuple` is `null_type`, which also means that our solution involves a specialization or function overload for `null_type`.

The remaining issue is getting the first element's value followed by the next, and so on, and then stopping at the end of the list. `tuples` provide the member functions `get_head` and `get_tail` to access the elements in them. As its name suggests, `get_head` returns the head of the sequence of values—that is, the first element's value. `get_tail` returns a `tuple` with all but the first value in the `tuple`. That leads to the following solution for `print_all`.

```
void print_all(const boost::tuples::null_type&) {}

template <typename Tuple> void print_all(const Tuple& t) {
  std::cout << t.get_head() << '\n';
  print_all(t.get_tail());
}
```

This solution is shorter than the original, and it prints the element values in the correct order. Each time the function template `print_all` executes, it prints one element from the beginning of the tuple and then recurses with a tuple of all but the first value in `t`. When there are no more values in the tuple, the tail is of type `null_type`, the overloaded function `print_all` is called, and the recursion terminates.

It can be useful to know the type of a particular element such as when declaring variables in generic code that are initialized from tuple elements. Consider a function that returns the sum of the first two elements of a tuple, with the additional requirement that the return type must correspond to the largest type (for example, with regards to range of integral types) of the two. Without somehow knowing the types of the elements, it would be impossible to create a general solution to this. This is what the helper template `element<N,Tuple>::type` does, as the following example shows. The problem we're facing not only involves calculating which element has the largest type, but declaring that type as the return value of a function. This is somewhat complicated, but we can solve it using an extra level of indirection. This indirection comes in the form of an additional helper template with one responsibility: to provide a `typedef` that defines the larger of two types. The code may seem a little hairy, but it does the job.

```cpp
#include <iostream>
#include "boost/tuple/tuple.hpp"
#include <cassert>
template <bool B,typename Tuple> struct largest_type_helper {
   typedef typename boost::tuples::element<1,Tuple>::type type;
};

template<typename Tuple> struct largest_type_helper<true,Tuple> {
   typedef typename boost::tuples::element<0,Tuple>::type type;
};

template<typename Tuple> struct largest_type {
   typedef typename largest_type_helper<
     (sizeof(boost::tuples::element<0,Tuple>) >
      sizeof(boost::tuples::element<1,Tuple>)),Tuple>::type type;
};

template <typename Tuple>
  typename largest_type<Tuple>::type sum(const Tuple& t) {
    typename largest_type<Tuple>::type
      result=boost::tuples::get<0>(t)+
```

```
        boost::tuples::get<1>(t);

    return result;
}

int main() {
    typedef boost::tuple<short,int,long> my_tuple;

    boost::tuples::element<0,my_tuple>::type first=14;
    assert(type_id(first) == typeid(short));
    boost::tuples::element<1,my_tuple>::type second=27;
    assert(type_id(second) == typeid(int));
    boost::tuples::element<
        boost::tuples::length<my_tuple>::value-1,my_tuple>::type
            last;

    my_tuple t(first,second,last);

    std::cout << "Type is int? " <<
        (typeid(int)==typeid(largest_type<my_tuple>::type)) << '\n';

    int s=sum(t);
}
```

If you didn't quite follow the exercise in template metaprogramming, don't worry—it's absolutely not a requirement for utilizing the Tuple library. Although this type of coding takes some time getting used to, the idea is really quite simple. largest_type gets the typedef from one of the two helper class templates, largest_type_helper, where one version is partially specialized on the Boolean parameter. This parameter is determined by comparing the size of the two first elements of the tuple (the second template parameter). The result of this is a typedef that represents the larger of the two types. Our function sum uses that type as the return value, and the rest is simply a matter of adding the two elements.

The rest of the example shows how to use the function sum, and also how to declare variables with types from certain tuple elements. The first two use a hardcoded index into the tuple.

```
boost::tuples::element<0,my_tuple>::type first=14;
boost::tuples::element<1,my_tuple>::type second=27;
```

The last declaration retrieves the index of the last element of the `tuple`, and uses that as input to the element helper to (generically) declare the type.

```
boost::tuples::element<
boost::tuples::length<my_tuple>::value-1,my_tuple>::type last;
```

Tuples and *for_each*

The method that we used to create the `print_all` function can be extended to create a more general mechanism like `std::for_each`. For example, what if we didn't want to print the elements, but rather wanted to sum them or copy them, or what if we wanted to print only some of them? Sequential access to the tuple elements isn't straightforward, as we discovered when we developed the preceding examples. It makes sense to create a general solution that accepts a function or function object argument to invoke on the tuple elements. This enables not only the (rather limited) `print_all` function's behavior, but also that of any function that can accept the types of elements from a `tuple`. The following example creates a function template called `for_each_element` to do just that. For the sake of argument, the example shows two function objects to show the workings of `for_each_element`.

```
#include <iostream>
#include <string>
#include <functional>
#include "boost/tuple/tuple.hpp"

template <typename Function> void for_each_element(
  const boost::tuples::null_type&, Function) {}

template <typename Tuple, typename Function> void
  for_each_element(Tuple& t, Function func) {
    func(t.get_head());
    for_each_element(t.get_tail(),func);
}

struct print {
  template <typename T> void operator()(const T& t) {
    std::cout << t << '\n';
  }
};
```

```
template <typename T> struct print_type {
  void operator()(const T& t) {
    std::cout << t << '\n';
  }

  template <typename U> void operator()(const U& u) {}
};

int main() {
  typedef boost::tuple<short,int,long> my_tuple;

  boost::tuple<int,short,double> nums(1,2,3.01);

  for_each_element(nums, print());
  for_each_element(nums, print_type<double>());
}
```

The function `for_each_element` reuses the strategy from earlier examples, by overloading the function with a version that accepts an argument of type `null_type` that signals the end of the tuple's elements, to do nothing. Let's look at the function where the work is done.

```
template <typename Tuple, typename Function> void
  for_each_element(Tuple& t, Function func) {
    func(t.get_head());
    for_each_element(t.get_tail(),func);
}
```

The second template and function parameter specifies the function (or function object) to call with the tuple elements as argument. `for_each_element` first invokes the function (object) with the element returned from `get_head`. One way to think of it is that `get_head` returns the current element of the tuple. Then, it recursively calls itself with the tail or remaining elements of the tuple. The next call extracts the head element and calls the function (object) with it and recurses again, and so on. Eventually, `get_tail` finds no more elements and returns an instance of `null_type`, which ends the recursion by matching the non-recursive `for_each_element` overload. That's all there is to `for_each_element`!

Next, the example illustrates two function objects that contain nice techniques for reuse in other contexts. One is the `print` function object.

```
struct print {
  template <typename T> void operator()(const T& t) {
```

```
      std::cout << t << '\n';
   }
};
```

There is nothing fancy about this `print` function object, but as it turns out, many programmers are unaware of the fact that the function call operator can be templated! Typically, function objects are parameterized on one or more types that they should work with, but that doesn't work for `tuples` because the elements are typically of different types. Thus, the parameterization is not on the function object itself, but on the function call operator, with the added benefit that using it is much simpler, as shown here.

```
for_each_element(nums, print());
```

There's no need to specify the type, which would have been required with a parameterized function object. Pushing the template parameters onto the member functions of a class is sometimes useful and often user-friendly.

The second function object prints all elements of a certain type. This kind of filtering can be used to extract elements of compatible types, too.

```
template <typename T> struct print_type {
   void operator()(const T& t) {
     std::cout << t << '\n';
   }

   template <typename U> void operator()(const U& u) {}
};
```

This function object displays another useful technique, which I refer to as the *discarding overload*. It's used to ignore the elements passed to it except those of type `T` untouched. The trick involves an overload with a better match for all but a certain type. That bell you hear ringing is probably from the close connection this technique has with the `sizeof` trick and the ellipsis (...) construct, which is used to make decisions at compile time, but that doesn't work here, where the function is actually called but doesn't do anything. The function object is used like this:

```
for_each_element(print_type<double>(),nums);
```

Easy to use, easy to write, and it adds value. That's probably not as much a property of the function object as it is of the Tuple library that enables the use of these and other idioms.

Tuple Summary

The Tuple library brings the concept of tuples to C++. It is intuitive and concise, and although its primary use seems to be for multiple return value from functions, it is also very useful for creating all sorts of logical groupings such as storing sets of elements (as elements) in Standard Library containers. The alternative for achieving the same level of coherency is to create unique `structs` for every different return type (groupings), which is not only tedious work, it also removes the possibility of generic solutions for recurring tasks. These problems are alleviated with the use of the Boost.Tuple.

In this chapter, we've seen how to use the Tuple library and how to extend it in the form of function objects and algorithms that can work with any tuple. Accessing elements by index, and the `get_head`/`get_tail` member functions, provides consistency in working with `tuples` that enables many solutions that are impossible with other forms of user-defined types (UDTs).

The creator of Boost.Tuple, Jaakko Järvi, deserves credit for this great library. This creation goes a long way to prove that nearly anything lacking in C++ can be added through libraries by talented designers.

Part III
Function Objects and Higher-Order Programming

The following four libraries have the potential of changing the way you look at programming in C++ forever. Although function objects are not a novel concept, especially for people who have long been using and customizing the algorithms in the Standard Library, the libraries covered in this part of the book take function objects to a whole new level of abstraction. There are areas in C++ that are sometimes considered to be shortcomings when employing certain designs, such as the seemingly unavoidable proliferation of small function objects when using Standard Library algorithms. One must never forget that in C++, it's best to not be (too) judgmental of the language itself, for it was designed to handle its own shortcomings through libraries; and that's exactly what the libraries Boost.Bind and Boost.Lambda try to do for the aforementioned problem. Callback functions are another problematic area that is addressed here; the root of the problem is accentuated by using libraries for higher-order programming, because storing and invoking delayed function-like objects becomes an important feature. That's what Boost.Function does, and of course, it plays very nicely with the other two libraries mentioned here (and others, too). The final chapter discusses Boost.Signals, a library that reifies the *Observer* pattern. There is fantastic power in these libraries—enabling programmers to write less code, more expressive statements, and really compact expressions that make code easier to read and maintain. With this power comes responsibility, because it's also quite possible to write virtually unparseable expressions. For many programmers, the acquaintance with these libraries has been an epiphany—I hope that it will be for you too.

Library 9
Bind

How Does the Bind Library Improve Your Programs?

- Adapts functions and function objects for use with Standard Library algorithms

- Consistent syntax for creating binders

- Powerful functional composition

When using the algorithms from the Standard Library, you often need to supply them with a function or a function object. This is an excellent way of customizing the behavior of algorithms, but you often end up writing new function objects because you don't have the tools necessary for functional composition and adaptation of argument order or arity. Although the Standard Library does offer some productive tools, such as `bind1st` and `bind2nd`, this is rarely enough. Even when the functionality suffices, that often implies suffering from awkward syntax that obfuscates the code for programmers who are not familiar with those tools. What you need, then, is a solution that both adds functionality and normalizes the syntax for creating function objects on-the-fly, and this is what Boost.Bind does.

In effect, a generalized binder is a sort of lambda expression, because through functional composition we can more or less construct local, unnamed functions at the call site. There are many cases where this is desirable, because it serves three purposes—reducing the amount of code, making the code easier to understand, and localizing behavior, which in turn implies more effective maintenance. Note that there is another Boost library, Boost.Lambda, which takes these properties even further. Boost.Lambda is covered in the next chapter. Why shouldn't you just skip ahead to that library? Because most of the time, Boost.Bind does everything you need when it comes to binding, and the learning curve isn't as steep.

One of the keys to the success of Bind is the uniform syntax for creating function objects and the few requirements on types that are to be used with the library. The design takes focus away from how to write the code that works with your types, and sets it to where we are all most interested—how the code works and what it actually does. When using adaptors from the Standard Library, such as `ptr_fun` and `mem_fun_ref`, code quickly becomes unnecessarily verbose because we have to provide these adaptors in order for the arguments to adhere to the requirements of the algorithms. This is not the case with Boost.Bind, which uses a much more sophisticated deduction system, and a straightforward syntax when the automatic deduction cannot be applied. The net effect of using Bind is that you'll write less code that is easier to understand.

How Does Bind Fit with the Standard Library?

Conceptually, Bind is a generalization of the existing Standard Library functions `bind1st` and `bind2nd`, with additional functionality that allows for more sophisticated functional composition. It also alleviates the need to use adaptors for pointers to functions and pointers to class members, which saves coding and potential errors. Boost.Bind also covers some of the popular extensions to the C++ Standard Library, such as the SGI extensions `compose1` and `compose2`, and also the `select1st` and `select2nd` functions. So, Bind does fit with the Standard Library, and it does so very well indeed. The need for such functionality is acknowledged, and at last in part addressed by the Standard Library, and also in popular extensions to the STL. Boost.Bind has been accepted for the upcoming Library Technical Report.

Bind

Header: `"boost/bind.hpp"`

The Bind library creates function objects that bind to a function (free function or member function). Rather than supplying all of the arguments to the function directly, arguments can be delayed, meaning that a binder can be used to create a function object with changed arity (number of arguments) for the function it binds to, or to reorder the arguments any way you like.

The return types of the overloaded versions of the function `bind` are unspecified—that is, there is no guarantee for what the signature of a returned function object is. Sometimes, you need to store that object somewhere, rather than just passing it directly to another function—when this need arises, you want to use Boost.Function, which is covered in "Library 11: Function." The key to understanding what the `bind`-functions return is to grok the transformation that is taking place. Using one of the overloaded `bind` functions—`template<class R, class F> unspecified-1 bind(F f)`—as an example, this would be (quoting from the online documentation), "A function object λ such that the expression $\lambda(v1, v2, ..., vm)$ is equivalent to f(), implicitly converted to R." Thus, the function that is bound is stored inside the binder, and the result of subsequent invocations on that function object yields the return value from the function (if any)—that is, the template parameter `R`. The implementation that we're covering here supports up to nine function arguments.

The implementation of Bind involves a number of functions and classes, but as users, we do not directly use anything other than the overloaded function `bind`. All binding takes place through the `bind` function, and we can never depend on the type of the return value. When using `bind`, the placeholders for arguments (called `_1`, `_2`, and so on) do not need to be introduced with a using declaration or directive, because they reside in an unnamed namespace. Thus, there is rarely a reason for writing one of the following lines when using Boost.Bind.

```
using boost::bind;
using namespace boost;
```

As was mentioned before, the current implementation of Boost.Bind supports nine placeholders (`_1`, `_2`, `_3`, and so forth), and therefore also up to nine arguments. It's instructive to at least browse through the synopsis for a high-level understanding of how the type deduction is performed, and when/why this does not always work. Parsing the signatures for member function pointers and free functions takes a while for the eye to get used to, but it's useful. You'll see that there are overloads for both free functions and class member functions. Also, there are overloads for each distinct number of arguments. Rather than listing the synopsis here, I encourage you to visit Boost.Bind's documentation at www.boost.org.

Usage

Boost.Bind offers a consistent syntax for both functions and function objects, and even for value semantics and pointer semantics. We'll start with some simple examples to get to grips with the usage of vanilla bindings, and then move on to functional composition through nested binds. One of the keys to understanding how to use bind is the concept of placeholders. Placeholders denote the arguments that are to be supplied to the resulting function object, and Boost.Bind supports up to nine such arguments. The placeholders are called _1, _2, _3, _4, and so on up to _9, and you use them in the places where you would ordinarily add the argument. As a first example, we shall define a function, nine_arguments, which is then called using a bind expression.

```
#include <iostream>
#include "boost/bind.hpp"

void nine_arguments(
    int i1,int i2,int i3,int i4,
      int i5,int i6,int i7,int i8, int i9) {
    std::cout << i1 << i2 << i3 << i4 << i5
        << i6 << i7 << i8 << i9 << '\n';
}

int main() {
    int i1=1,i2=2,i3=3,i4=4,i5=5,i6=6,i7=7,i8=8,i9=9;
    (boost::bind(&nine_arguments,_9,_2,_1,_6,_3,_8,_4,_5,_7))
      (i1,i2,i3,i4,i5,i6,i7,i8,i9);
}
```

In this example, you create an unnamed temporary binder and immediately invoke it by passing arguments to its function call operator. As you can see, the order of the placeholders is scrambled—this illustrates the reordering of arguments. Note also that placeholders can be used more than once in an expression. The output of this program is as follows.

```
921638457
```

This shows that the placeholders correspond to the argument with the placeholder's number—that is, _1 is substituted with the first argument, _2 with the second argument, and so on. Next, you'll see how to call member functions of a class.

Calling a Member Function

Let's take a look at calling member functions using bind. We'll start by doing something that also can be done with the Standard Library, in order to compare and contrast that solution with the one using Boost.Bind. When storing elements of some class type in Standard Library containers, a common need is to call a member function on some or all of these elements. This can be done in a loop, and is all-too-often implemented thusly, but there are better solutions. Consider the following simple class, status, which we'll use to show that the ease of use and power of Boost.Bind is indeed tremendous.

```cpp
class status {
  std::string name_;
  bool ok_;
public:
  status(const std::string& name):name_(name),ok_(true) {}

  void break_it() {
    ok_=false;
  }

  bool is_broken() const {
    return ok_;
  }

  void report() const {
    std::cout << name_ << " is " <<
      (ok_ ? "working nominally":"terribly broken") << '\n';
  }
};
```

If we store instances of this class in a vector, and we need to call the member function report, we might be tempted to do it as follows.

```cpp
std::vector<status> statuses;
statuses.push_back(status("status 1"));
statuses.push_back(status("status 2"));
statuses.push_back(status("status 3"));
statuses.push_back(status("status 4"));

statuses[1].break_it();
statuses[2].break_it();
```

```
for (std::vector<status>::iterator it=statuses.begin();
        it!=statuses.end();++it) {
  it->report();
}
```

This loop does the job correctly, but it's verbose, inefficient (due to the multiple calls to `statuses.end()`), and not as clear as using the algorithm from the Standard Library that exists for exactly this purpose, `for_each`. To use `for_each` to replace the loop, we need to use an adaptor for calling the member function `report` on the `vector` elements. In this case, because the elements are stored by value, what we need is the adaptor `mem_fun_ref`.

```
std::for_each(
  statuses.begin(),
  statuses.end(),
  std::mem_fun_ref(&status::report));
```

This is a correct and sound way to do it—it is quite terse, and there can be no doubt as to what the code is doing. The equivalent code for doing this using `Boost.Bind` follows.[1]

```
std::for_each(
  statuses.begin(),
  statuses.end(),
  boost::bind(&status::report,_1));
```

This version is equally clear and understandable. This is the first real use of the aforementioned placeholders of the Bind library, and what we're telling both the compiler and the reader of our code is that `_1` is to be substituted for an actual argument by the function invoking the binder. Although this code does save a few characters when typing, there is no big difference between the Standard Library `mem_fun_ref` and `bind` for this particular case, but let's reuse this example and change the container to hold pointers instead.

```
std::vector<status*> p_statuses;
p_statuses.push_back(new status("status 1"));
p_statuses.push_back(new status("status 2"));
p_statuses.push_back(new status("status 3"));
p_statuses.push_back(new status("status 4"));
```

1. It should be noted that `boost::mem_fn`, which has also been accepted for the Library Technical Report, would work just as well for the cases where there are no arguments. `mem_fn` supersedes `std::mem_fun` and `std::mem_fun_ref`.

```
p_statuses[1]->break_it();
p_statuses[2]->break_it();
```

We can still use both the Standard Library, but we can no longer use mem_fun_ref. We need help from the adaptor mem_fun, which is considered a bit of a misnomer, but again does the job that needs to be done.

```
std::for_each(
  p_statuses.begin(),
  p_statuses.end(),
  std::mem_fun(&status::report));
```

Although this works too, the syntax has changed, even though we are trying to do something very similar. It would be nice if the syntax was identical to the first example, so that the focus is on *what* the code really does rather than *how* it does it. Using bind, we do not need to be explicit about the fact that we are dealing with elements that are pointers (this is already encoded in the type of the container, and redundant information of this kind is typically unnecessary for modern libraries).

```
std::for_each(
  p_statuses.begin(),
  p_statuses.end(),
  boost::bind(&status::report,_1));
```

As you can see, this is exactly what we did in the previous example, which means that if we understood bind then, we should understand it now, too. Now that we have decided to switch to using pointers, we are faced with another problem, namely that of lifetime control. We must manually deallocate the elements of p_statuses, and that is both error prone and unnecessary. So, we may decide to start using smart pointers, and (again) change our code.

```
std::vector<boost::shared_ptr<status> > s_statuses;
s_statuses.push_back(
  boost::shared_ptr<status>(new status("status 1")));
s_statuses.push_back(
  boost::shared_ptr<status>(new status("status 2")));
s_statuses.push_back(
  boost::shared_ptr<status>(new status("status 3")));
s_statuses.push_back(
  boost::shared_ptr<status>(new status("status 4")));
```

```
s_statuses[1]->break_it();
s_statuses[2]->break_it();
```

Now, which adaptor from the Standard Library do we use? `mem_fun` and `mem_fun_ref` do not apply, because the smart pointer doesn't have a member function called `report`, and thus the following code fails to compile.

```
std::for_each(
  s_statuses.begin(),
  s_statuses.end(),
  std::mem_fun(&status::report));
```

The fact of the matter is that we lucked out—the Standard Library cannot help us with this task.[2] Thus, we have to resort to the same type of loop that we wanted to get rid of—or use Boost.Bind, which doesn't complain at all, but delivers exactly what we want.

```
std::for_each(
  s_statuses.begin(),
  s_statuses.end(),
  boost::bind(&status::report,_1));
```

Again, this example code is identical to the example before (apart from the different name of the container). The same syntax is used for binding, regardless of whether value semantics or pointer semantics apply, and even when using smart pointers. Sometimes, having a different syntax helps the understanding of the code, but in this case, it doesn't—the task at hand is to call a member function on elements of a container, nothing more and nothing less. The value of a consistent syntax should not be underestimated, because it helps both the person who is writing the code and all who later need to maintain the code (of course, we don't write code that actually needs maintenance, but for the sake of argument, let's pretend that we do).

These examples have demonstrated a very basic and common use case where Boost.Bind excels. Even though the Standard Library does offer some basic tools that do the same thing, we have seen that Bind offers both the consistency of syntax and additional functionality that the Standard Library currently lacks.

---

2. It will do so in the future, because both mem_fn and bind will be part of the future Standard Library.

A Look Behind the Curtain

After you start using Boost.Bind, it is inevitable; you will start to wonder how it actually works. It seems as magic when bind deduces the types of the arguments and return type, and what's the deal with the placeholders, anyway? We'll have a quick look on some of the mechanisms that drives such a beast. It helps to know a little about how bind works, especially when trying to decipher the wonderfully succinct and direct error messages the compiler emits at the slightest mistake. We will create a very simple binder that, at least in part, mimics the syntax of Boost.Bind. To avoid stretching this digression over several pages, we shall only support one type of binding, and that is for a member function taking a single argument. Moreover, we won't even get bogged down with the details of how to handle cv-qualification and its ilk; we'll just keep it simple.

First of all, we need to be able to deduce the return type, the class type, and the argument type for the function that we are to bind. We do this with a function template.

```
template <typename R, typename T, typename Arg>
   simple_bind_t<R,T,Arg> simple_bind(
     R (T::*fn)(Arg),
     const T& t,
     const placeholder&) {
       return simple_bind_t<R,T,Arg>(fn,t);
}
```

The preceding might seem a little intimidating at first, and by all rights it is because we have yet to define part of the machinery. However, the part to focus on here is where the type deduction takes place. You'll note that there are three template parameters to the function, R, T, and Arg. R is the return type, T is the class type, and Arg is the type of the (single) argument. These template parameters are what makes up the first argument to our function—that is, R (T::*f)(Arg). Thus, passing a member function with a single formal parameter to simple_bind permits the compiler to deduce R as the member function's return type, T as the member function's class, and Arg as the member function's argument type. simple_bind's return type is a function object that is parameterized on the same types as simple_bind, and whose constructor receives a pointer to the member function and an instance of the class (T). simple_bind simply ignores the placeholder (the last argument to the function), and the reason why I've included it in the first place is to simulate the syntax of Boost.Bind. In a better implementation of this concept, we would obviously need to make use of that argument, but now we allow ourselves the luxury of letting it pass into oblivion. The implementation of the function object is fairly straightforward.

```
template <typename R,typename T, typename Arg>
  class simple_bind_t {
  typedef R (T::*fn)(Arg);
  fn fn_;
  T t_;
public:
  simple_bind_t(fn f,const T& t):fn_(f),t_(t) {}

  R operator()(Arg& a) {
    return (t_.*fn_)(a);
  }
};
```

As we saw in `simple_bind`'s implementation, the constructor accepts two arguments: the first is the pointer to a member function and the second is a reference to const T that is copied and later used to invoke the function with a user-supplied argument. Finally, the function call operator returns R, the return type of the member function, and accepts an Arg argument, which is the type of the argument to be passed to the member function. The somewhat obscure syntax for invoking the member function is this:

```
(t_.*fn_)(a);
```

.* is the pointer-to-member operator, used when the first operand is of class T; there's also another pointer-to-member operator, ->*, which is used when the first operand is a pointer to T. What remains is to create a placeholder—that is, a variable that is used in place of the actual argument. We can create such a placeholder by using an unnamed namespace containing a variable of some type; let's call it `placeholder`:

```
namespace {
  class placeholder {};
  placeholder _1;
}
```

Let's create a simple class and a small application for testing this.

```
class Test {
public:
  void do_stuff(const std::vector<int>& v) {
    std::copy(v.begin(),v.end(),
      std::ostream_iterator<int>(std::cout," "));
  }
};

int main() {
  Test t;
  std::vector<int> vec;
  vec.push_back(42);
  simple_bind(&Test::do_stuff,t,_1)(vec);
}
```

When we instantiate the function `simple_bind` with the preceding arguments, the types are automatically deduced; R is void, T is Test, and Arg is a reference to const std::vector<int>. The function returns an instance of `simple_bind_t<void,Test,Arg>`, on which we immediately invoke the function call operator by passing the argument vec.

Hopefully, `simple_bind` has given you an idea of how binders work. Now, it's time to get back to Boost.Bind!

More on Placeholders and Arguments

The first example demonstrated that `bind` supports up to nine arguments, but it will serve us well to look a bit more closely at how arguments and placeholders work. First of all, it's important to note that there is an important difference between free functions and member functions—when binding to a member function, the first argument to the `bind` expression must be an instance of the member function's class! The easiest way to think about this rule is that this explicit argument substitutes the implicit `this` that is passed to all non-static member functions. The diligent reader will note that, in effect, this means that for binders to member functions, only (sic!) eight arguments are supported, because the first will be used for the actual object. The following example defines a free function `print_string` and a class `some_class` with a member function `print_string`, soon to be used in `bind` expressions.

```
#include <iostream>
#include <string>
#include "boost/bind.hpp"
```

```
class some_class {
public:
  typedef void result_type;
  void print_string(const std::string& s) const {
    std::cout << s << '\n';
  }
};

void print_string(const std::string s) {
  std::cout << s << '\n';
}

int main() {
  (boost::bind(&print_string,_1))("Hello func!");
  some_class sc;
  (boost::bind(&some_class::print_string,_1,_2))
    (sc,"Hello member!");
}
```

The first `bind` expression binds to the free function `print_string`. Because the function expects one argument, we need to use one placeholder (`_1`) to tell `bind` which of its arguments will be passed as the first argument of `print_string`. To invoke the resulting function object, we must pass the `string` argument to the function call operator. The argument is a `const std::string&`, so passing a string literal triggers invocation of `std::string`'s converting constructor.

```
(boost::bind(&print_string,_1))("Hello func!");
```

The second binder adapts a member function, `print_string` of `some_class`. The first argument to `bind` is a pointer to the member function. However, a pointer to a non-static member function isn't really a pointer.[3] We must have an object before we can invoke the function. That's why the `bind` expression must state that there are two arguments to the binder, both of which are to be supplied when invoking it.

```
boost::bind(&some_class::print_string,_1,_2);
```

---

3. Yes, I know how weird this sounds. It's still true, though.

To see why this makes sense, consider how the resulting function object can be used. We must pass to it both an instance of `some_class` and the argument to `print_string`.

```
(boost::bind(&some_class::print_string,_1,_2))(sc,"Hello member!");
```

The first argument to the function call operator is `this` —that is, the instance of `some_class`. Note that the first argument can be a pointer (smart or raw) or a reference to an instance; `bind` is very accommodating. The second argument to the function call operator is the member function's one argument. In this case, we've "delayed" both arguments—that is, we defined the binder such that it expects to get both the object and the member function's argument via its function call operator. We didn't have to do it that way, however. For example, we could create a binder that invokes `print_string` on the same object each time it is invoked, like so:

```
(boost::bind(&some_class::print_string,some_class(),_1))
  ("Hello member!");
```

The resulting function object already contains an instance of `some_class`, so there's only need for one placeholder (`_1`) and one argument (a string) for the function call operator. Finally, we could also have created a so-called *nullary* function object by also binding the string, like so:

```
(boost::bind(&some_class::print_string,
  some_class(),"Hello member!"))();
```

These examples clearly show the versatility of `bind`. It can be used to delay all, some, or none of the arguments required by the function it encapsulates. It can also handle reordering arguments any way you see fit; just order the placeholders according to your needs. Next, we'll see how to use `bind` to create sorting predicates on-the-fly.

Dynamic Sorting Criteria

When sorting the elements of a container, we sometimes need to create function objects that define the sorting criteria—we need to do so if we are missing relational operators, or if the existing relational operators do not define the sorting criteria we are interested in. We can sometimes use the comparison function objects from the Standard Library (std::greater, std::greater_equal, and so forth), but only use comparisons that already exist for the types—we cannot define new ones at the call site. We'll use a class called personal_info for the purpose of showing how Boost.Bind can help us in this quest. personal_info contains the first name, last name, and age, and it doesn't provide any comparison operators. The information is immutable upon creation, and can be retrieved using the member functions name, surname, and age.

```cpp
class personal_info {
  std::string name_;
  std::string surname_;
  unsigned int age_;

public:
  personal_info(
      const std::string& n,
      const std::string& s,
      unsigned int age) :name_(n),surname_(s),age_(age) {}

  std::string name() const {
    return name_;
  }

  std::string surname() const {
    return surname_;
  }

  unsigned int age() const {
    return age_;
  }
};
```

We make the class *OutputStreamable* by supplying the following operator:

```cpp
std::ostream& operator<<(
    std::ostream& os,const personal_info& pi) {
  os << pi.name() << ' ' <<
    pi.surname() << ' ' << pi.age() << '\n';
  return os;
}
```

If we are to sort a container with elements of type personal_info, we need to supply a sorting predicate for it. Why would we omit the relational operators from `personal_info` in the first place? One reason is because there are several possible sorting options, and we cannot know which is appropriate for different users. Although we could also opt to provide different member functions for different sorting criteria, this would add the burden of having all relevant sorting criteria encoded in the class, which is not always possible. Fortunately, it is easy to create the predicate at the call site by using `bind`. Let's say that we need the sorting to be performed based on the age (available through the member function `age`). We could create a function object just for that purpose.

```cpp
class personal_info_age_less_than :
  public std::binary_function<
    personal_info,personal_info,bool> {
public:
  bool operator()(
    const personal_info& p1,const personal_info& p2) {
    return p1.age()<p2.age();
  }
};
```

We've made the `personal_info_age_less_than` adaptable by publicly inheriting from `binary_function`. Deriving from `binary_function` provides the appropriate `typedefs` needed when using, for example, `std::not2`. Assuming a vector, `vec`, containing elements of type `personal_info`, we would use the function object like this:

```cpp
std::sort(vec.begin(),vec.end(),personal_info_age_less_than());
```

This works fine as long as the number of different comparisons is limited. However, there is a potential problem in that the logic is defined in a different place, which can make the code harder to understand. With a long and descriptive name such as the one we've chosen here, there shouldn't be a problem, but not all cases are so clear-cut, and there is a real chance that we'd need to supply a slew of function objects for greater than, less than or equal to, and so on.

So, how can Boost.Bind help? Actually, it helps us out three times for this example. If we examine the problem at hand, we find that there are three things we need to do, the first being to bind a logical operation, such as `std::less`. This is easy, and gives us the first part of the code.

```cpp
boost::bind<bool>(std::less<unsigned int>(),_1,_2);
```

Note that we are explicitly adding the return type by supplying the `bool` parameter to `bind`. This is sometimes necessary, both on broken compilers and in contexts where the return type cannot be deduced. If a function object contains a `typedef`, `result_type`, there is no need to explicitly name the return type.[4] Now, we have a function object that accepts two arguments, both of type `unsigned int`, but we can't use it just yet, because the elements have the type `personal_info`, and we need to extract the age from those elements and pass the age as arguments to `std::less`. Again, we can use `bind` to do that.

```
boost::bind(
  std::less<unsigned int>(),
  boost::bind(&personal_info::age,_1),
  boost::bind(&personal_info::age,_2));
```

Here, we create two more binders. The first one calls `personal_info::age` with the main binder's function call operator's first argument (`_1`). The second one calls `personal_info::age` with the main binder's function call operator's second argument (`_2`). Because `std::sort` passes two `personal_info` objects to the main binder's function call operator, the result is to invoke `personal_info::age` on each of two `personal_info` objects from the `vector` being sorted. Finally, the main binder passes the ages returned by the two new, inner binders' function call operator to `std::less`. This is exactly what we need! The result of invoking this function object is the result of `std::less`, which means that we have a valid comparison function object easily used to sort a container of `personal_info` objects. Here's how it looks in action:

```
std::vector<personal_info> vec;
vec.push_back(personal_info("Little","John",30));
vec.push_back(personal_info("Friar", "Tuck",50));
vec.push_back(personal_info("Robin", "Hood",40));

std::sort(
  vec.begin(),
  vec.end(),
  boost::bind(
    std::less<unsigned int>(),
    boost::bind(&personal_info::age,_1),
    boost::bind(&personal_info::age,_2)));
```

---

4. The Standard Library function objects all have `result_type` defined, so they work with `bind`'s return type deduction mechanism.

We could sort differently simply by binding to another member (variable or function) from `personal_info`—for example, the last name.

```
std::sort(
  vec.begin(),
  vec.end(),
  boost::bind(
    std::less<std::string>(),
    boost::bind(&personal_info::surname,_1),
    boost::bind(&personal_info::surname,_2)));
```

This is a great technique, because it offers an important property: simple functionality implemented at the call site. It makes the code easy to understand and maintain. Although it is technically possible to sort using binders based upon complex criteria, it is not wise. Adding more logic to the `bind` expressions quickly loses clarity and succinctness. Although it is sometimes tempting to do more in terms of binding, strive to write binders that are as clever as the people who must maintain it, but no more so.

Functional Composition, Part I

One problem that's often looking for a solution is to compose a function object out of other functions or function objects. Suppose that you need to test an `int` to see whether it is greater than 5 and less than, or equal to, 10. Using "regular" code, you would do something like this:

```
if (i>5 && i<=10) {
  // Do something
}
```

When processing elements of a container, the preceding code only works if you put it in a separate function. When this is not desirable, using a nested `bind` can express the same thing (note that this is typically not possible using `bind1st` and `bind2nd` from the Standard Library). If we decompose the problem, we find that we need operations for *logical and* (`std::logical_and`), *greater than* (`std::greater`), and *less than or equal to* (`std::less_equal`). The *logical and* should look something like this:

```
boost::bind(std::logical_and<bool>(),_1,_2);
```

Then, we need another predicate that answers whether _1 is *less than* or *equal to* 10.

```
boost::bind(std::greater<int>(),_1,5);
```

Then, we need another predicate that answers whether _1 is *less than* or *equal to* 10.

```
boost::bind(std::less_equal<int>(),_1,10);
```

Finally, we need to logically *and* those two together, like so:

```
boost::bind(
  std::logical_and<bool>(),
  boost::bind(std::greater<int>(),_1,5),
  boost::bind(std::less_equal<int>(),_1,10));
```

A nested `bind` such as this is relatively easy to understand, though it has post-fix order. Still, one can almost read the code literally and determine the intent. Let's put this binder to the test in an example.

```
std::vector<int> ints;

ints.push_back(7);
ints.push_back(4);
ints.push_back(12);
ints.push_back(10);

int count=std::count_if(
  ints.begin(),
  ints.end(),
  boost::bind(
    std::logical_and<bool>(),
    boost::bind(std::greater<int>(),_1,5),
    boost::bind(std::less_equal<int>(),_1,10)));

std::cout << count << '\n';

std::vector<int>::iterator int_it=std::find_if(
  ints.begin(),
  ints.end(),
  boost::bind(std::logical_and<bool>(),
    boost::bind(std::greater<int>(),_1,5),
```

```
        boost::bind(std::less_equal<int>(),_1,10)));

if (int_it!=ints.end()) {
  std::cout << *int_it << '\n';
}
```

It is important to carefully indent the code properly when using nested `binds`, because the code can quickly become hard to understand if one neglects sensible indentation. Consider the preceding clear code, and then look at the following obfuscated example.

```
std::vector<int>::iterator int_it=
  std::find_if(ints.begin(),ints.end(),
    boost::bind<bool>(
    std::logical_and<bool>(),
    boost::bind<bool>(std::greater<int>(),_1,5),
      boost::bind<bool>(std::less_equal<int>(),_1,10)));
```

This is a general problem with long lines, of course, but it becomes apparent when using constructs such as those described here, where long statements are the rule rather than the exception. So, please be nice to your fellow programmers by making sure that your lines wrap in a way that makes them easy to read.

One of the hard-working reviewers for this book asked why, in the previous example, two equivalent binders were created, and if it wouldn't make more sense to create a binder object and use it two times. The answer is that because we can't know the exact type of the binder (it's implementation defined) that's created when we call `bind`, we have no way of declaring a variable for it. Also, the type typically is very complex, because its signature includes all of the type information that's been captured (and deduced automatically) in the function `bind`. However, it is possible to store the resulting function objects using other facilities—for example, those from Boost.Function. See "Library 11: Function" for details on how this is accomplished.

The composition outlined here corresponds to a popular extension to the Standard Library, namely the function `compose2` from the SGI STL, also known as `compose_f_gx_hx` in the (now deprecated) Boost.Compose library.

Functional Composition, Part II

Another useful functional composition is known as `compose1` in SGI STL, and `compose_f_gx` in Boost.Compose. These functionals offer a way to call two functions with an argument, and have the result of the innermost function passed to the first function. An example sometimes says more than a thousand contrived words, so consider the scenario where you need to perform two arithmetic operations on container elements of floating point type. We first add 10% to the values, and then reduce the values with 10%; the example could also serve as a useful lesson to quite a few people working in the financial sector.

```
std::list<double> values;
values.push_back(10.0);
values.push_back(100.0);
values.push_back(1000.0);

std::transform(
  values.begin(),
  values.end(),
  values.begin(),
  boost::bind(
 std::multiplies<double>(),0.90,
   boost::bind<double>(
      std::multiplies<double>(),_1,1.10)));

std::copy(
  values.begin(),
  values.end(),
  std::ostream_iterator<double>(std::cout," "));
```

How do you know which of the nested binds will be called first? As you've probably already noticed, it is always the innermost bind that is evaluated first. This means that we could write the equivalent code somewhat differently.

```
std::transform(
  values.begin(),
  values.end(),
  values.begin(),
  boost::bind<double>(
 std::multiplies<double>(),
   boost::bind<double>(
      std::multiplies<double>(),_1,1.10),0.90));
```

Here, we change the order of the arguments passed to the bind, tacking on the argument to the first bind last in the expression. Although I do not recommend this practice, it is useful for understanding how arguments are passed to bind functions.

Value or Pointer Semantics in *bind* Expressions?

When we pass an instance of some type to a `bind` expression, it is copied, unless we explicitly tell `bind` not to copy it. Depending on what we are doing, this can be of vital importance. To see what goes on behind our backs, we will create a `tracer` class that will tell us when it is default constructed, copy constructed, assigned to, and destructed. That way, we can easily see how different uses of `bind` affect the instances that we pass. Here is the `tracer` class in its entirety.

```cpp
class tracer {
public:
  tracer() {
    std::cout << "tracer::tracer()\n";
  }

tracer(const tracer& other) {
    std::cout << "tracer::tracer(const tracer& other)\n";
  }

tracer& operator=(const tracer& other) {
    std::cout <<
      "tracer& tracer::operator=(const tracer& other)\n";
    return *this;
  }

~tracer() {
    std::cout << "tracer::~tracer()\n";
  }

void print(const std::string& s) const {
    std::cout << s << '\n';
    }
};
```

We put our `tracer` class to work with a regular `bind` expression like the one that follows.

```cpp
tracer t;
boost::bind(&tracer::print,t,_1)
  (std::string("I'm called on a copy of t\n"));
```

Running this code produces the following output, which clearly shows that there is copying involved.

```
tracer::tracer()
tracer::tracer(const tracer& other)
tracer::tracer(const tracer& other)
tracer::tracer(const tracer& other)
tracer::~tracer()
tracer::tracer(const tracer& other)
tracer::~tracer()
tracer::~tracer()
I'm called on a copy of t

tracer::~tracer()
```

If we had been using objects where copying was expensive, we probably could not afford to use bind this way. There is an advantage to the copying, however. It means that the bind expression and its resulting binder are not dependent on the lifetime of the original object (t in this case), which is often the exact behavior desired. To avoid the copies, we must tell bind that we intend to pass it a reference that it is supposed to use rather than a value. We do this with boost::ref and boost::cref (for reference and reference to const, respectively), which are also part of the Boost.Bind library. Using boost::ref with our tracer class, the testing code now looks like this:

```
tracer t;
boost::bind(&tracer::print,boost::ref(t),_1)(
  std::string("I'm called directly on t\n"));
```

Executing the code gives us this:

```
tracer::tracer()
I'm called directly on t
tracer::~tracer
```

That's exactly what's needed to avoid unnecessary copying. The bind expression uses the original instance, which means that there are no copies of the tracer object. Of course, it also means that the binder is now dependent upon the lifetime of the tracer instance. There's also another way of avoiding copies; just pass the argument by pointer rather than by value.

```
tracer t;
boost::bind(&tracer::print,&t,_1)(
  std::string("I'm called directly on t\n"));
```

So, `bind` always copies. If you pass by value, the object is copied and that may be detrimental on performance or cause unwanted effects. To avoid copying the object, you can either use `boost::ref`/`boost::cref` or use pointer semantics.

Virtual Functions Can Also Be Bound

So far, we've seen how `bind` can work with non-member functions and non-virtual member functions, but it is, of course, also possible to bind a virtual member function. With Boost.Bind, you use virtual functions as you would non-virtual functions—that is, just bind to the virtual function in the base class that first declared the member function virtual. That makes the binder useful with all derived types. If you bind against a more derived type, you restrict the classes with which the binder can be used.[5] Consider the following classes named `base` and `derived`:

```
class base {
public:
  virtual void print() const {
    std::cout << "I am base.\n";
  }
  virtual ~base() {}
};

class derived : public base {
public:
  void print() const {
    std::cout << "I am derived.\n";
  }
};
```

Using these classes, we can test the binding of a virtual function like so:

```
derived d;
base b;
boost::bind(&base::print,_1)(b);
boost::bind(&base::print,_1)(d);
```

---

5. This is no different than when declaring a pointer to a class in order to invoke a virtual member function. The more derived the type pointed to, the fewer classes can be bound to the pointer.

Running this code clearly shows that this works as one would hope and expect.

```
I am base.
I am derived.
```

The fact that virtual functions are supported should come as no surprise to you, but now we've shown that it works just like other functions. On a related note, what would happen if you `bind` a member function that is later redefined by a derived class, or a virtual function that is public in the base class but private in the derived? Will things still work? If so, which behavior would you expect? Well, the behavior does not change whether you are using Boost.Bind or not. Thus, if you `bind` to a function that is redefined in another class—that is, it's not virtual and the derived class adds a member function with an identical signature—the version in the base class is called. If a function is hidden, the binder can still be invoked, because it explicitly accesses the function in the base class, which works even for hidden member functions. Finally, if the virtual function is declared public in the base class, but is private in a derived class, invoking the function on an instance of the derived class succeeds, because the access is through a base instance, where the member is public. Of course, such a case indicates a seriously flawed design.

Binding to Member Variables

There are many occasions when you need to `bind` data members rather than member functions. For example, when using `std::map` or `std::multimap`, the element type is `std::pair<key const,data>`, but the information you want to use is often not the key, but the data. Suppose you want to pass the data from each element in a `map` to a function that takes a single argument of the data type. You need to create a binder that forwards the `second` member of each element (of type `std::pair`) to the bound function. Here's code that illustrates how to do that:

```cpp
void print_string(const std::string& s) {
  std::cout << s << '\n';
}

std::map<int,std::string> my_map;
my_map[0]="Boost";
my_map[1]="Bind";
```

```
std::for_each(
  my_map.begin(),
  my_map.end(),
    boost::bind(&print_string, boost::bind(
      &std::map<int,std::string>::value_type::second,_1)));
```

You can `bind` to a member variable just as you can with a member function, or a free function. It should be noted that to make the code easier to read (and write), it's a good idea to use short and convenient names. In the previous example, the use of a `typedef` for the `std::map` helps improve readability.

```
typedef std::map<int,std::string> map_type;
boost::bind(&map_type::value_type::second,_1)));
```

Although the need to `bind` to member variables does not arise as often as for member functions, it is still very convenient to be able to do so. Users of SGI STL (and derivatives thereof) are probably familiar with the `select1st` and `select2nd` functions. They are used to select the `first` or the `second` member of `std::pair`, which is the same thing that we're doing in this example. Note that `bind` works with arbitrary types and arbitrary names, which is definitively a plus.

To Bind or Not to Bind

The great flexibility brought by the Boost.Bind library also offers a challenge for the programmer, because it is sometimes very tempting to use a binder, although a separate function object is warranted. Many tasks can and should be accomplished with the help of Bind, but it's an error to go too far—and the line is drawn where the code becomes hard to read, understand, and maintain. Unfortunately, the position of the line greatly depends on the programmers that share (by reading, maintaining, and extending) the code, as their experience must dictate what is acceptable and what is not. The advantage of using specialized function objects is that they can typically be made quite self-explanatory, and to provide the same clear message using binders is a challenge that we must diligently try to overcome. For example, if you need to create a nested `bind` that you have trouble understanding, chances are that you have gone too far. Let me explain this with code.

```
#include <iostream>
#include <string>
```

```
#include <map>
#include <vector>
#include <algorithm>
#include "boost/bind.hpp"

void print(std::ostream* os,int i) {
  (*os) << i << '\n';
}

int main() {
  std::map<std::string,std::vector<int> > m;
  m["Strange?"].push_back(1);
  m["Strange?"].push_back(2);
  m["Strange?"].push_back(3);
  m["Weird?"].push_back(4);
  m["Weird?"].push_back(5);

  std::for_each(m.begin(),m.end(),
    boost::bind(&print,&std::cout,
    boost::bind(&std::vector<int>::size,
    boost::bind(
      &std::map<std::string,
        std::vector<int> >::value_type::second,_1))));
}
```

What does the preceding code actually do? There are people who read code like this fluently,[6] but for many of us mortals, it takes some time to figure out what's going on. Yes, the binder calls the member function `size` on whatever exists as the `pair` member `second` (the `std::map<std::string,std::vector<int> >::value_type`). In cases like this, where the problem is simple yet complex to express using a binder, it often makes sense to create a small function object instead of a complex binder that some people will definitely have a hard time understanding. A simple function object that does the same thing could look something like this:

```
class print_size {
  std::ostream& os_;
  typedef std::map<std::string,std::vector<int> > map_type;
public:
  print_size(std::ostream& os):os_(os) {}
```

---

6. Hello, Peter Dimov.

```
  void operator()(
    const map_type::value_type& x) const {
      os_ << x.second.size() << '\n';
  }
};
```

The great advantage in this case comes when we are using the function object, whose name is self-explanatory.

```
std::for_each(m.begin(),m.end(),print_size(std::cout));
```

This (the source for the function object and the actual invocation) is to be compared with the version using a binder.

```
std::for_each(m.begin(),m.end(),
  boost::bind(&print,&std::cout,
  boost::bind(&std::vector<int>::size,
  boost::bind(
    &std::map<std::string,
      std::vector<int> >::value_type::second,_1))));
```

Or, if we had been a bit more responsible and created terse `typedefs` for the `vector` and `map`:

```
std::for_each(m.begin(),m.end(),
  boost::bind(&print,&std::cout,
  boost::bind(&vec_type::size,
  boost::bind(&map_type::value_type::second,_1))));
```

That's a bit easier to parse, but it's still a bit too much.

Although there may be some good arguments for using the `bind` version, I think that the point is clear—binders are incredibly useful tools that should be used responsibly, where they add value. This is very, very common when using the Standard Library containers and algorithms. But when things get too complicated, do it the old fashioned way.

Let Binders Handle State

There are several options available to use when creating a function object like `print_size`. The version that we created in the previous section stored a reference to a `std::ostream`, and used that `ostream` to print the return value of `size` for the member `second` on the `map_type::value_type` argument. Here's the original `print_size` again:

```
class print_size {
  std::ostream& os_;
  typedef std::map<std::string,std::vector<int> > map_type;
public:
  print_size(std::ostream& os):os_(os) {}

  void operator()(
    const map_type::value_type& x) const {
      os_ << x.second.size() << '\n';
  }
};
```

An important observation for this class is that is has state, through the stored `std::ostream`. We could remove the state by adding the `ostream` as an argument to the function call operator. This would mean that the function object becomes stateless.

```
class print_size {
  typedef std::map<std::string,std::vector<int> > map_type;
public:
  typedef void result_type;
  result_type operator()(std::ostream& os,
    const map_type::value_type& x) const {
      os << x.second.size() << '\n';
  }
};
```

Note that this version of `print_size` is well behaved when used with `bind`, through the addition of the `result_type` typedef. This relieves users from having to explicitly state the return type of the function object when using `bind`. In this new version of `print_size`, users need to pass an `ostream` as an argument when invoking it. That's easy when using binders. Rewriting the example from the previous section with the new `print_size` gives us this:

```
#include <iostream>
#include <string>
#include <map>
#include <vector>
#include <algorithm>
```

```
#include "boost/bind.hpp"

// Definition of print_size omitted

int main() {
  typedef std::map<std::string,std::vector<int> > map_type;
  map_type m;
  m["Strange?"].push_back(1);
  m["Strange?"].push_back(2);
  m["Strange?"].push_back(3);
  m["Weird?"].push_back(4);
  m["Weird?"].push_back(5);

  std::for_each(m.begin(),m.end(),
    boost::bind(print_size(),boost::ref(std::cout),_1));
}
```

The diligent reader might wonder why print_size isn't a free function now, because it doesn't carry state anymore. In fact, it can be

```
void print_size(std::ostream& os,
  const std::map<std::string,std::vector<int> >::value_type& x) {
  os << x.second.size() << '\n';
}
```

But there are more generalizations to consider. Our current version of print_size requires that the second argument to the function call operator be a reference to const std::map<std::string,std::vector<int> >, which isn't very general. We can do better, by parameterizing the function call operator on the type. This makes print_size usable with any argument that contains a public member called second, which in turn has a member function size. Here's the improved version:

```
class print_size {
public:
  typedef void result_type;
  template <typename Pair> result_type operator()
    (std::ostream& os,const Pair& x) const {
    os << x.second.size() << '\n';
  }
};
```

Usage is the same with this version as the previous, but it's much more flexible. This kind of generalization becomes more important than usual when creating function objects that can be used in `bind` expressions. Because the number of cases where the function objects can be used increase markedly, most any potential generalization is worthwhile. In that vein, there is one more change that we could make to further relax the requirements for types to be used with `print_size`. The current version of `print_size` requires that the second argument of the function call operator be a pair-like object—that is, an object with a member called `second`. If we decide to require only that the argument contain a member function `size`, the function object starts to really deserve its name.

```
class print_size {
public:
  typedef void result_type;
  template <typename T> void operator()
    (std::ostream& os,const T& x) const {
    os << x.size() << '\n';
  }
};
```

Of course, although `print_size` is now true to its name, we require more of the user for the use case that we've already considered. Usage now includes "manually" binding to `map_type::value_type::second`.

```
std::for_each(m.begin(),m.end(),
  boost::bind(print_size(),boost::ref(std::cout),
    boost::bind(&map_type::value_type::second,_1)));
```

Such are often the tradeoffs when using `bind`—generalizations can only take you so far before starting to interfere with usability. Had we taken things to an extreme, and removed even the requirement that there be a member function `size`, we'd complete the circle and be back where we started, with a `bind` expression that's just too complex for most programmers.

```
std::for_each(m.begin(),m.end(),
  boost::bind(&print⁷,&std::cout,
  boost::bind(&vec_type::size,
  boost::bind(&map_type::value_type::second,_1))));
```

---

7. The `print` function would obviously be required, too, without some lambda facility.

A Boost.Bind and Boost.Function Teaser

Although the material that we have covered in this chapter shouldn't leave you wanting for more, there is actually a very useful synergy between Boost.Bind and another library, Boost.Function, that provides still more functionality. We shall see more of the added value in "Library 11: Function," but I'd like to give you a hint of what's to come. As we've seen, there is no apparent way of storing our binders for later use—we only know that they are compatible function objects with some (unknown) signature. But, when using Boost.Function, storing functions for later invocation is exactly what the library does, and thanks to the compatibility with Boost.Bind, it's possible to assign binders to functions, saving them for later invocation. This is an enormously useful concept, which enables adaptation and promotes loose coupling.

Bind Summary

Use Bind when

- You need to bind a call to a free function, and some or all of its arguments

- You need to bind a call to a member function, and some or all of its arguments

- You need to compose nested function objects

The existence of a generalized binder is a tremendously useful tool when it comes to writing terse, coherent code. It reduces the number of small function objects created for adapting functions/function objects, and combinations of functions. Although the Standard Library already offers a small part of the functionality found in Boost.Bind, there are significant improvements that make Boost.Bind the better choice in most places. In addition to the simplification of existing features, Bind also offers powerful functional composition features, which provide the programmer with great power without negative effects on maintenance. If you've taken the time to learn about `bind1st`, `bind2nd`, `ptr_fun`, `mem_fun_ref`, and so forth, you'll have little or no trouble transitioning to Boost.Bind. If you've yet to start using the current binder offerings from the C++ Standard Library, I strongly suggest that you start by using Bind, because it is both easier to learn and more powerful.

I know many programmers who have yet to experience the wonders of binders in general, and function composition in particular. If you used to be one of them, I'm hoping that this chapter has managed to convey some of the tremendous power that is brought forth by the concept as such. Moreover, think about the implications this type of function, declared and defined at the call site, will have on maintenance. It's going to be a breeze compared to the dispersion of code that can easily be caused by small, innocent-looking[8] function objects that are scattered around the classes merely to provide the correct signature and perform a trivial task.

The Boost.Bind library is created and maintained by Peter Dimov, who has, besides making it such a complete facility for binding and function composition, also managed to make it work cleanly for most compilers.

---

8. But they're not.

Library 10
Lambda

How Does the Lambda Library Improve Your Programs?

- Adapts functions and function objects for use with Standard Library algorithms

- Binds arguments to function calls

- Transforms arbitrary expressions into function objects compatible with the Standard Library algorithms

- Defines unnamed functions at the call site, thereby improving readability and maintainability of the code

- Implements predicates when and where needed

When using the Standard Library, or any library employing a similar design that relies on algorithmic configuration by the means of functions and function objects, one often ends up writing lots of small function objects that perform quite trivial operations. As we saw in "Library 9: Bind," this can quickly become a problem, because an explosion of small classes that are scattered through the code base is not easily maintained. Also, understanding the code where the function objects are actually invoked is harder, because part of the functionality is defined elsewhere. A perfect solution to this problem is a way to define these functions or function objects directly at the call site. This typically makes the code faster to write, easier to read, and more readily maintained, as the definition of the functionality then resides in the location where it is used. This is what the Boost.Lambda library offers, unnamed functions defined at the call site. Boost.Lambda works by creating function objects that can be defined and invoked directly, or stored for later invocation. This is similar to the offerings from the Boost.Bind library, but Boost.Lambda does both argument binding and much more, by adding control structures, automatic conversions of expressions into function objects, and even support for exception handling in lambda expressions.

The term lambda expression, or lambda function, originates from functional programming and lambda calculus. A lambda abstraction defines an unnamed function. Although lambda abstractions are ubiquitous in functional programming languages, that's not the case for most imperative programming languages, such as C++. But, using advanced techniques such as expression templates, C++ makes it possible to augment the language with a form of lambda expressions.

The first and foremost motivation for creating the Lambda library is to enable unnamed functions for use with the Standard Library algorithms. Because the use of the Standard Library has virtually exploded since the first C++ Standard in 1998, our knowledge of what's good and what's missing has rapidly increased—and one of the parts that can be problematic is the definition of numerous small function objects, where a simple expression would seem to suffice. The function object issue is obviously addressed by this library, but there is still room for exploration of the uses of lambda functions. Now that lambda functions are available, we have the opportunity to apply them to problems that previously required totally different solutions. It's both fascinating and exciting that it is possible to explore new programming techniques in a language as mature as C++. What new idioms and ways of solving problems will arise from the presence of unnamed functions and expression templates? The truth is that we don't know, because we have yet to try them all out! Still, the focus here is on the practical problems that the library explicitly addresses—avoiding code bloat and scattered functionality through lambda expressions—functions defined at the call site. We can do many wonderful things with this—and we can be really terse about it, which should satisfy both programmers, who can focus more on the problem at hand, and their managers, who can reap the benefits of a higher production rate (and, hopefully, more easily maintained code!).

How Does Lambda Fit with the Standard Library?

The library addresses a problem that is often encountered when using the Standard Library algorithms—the need to define many simple function objects just to comply with the requirements of the algorithms. Almost all of the

Standard Library algorithms also come in a version that accepts a function object, to perform operations such as ordering, equality, transformations, and so on. To a limited extent, the Standard Library supports functional composition, through the binders `bind1st` and `bind2nd`. However, these are very limited in what they can produce, and they provide only argument binding, not bindings for expressions. Given that both flexible support for binding arguments and for creating function objects directly from expressions are available in the Boost.Lambda library, it is an excellent companion to the C++ Standard Library.

Lambda

Header: `"boost/lambda/lambda.hpp"`

This includes the core of the library.

`"boost/lambda/bind.hpp"`

defines `bind` functions.

`"boost/lambda/if.hpp"`

defines the lambda equivalent of `if`, and the conditional operator.

`"boost/lambda/loops.hpp"`

defines looping constructs (for example, `while_loop` and `for_loop`).

`"boost/lambda/switch.hpp"`

defines the lambda equivalent of switch statements.

`"boost/lambda/construct.hpp"`

defines tools for adding construction/destruction and `new`/`delete` to lambda expressions.

`"boost/lambda/casts.hpp"`

provides cast operators for lambda expressions.

`"boost/lambda/exceptions.hpp"`

defines tools for exception handling in lambda expressions.

`"boost/lambda/algorithm.hpp"` and `"boost/lambda/numeric.hpp"`

defines lambda versions (essentially function objects) of C++ Standard library algorithms to be used in nested function invocations.

Usage

This library, like most other Boost libraries, is purely defined in header files, which means that you don't have to build anything to get started. However, understanding a little something about lambda expressions is definitely helpful. The following sections will walk you through this library, even including how to perform exception handling in lambda expressions! The library is quite extensive, and there's a lot of power waiting ahead. A lambda expression is often called an *unnamed function*. It is declared and defined when it's needed—that is, at the call site. This is very useful, because we often need to define an algorithm in another algorithm, something that isn't really supported by the language. Instead, we externalize behavior by bringing in functions and function objects from a wider scope, or use nested loop constructs with the algorithmic expressions encoded in the loops. As we shall see, this is where lambda expressions come to the rescue. This section consists of many examples, and there is often one part of the example that demonstrates how the solution would be coded using "traditional" tools. The intent is to show when and how lambda expressions help programmers write more logic with less code. There is a certain learning curve associated with lambda expressions, and the syntax may seem daunting at first glance. Like every new paradigm or tool, this one must be learned—but trust me when I say that the profit definitely outweighs the cost.

A Little Teaser

The first program using Boost.Lambda should whet your appetite for lambda expressions. First of all, note that the lambda types are declared in the namespace `boost::lambda`—typically, you bring these declarations into scope with a using directive or using declarations. The core functionality of the library is available when including the file `"boost/lambda/lambda.hpp"`, which is sufficient for our first program.

```
#include <iostream>
#include "boost/lambda/lambda.hpp"
#include "boost/function.hpp"

int main() {
  using namespace boost::lambda;

  (std::cout << _1 << " " << _3 << " " << _2 << "!\n")
    ("Hello","friend","my");

  boost::function<void(int,int,int)> f=
    std::cout << _1 << "*" << _2 << "+" << _3
      << "=" <<_1*_2+_3 << "\n";

  f(1,2,3);
  f(3,2,1);
}
```

The first expression looks peculiar at first glance, but it helps to mentally divide the expression as the parentheses do; the first part is a lambda expression that basically says, "print these arguments to `std::cout`, but don't do it right now, because I don't yet know the first, second, and third arguments." The second part of the expression actually invokes the function by saying, "Hey! Here are the three arguments that you need." Look at the first part of the expression again.

```
std::cout << _1 << " " << _3 << " " << _2 << "!\n"
```

You'll note that there are three *placeholders*, aptly named _1, _2, and _3, in the expression.[1] These placeholders denote the delayed arguments to the lambda expression. Note that unlike the syntax of many functional programming languages, there's no keyword or name for creating lambda expressions; it is the presence of the placeholders that signal that this is a lambda expression. So, this is a lambda expression that accepts three arguments of any type that support streaming through `operator<<`. The arguments are printed to `cout` in the order

---

1. It may not have occurred to you before that identifiers like _1 are legal, but they are. Identifiers may not start with a number, but they may start with an underscore, and numbers can appear anywhere else in an identifier.

1-3-2. Now, in the example, we enclose this expression in parentheses, and then invoke the resulting function object by passing three arguments to it: `"Hello"`, `"friend"`, and `"my"`. This results in the following output:

```
Hello my friend!
```

Typically, we use function objects to pass into algorithms, which we shall investigate further, but to try something a little more useful, let's store the lambda expression in another delayed function, namely `boost::function`. These useful creatures are described in the following chapter, "Library 11: Function," but for now, it suffices to know that you can pass a function or a function object to an instance of `boost::function`, and store it there for later invocation. In the example, we define such a function, `f`, like so:

```
boost::function<void(int,int,int)> f;
```

This declaration states that `f` can store functions and function objects that can be invoked with three arguments, all of the type `int`. Then, we assign such a function object using a lambda expression that captures the algorithm $X=S*T+U$, and then prints the expression and the result to `cout`.

```
boost::function<void(int,int,int)> f=
std::cout <<
    _1 << "*" << _2 << "+" << _3 << "=" <<_1*_2+_3 << "\n";
```

The placeholders can be used several times in an expression, as shown here. Our function `f` can now be invoked just like an ordinary function, like so:

```
f(1,2,3);
f(3,2,1);
```

The output of running this code follows.

```
1*2+3=5
3*2+1=7
```

Any expression where standard operators (the ones that can be overloaded!) are used can be captured in a lambda expression, and stored for later invocation, or passed directly to an algorithm. You will note that when no placeholder is used in a lambda expression (we haven't yet seen how to do that, but it can be done), the result is a nullary function (object). For comparison, when only _1 is used, the result is a unary function object; when just _1 and _2 are used, the result is a binary function object; and when just _1, _2, and _3 are used, the result is a ternary function object. These first lambda expressions have all benefited from the fact that the expression uses only built-in or common C++ operators, which allows coding the algorithms directly. Read on to see how to bind expressions to other functions, class member functions, and even to data members!

Bind—When Operators Aren't Enough

What we've seen so far is great when there are operators available to support our expressions, but that's not always the case. Sometimes, we need to call another function as part of the expression, and that's often referred to as *binding*; the difference between the binding that we've already seen when creating lambda expressions is that this type of binding requires a separate keyword, bind (hey, that's a clever name!). A bind expression is a delayed function call, either to a free function or a member function. There can be zero or more arguments to the function, some of these can be set directly, some supplied when the function is invoked. With the current version of Boost.Lambda, up to nine arguments are supported (three of which can be applied later through the use of placeholders). To use the binders, you need to include the header "boost/lambda/bind.hpp".

When binding to a function, the first argument is the address of the function, and the subsequent arguments are the arguments. For a non-static class member function, there is always an implicit this argument; in a bind expression, the this argument must be explicitly added. For convenience, the syntax is the same regardless of whether the object is passed by reference or by pointer. So, when binding to a member function, the second argument (that is, the first after the function pointer) is the actual object to which the function should be invoked. It's even possible to bind to data members, which is also demonstrated in the following example:

```
#include <iostream>
#include <string>
#include <map>
#include <algorithm>
#include "boost/lambda/lambda.hpp"
#include "boost/lambda/bind.hpp"
```

```
int main() {
  using namespace boost::lambda;

  typedef std::map<int,std::string> type;
  type keys_and_values;
  keys_and_values[3]="Less than pi";
  keys_and_values[42]="You tell me";
  keys_and_values[0]="Nothing, if you ask me";

  std::cout << "What's wrong with the following expression?\n";
  std::for_each(
    keys_and_values.begin(),
    keys_and_values.end(),
    std::cout << "key=" <<
      bind(&type::value_type::first,_1) << ", value="
        << bind(&type::value_type::second,_1) << '\n');

  std::cout << "\n...and why does this work as expected?\n";
  std::for_each(
    keys_and_values.begin(),
    keys_and_values.end(),
    std::cout << constant("key=") <<
      bind(&type::value_type::first,_1) << ", value="
        << bind(&type::value_type::second,_1) << '\n');

  std::cout << '\n';
  // Print the size and max_size of the container
  (std::cout << "keys_and_values.size()=" <<
    bind(&type::size,_1) << "\nkeys_and_values.max_size()="
      << bind(&type::max_size,_1))(keys_and_values);
}
```

This example starts out with the creation of a `std::map` with keys of type `int` and values of type `std::string`. Remember that the `value_type` of `std::map` is a `std::pair` with the key type and the value type as members. Thus, for our map, the `value_type` is `std::pair<int,std::string>`, so in the `for_each` algorithm, the function object that we pass will receive such a type. Given this `pair`, it would be nice to be able to extract the two members (the key and the value), and that's exactly what our first `bind` expression does.

```
bind(&type::value_type::first,_1)
```

This expression yields a function object that, when invoked, retrieves the data member `first`, of the nested type `value_type`, of its argument, the `pair` we discussed earlier. In our example, `first` is the key type of the `map`, and is thus a `const int`. This is exactly the same syntax as for member functions. But you'll note that our lambda expression does a bit more; the first part of the expression is

```
std::cout << "key=" << ...
```

This compiles, and it works, but it's probably not what's intended. This expression is not a lambda expression; it's just an expression, period. When invoked, it prints `key=`, but it is only invoked once when the expression is evaluated, not once for each element visited by `std::for_each`. In the example, the intention is for `key=` to be the prefix for each key/value pair of our `keys_and_values`. In earlier examples, we wrote code similar to this, but it didn't exhibit this problem. The reason is that we used a placeholder as the first argument to the `operator<<`, which made it a valid lambda expression. Here, we must somehow tell Boost.Lambda that it's supposed to create a function object including the `"key="`. This is done with the function `constant`, which creates a nullary function object, one that takes no arguments; it merely stores its argument, and then returns it when invoked.

```
std::cout << constant("key=") << ...
```

This little change makes all the difference, as shown by the output when running this program.

```
What's wrong with the following expression?
key=0, value=Nothing, if you ask me
3, value=Less than pi
42, value=You tell me

...and why does this work as expected?
key=0, value=Nothing, if you ask me
key=3, value=Less than pi
key=42, value=You tell me

keys_and_values.size()=3
keys_and_values.max_size()=4294967295
```

The final part of the example is a binder that binds to a member function rather than a data member; the syntax is identical, and you'll note that in both cases, there's no need to explicitly state the return type of the function. This magic is

Library 10: Lambda

achieved by automatically deducing the return type of the function or member function, and the type if the binder refers to a data member. However, there is a case where the return type cannot be deduced, and that's when a function object is to be bound; for free functions and member functions, it's a straightforward task to deduce the return type,[2] but for function objects it's impossible. There are two ways around this limitation of the language, and the first is brought forth by the Lambda library itself: overriding the return type deduction by explicitly stating it as a template parameter to the call to `bind`, as demonstrated by the following program.

```
class double_it {
public:
   int operator()(int i) const {
      return i*2;
   }
};

int main() {
   using namespace boost::lambda;

   double_it d;
   int i=12;
   // If you uncomment the following expression,
   // the compiler will complain;
   // it's just not possible to deduce the return type
   // of the function call operator of double_it.
   // (std::cout << _1 << "*2=" << (bind(d,_1)))(i);
   (std::cout << _1 << "*2=" << (bind<int>(d,_1)))(i);
   (std::cout << _1 << "*2=" << (ret<int>(bind(d,_1))))(i);
}
```

There are two versions of the mechanism that disables the return type deduction system—the shorthand version is simply passing the return type as a parameter to `bind`, the second is by using `ret`, which must enclose any lambda/bind expression where the automatic deduction would otherwise fail. This can quickly become tedious in nested lambda expressions, but there is an even better way, which allows the deduction to succeed. We'll cover that later in this chapter.

Also note that a bind expression can consist of another bind expression, which makes binders a great tool for functional composition. There's plenty of power in

---

2. Your mileage may wary. Let's just say that it's technically doable.

nested binds, but tread carefully, because with the power comes additional complexity when reading, writing, and understanding the code.

I Don't Like _1, _2, and _3—Can I Rename Them?

Some people aren't comfortable with the predefined placeholder names, so the library offers a convenient way to change them[3] to anything the user wants. This is accomplished by declaring variables of the type `boost::lambda::placeholderX_type`, where x is 1, 2, or 3. For example, assuming one prefers the names `Arg1`, `Arg2`, and `Arg3` as names for the placeholders:

```cpp
#include <iostream>
#include <vector>
#include <string>
#include "boost/lambda/lambda.hpp"

boost::lambda::placeholder1_type Arg1;
boost::lambda::placeholder2_type Arg2;
boost::lambda::placeholder3_type Arg3;

template <typename T,typename Operation>
  void for_all(T& t,Operation Op) {
    std::for_each(t.begin(),t.end(),Op);
  }

int main() {
  std::vector<std::string> vec;
  vec.push_back("What are");
  vec.push_back("the names");
  vec.push_back("of the");
  vec.push_back("placeholders?");

  for_all(vec,std::cout << Arg1 << " ");
  std::cout << "\nArg1, Arg2, and Arg3!";
}
```

The placeholder variables you declare this way work just like _1, _2, and _3. As an aside, note the function `for_all` that is introduced here—it offers a convenient way of avoiding some redundant typing when frequent operations are to

---

3. Technically, to add new ones.

be applied to all elements of a container—that is, when one would typically use
`for_each`. The function accepts two arguments: a reference to a container, and a
function or function object. For each element of this container, the element is
applied to the function or function objects. I tend to find it quite useful from time
to time—perhaps you will too. Running the program produces the following
output:

```
What are the names of the placeholders?
Arg1, Arg2, and Arg3!
```

Creating your own placeholder names can be a liability for others reading your
code; most programmers who know Boost.Lambda (or Boost.Bind) will be
familiar with the placeholder names _1, _2, and _3. If you decide to call them q,
w, and e, you'll most likely need to explain what they mean to your coworkers.
(And you'll probably have to repeat the explanation often!)

I Want to Give My Constants and Variables Names!

Sometimes, the readability of the code can be improved by giving names to
constants and variables. As you'll recall, we must sometimes create a lambda
expression out of an expression that would otherwise be evaluated immediately.
This is done using either `constant` or `var`; they operate on constant and mutable
variables, respectively. We've already used `constant`, and `var` basically works
the same way. In complex or long lambda expressions, giving a name to one or
more constants can make the expression significantly easier to understand; the
same goes for variables. To create named constants and variables, one simply has
to define a variable of the type `boost::lambda::constant_type<T>::type` and
`boost::lambda::var_type<T>::type`, where `T` is the type of the wrapped constant or variable. Consider this use of a lambda expression:

```
for_all(vec,
   std::cout << constant(' ') << _ << constant('\n'));
```

It can be rather tedious to use `constant` all of the time. Following is a sample
program that names two constants, `newline` and `space`, and uses them in a lambda expression.

```
#include <iostream>
#include <vector>
```

```
#include <algorithm>
#include "boost/lambda/lambda.hpp"

int main() {

   using boost::lambda::constant;
   using boost::lambda::constant_type;

   constant_type<char>::type newline(constant('\n'));
   constant_type<char>::type space(constant(' '));

   boost::lambda::placeholder1_type _;

   std::vector<int> vec;
   vec.push_back(0);
   vec.push_back(1);
   vec.push_back(2);
   vec.push_back(3);
   vec.push_back(4);

   for_all(vec,std::cout << space << _ << newline);
   for_all(vec,
      std::cout << constant(' ') << _ << constant('\n'));
}
```

This is a convenient way of avoiding repetitious typing, and making the lambda expressions a little bit clearer. Following is a similar example, which first defines a type memorizer, which keeps track of all the values that have been assigned to it. Then, a named variable is created using var_type, to be used in a subsequent lambda expression. You'll soon see that named constants tend to be needed much more often than named variables, but there are situations where it makes perfect sense to use named variables, too.[4]

```
#include <iostream>
#include <vector>
#include <algorithm>
#include "boost/lambda/lambda.hpp"

template <typename T> class memorizer {
   std::vector<T> vec_;
public:
```

---

4. Especially when using the lambda looping constructs.

```
    memorizer& operator=(const T& t) {
      vec_.push_back(t);
      return *this;
    }
    void clear() {
      vec_.clear();
    }

    void report() const {
      using boost::lambda::_1;
      std::for_each(
        vec_.begin(),
        vec_.end(),
        std::cout << _1 << ",");
    }
};

int main() {
  using boost::lambda::var_type;
  using boost::lambda::var;
  using boost::lambda::_1;

  std::vector<int> vec;
  vec.push_back(0);
  vec.push_back(1);
  vec.push_back(2);
  vec.push_back(3);
  vec.push_back(4);

  memorizer<int> m;
  var_type<memorizer<int> >::type mem(var(m));

  std::for_each(vec.begin(),vec.end(),mem=_1);
  m.report();
  m.clear();
  std::for_each(vec.begin(),vec.end(),var(m)=_1);
  m.report();
}
```

That's all there is to it, but before you think that you've got all this nailed down, answer this: What should be the type T in the following declaration?

```
constant_type<T>::type hello(constant("Hello"));
```

Is it a `char*`? A `const char*`? No, it's actually a constant reference to an array of six characters (the terminating null counts, too), which gives us this:

```
constant_type<const char (&)[6]>::type
   hello(constant("Hello"));
```

This isn't a pretty sight, and it's a pain for anyone who needs to update the literal—which is why I find it much cleaner to use the good old `std::string` to get the job done.

```
constant_type<std::string>::type
   hello_string(constant(std::string("Hello")));
```

This way, you have to type a little bit more the first time, but you don't need to count the characters, and if there's ever a need to change the string, it just works.

Where Did *ptr_fun* and *mem_fun* Go?

Perhaps you've already thought of this—because Boost.Lambda creates standard-conforming function objects, there's actually no need to remember the adaptor types from the Standard Library. A lambda expression that binds the function or member function works just as well, and the syntax is the same regardless of the type that's being bound to. This allows the code to stay focused on the task, rather than on some syntactic peculiarity. Here's an example that illustrates these benefits:

```
#include <iostream>
#include <vector>
#include <algorithm>
#include <functional>
#include "boost/lambda/lambda.hpp"
#include "boost/lambda/bind.hpp"

void plain_function(int i) {
   std::cout << "void plain_function(" << i << ")\n";
}

class some_class {
public:
   void member_function(int i) const {
```

```
      std::cout <<
        "void some_class::member_function(" << i << ") const\n";

  }
};

int main() {
  std::vector<int> vec(3);
  vec[0]=12;
  vec[1]=10;
  vec[2]=7;

  some_class sc;
  some_class* psc=&sc;

  // Bind to a free function using ptr_fun
  std::for_each(
    vec.begin(),
    vec.end(),
    std::ptr_fun(plain_function));

  // Bind to a member function using mem_fun_ref
  std::for_each(vec.begin(),vec.end(),
    std::bind1st(
      std::mem_fun_ref(&some_class::member_function),sc));

  // Bind to a member function using mem_fun
  std::for_each(vec.begin(),vec.end(),
    std::bind1st(
      std::mem_fun(&some_class::member_function),psc));

  using namespace boost::lambda;

  std::for_each(
    vec.begin(),
    vec.end(),
    bind(&plain_function,_1));

  std::for_each(vec.begin(),vec.end(),
    bind(&some_class::member_function,sc,_1));

  std::for_each(vec.begin(),vec.end(),
    bind(&some_class::member_function,psc,_1));
  }
```

There's really no need to make the case for lambda expressions and binders here, is there? Rather than using three different constructs for performing virtually the same thing, we'll let `bind` figure out what to do, and then be done with it. In the example, it was necessary to use `std::bind1st` to enable the instance of `some_class` to be bound to the invocation; with Boost.Lambda, that's part of the job description. So, the next time you are wondering whether to use `ptr_fun`, `mem_fun`, or `mem_fun_ref`—stop wondering and use Boost.Lambda instead!

Arithmetic Operations Without *<functional>*

We often perform arithmetic operations on elements from sequences, and the Standard Library helps out by providing a number of binary function objects for arithmetic operations, such as `plus`, `minus`, `divides`, `modulus`, and so on. However, these function objects require more typing than one likes, and often one argument needs to be bound, which in turn requires the use of binders. When nesting such arithmetic, expressions quickly become unwieldy, and this is yet another area where lambda expressions really shine. Because we are dealing with operators here, both in arithmetic and C++ terms, we have the power to directly code our algorithms as lambda expressions. To give a short motivation, consider the trivial problem of incrementing a numeric value by 4. Then, consider doing that same inside a Standard Library algorithm (such as `transform`). Although the first comes very naturally, the second is a totally different beast (which will drive you into the arms of handwritten loops). Using a lambda expression, focus remains on the arithmetic. In the following example, we'll first use `std::bind1st` and `std::plus` to add 4 to each element of a container—and then we'll use `lambda` to subtract 4.

```
#include <iostream>
#include <vector>
#include <algorithm>
#include <functional>
#include "boost/lambda/lambda.hpp"
#include "boost/lambda/bind.hpp"

int main() {
  using namespace boost::lambda;

  std::vector<int> vec(3);
  vec[0]=12;
  vec[1]=10;
```

```
    vec[2]=7;

    // Transform using std::bind1st and std::plus
    std::transform(vec.begin(),vec.end(),vec.begin(),
      std::bind1st(std::plus<int>(),4));

    // Transform using a lambda expression
    std::transform(vec.begin(),vec.end(),vec.begin(),_1-=4);
}
```

The difference is astounding! When adding 4 using "traditional" means, it's hard for the untrained eye to see what's going on. Reading the code, we see that we are binding the first argument of a default-constructed instance of std::plus to 4. The lambda expression spells it out—subtract 4 from the element. If you think that the version using bind1st and plus isn't that bad, try it with longer expressions.

Boost.Lambda supports all of the arithmetic operators in C++, so there's rarely a need to include <functional> just for the sake of arithmetic function objects. The following example demonstrates the use of some of those arithmetic operators. Each element in the vector vec is modified using the additive and multiplicative operators.

```
#include <iostream>
#include <vector>
#include <algorithm>
#include "boost/lambda/lambda.hpp"

int main() {
  using namespace boost::lambda;

  std::vector<int> vec(3);
  vec[0]=1;
  vec[1]=2;
  vec[2]=3;

  std::for_each(vec.begin(),vec.end(),_1+=10);
  std::for_each(vec.begin(),vec.end(),_1-=10);
  std::for_each(vec.begin(),vec.end(),_1*=3);
  std::for_each(vec.begin(),vec.end(),_1/=2);
  std::for_each(vec.begin(),vec.end(),_1%=3);
}
```

Terse, readable, and maintainable—that's the kind of code you get with Boost.Lambda. Skip `std::plus`, `std::minus`, `std::multiplies`, `std::divides`, and `std::modulus`; your code is always better with Boost.Lambda.

Writing Readable Predicates

Many of the algorithms in the Standard Library come in a version that accepts a unary or binary predicate. These predicates are free functions of function objects, but of course, a lambda expression also fits the bill. For predicates that are used often, it makes perfect sense to define function objects, but frequently, they are used once or twice and then never looked at again. In such cases, a lambda expression is a superior choice, both because the code becomes easier to understand (all functionality resides at the same location), and because the code isn't cluttered with function objects that are rarely used. As a concrete example, consider finding an element with a specific value in a container. If `operator==` is defined for the type, it's easy to use the algorithm `find` directly, but what if another criteria for the search is to be used? Given the type `search_for_me` in the following, how would you use `find` to search for the first element where the member function `a` returns `"apple"`?

```cpp
#include <iostream>
#include <algorithm>
#include <vector>
#include <string>

class search_for_me {
  std::string a_;
  std::string b_;
public:

  search_for_me() {}
  search_for_me(const std::string& a,const std::string& b)
    : a_(a),b_(b) {}

  std::string a() const {
    return a_;
  }

  std::string b() const {
    return b_;
```

```
      }
};

int main() {
  std::vector<search_for_me> vec;
  vec.push_back(search_for_me("apple","banana"));
  vec.push_back(search_for_me("orange","mango"));

  std::vector<search_for_me>::iterator it=
    std::find_if(vec.begin(),vec.end(),???);

  if (it!=vec.end())
    std::cout << it->a() << '\n';
}
```

First of all, note that we need to use `find_if`,[5] but how should the predicate marked with ??? in the preceding code be defined? Here's one way: a function object that implements the logic for the predicate.

```
class a_finder {
  std::string val_;
public:
  a_finder() {}
  a_finder(const std::string& val) : val_(val) {}

  bool operator()(const search_for_me& s) const {
    return s.a()==val_;
  }
};
```

This function object can be used like so:

```
std::vector<search_for_me>::iterator it=
  std::find_if(vec.begin(),vec.end(),a_finder("apple"));
```

That's fine, but two minutes (or days) later, we'll want another function object, this time one that tests the member function b. And so on...this sort of thing quickly becomes tedious. As you've no doubt guessed, this is another excellent case for lambda expressions; we need the flexibility of creating the predicate directly where and when it's needed. The preceding `find_if` could have been written like this.

---

5. `find` uses `operator==`; `find_if` requires an additional predicate function (or function object).

```
std::vector<search_for_me>::iterator it=
  std::find_if(vec.begin(),vec.end(),
    bind(&search_for_me::a,_1)=="apple");
```

We `bind` to the member function a, and we test it for equality with `"apple"`— and that's our unary predicate in full, defined right where it's used. But wait, as they say, there's more. When dealing with numeric types, we have the full range of arithmetic operators, comparisons, and logical operations to choose from. This means that even complex predicates are straightforward to define. Read the following code carefully, and see how well the predicates are expressed.

```
#include <iostream>
#include <algorithm>
#include <vector>
#include <string>
#include "boost/lambda/lambda.hpp"

int main() {
  using namespace boost::lambda;

  std::vector<int> vec1;
  vec1.push_back(2);
  vec1.push_back(3);
  vec1.push_back(5);
  vec1.push_back(7);
  vec1.push_back(11);

  std::vector<int> vec2;
  vec2.push_back(7);
  vec2.push_back(4);
  vec2.push_back(2);
  vec2.push_back(3);
  vec2.push_back(1);

  std::cout << *std::find_if(vec1.begin(),vec1.end(),
    (_1>=3 && _1<5) || _1<1) << '\n';

  std::cout << *std::find_if(vec2.begin(),vec2.end(),
    _1>=4 && _1<10) << '\n';

  std::cout << *std::find_if(vec1.begin(),vec1.end(),
    _1==4 || _1==5) << '\n';

  std::cout << *std::find_if(vec2.begin(),vec2.end(),
```

```
    _1!=7 && _1<10) << '\n';

std::cout << *std::find_if(vec1.begin(),vec1.end(),
    !(_1%3)) << '\n';

std::cout << *std::find_if(vec2.begin(),vec2.end(),
    _1/2<3) << '\n';
}
```

As you can see, creating such predicates is as easy as writing down the logic in the first place. This is one of my favorite uses for lambda expressions, because they can be understood by just about anyone. It's inevitable that we sometimes need to choose other mechanisms than lambda expressions simply because of the competence profiles of those who must understand the code; but here, there's nothing but added value.

Make Your Function Objects Play Nicely with Boost.Lambda

Not all expressions are suitable as lambda expressions—complex expressions are better suited for regular function objects, and expressions that are reused as-is many times should also be made first-class citizens of your code base. They should be collected in a library of reusable function objects. But, you'll likely want to use these function objects in lambda expressions, too, and you'll want them to play nicely with Lambda; not all function objects do. The problem is that the return type of function objects cannot be deduced the way ordinary functions can; this is an inherent limitation of the language. However, there is a well-defined way for providing this important information to the Lambda library, which in turn makes bind expressions much cleaner. To give an example of the problem, consider the following function object:

```
template <typename T> class add_prev {
  T prev_;
public:
  T operator()(T t) {
    prev_+=t;
    return prev_;
  }
};
```

Given such a function object, a lambda expression cannot deduce the return type, so the following example doesn't compile.

```
#include <iostream>
#include <algorithm>
#include <vector>
#include "boost/lambda/lambda.hpp"
#include "boost/lambda/bind.hpp"

int main() {
  using namespace boost::lambda;

  std::vector<int> vec;
  vec.push_back(5);
  vec.push_back(8);
  vec.push_back(2);
  vec.push_back(1);

  add_prev<int> ap;
  std::transform(
    vec.begin(),
    vec.end(),
    vec.begin(),
    bind(var(ap),_1));
}
```

The problem is the call to `transform`.

```
std::transform(vec.begin(),vec.end(),vec.begin(),bind(var(ap),_1));
```

When the binder is instantiated, the mechanism for return type deduction kicks in...and fails. Thus, the program does not compile, and you must explicitly tell `bind` the return type, like so:

```
std::transform(vec.begin(),vec.end(),vec.begin(),
  bind<int>(var(ap),_1));
```

This is a shorthand notation for the general form of explicitly setting the return types for lambda expression, and it's the equivalent of this code.

```
std::transform(vec.begin(),vec.end(),vec.begin(),
  ret<int>(bind<int>(var(ap),_1)));
```

This problem isn't new; it's virtually the same that applies for function objects used by the Standard Library algorithms. There, the solution is to add `typedefs` that state the return type and argument type(s) of the function objects. The Standard Library even provides helper classes for accomplishing this, through the class templates `unary_function` and `binary_function`—our example class `add_prev` could become a compliant function object by either defining the required `typedefs` (`argument_type` and `result_type` for unary function objects, `first_argument_type`, `second_argument_type`, and `result_type` for binary function objects), or inheriting from `unary_function`/`binary_function`.

```
template <typename T> class add_prev : public std::unary_function<T,T>
```

Is this good enough for lambda expressions, too? Can we simply reuse this scheme, and thus our existing function objects, too? Alas, the answer is no. There is a problem with this `typedef` approach: What happens when the result type or the argument type(s) is dependent on a template parameter to a parameterized function call operator? Or, when there are several overloaded function call operators? Had there been language support for template `typedefs`, much of the problem would be solved, but currently, that's not the case. That's why Boost.Lambda requires a different approach, through a nested parameterized class called `sig`. To enable the return type deduction to work with `add_prev`, we must define a nested type `sig` like this:

```
template <typename T> class add_prev :
  public std::unary_function<T,T> {
  T prev_;
public:
  template <typename Args> class sig {
  public:
    typedef T type;
  };
// Rest of definition
```

The template parameter `Args` is actually a tuple containing the function object (first element) and the types of the arguments to the function call operator. In our case, we have no need for this information, as the return type and the argument type are always `T`. Using this improved version of `add_prev`, there's no need to short-circuit the return type deduction in a lambda expression, so our original version of the code now compiles cleanly.

```
std::transform(vec.begin(),vec.end(),vec.begin(),bind(var(ap),_1));
```

To see how the tuple in the template parameter to `sig` works, consider another function object with two function call operators, one version accepting an `int` argument, the other accepting a reference to const `std::string`. The problem that we need to solve can be expressed as, "if the second element of the tuple passed to the `sig` template is of type `int`, set the return type to `std::string`; if the second element of the tuple passed to the `sig` template is of type `std::string`, set the return type to `double`." To do this, we'll add another class template that we can specialize and then use in `add_prev::sig`.

```cpp
template <typename T> class sig_helper {};;

// The version for the overload on int
template<> class sig_helper<int> {
public:
  typedef std::string type;
};

// The version for the overload on std::string
template<> class sig_helper<std::string> {
public:
  typedef double type;
};

// The function object
class some_function_object {

  template <typename Args> class sig {
    typedef typename boost::tuples::element<1,Args>::type
      cv_first_argument_type;

    typedef typename
      boost::remove_cv<cv_first_argument_type>::type
      first_argument_type;

  public:
  // The first argument helps us decide the correct version
    typedef typename
      sig_helper<first_argument_type>::type type;
  };

  std::string operator()(int i) const {
    std::cout << i << '\n';
    return "Hello!";
  }
```

```
double operator()(const std::string& s) const {
    std::cout << s << '\n';
    return 3.14159265353;
  }
};
```

There are two important parts to study here—first, the helper class sig_helper, which is class parameterized on a type T. This type is either int or std::string, depending on which of the overloaded versions of the function call operator is requested. By fully specializing this template, the correct typedef, type, is defined. The next interesting part is the sig class, where the first argument type (the second element of the tuple) is retrieved, any const or volatile qualifiers are removed, and the resulting type is used to instantiate the correct version of the sig_helper class, which has the correct typedef type. This is a rather complex (but necessary!) way of defining the return types for our classes, but most of the time, there's only one version of the function call operator; and then it's a trivial task to correctly add the nested sig class.

It's important that our function objects work without hassle in lambda expressions, and defining the nested sig class where it's needed is definitely a good idea; it helps a lot.

Control Structures in Lambda Expressions

We have seen that powerful lambda expressions can be created with ease, but many programming problems require that we be able to express conditions, which we do in C++ using if-then-else, for, while, and so on. There are lambda versions of all C++ control structures in Boost.Lambda. To use the selection statements, if and switch, include the files "boost/lambda/if.hpp" and "boost/lambda/switch.hpp", respectively. For the iteration statements, while, do, and for, include "boost/lambda/loops.hpp". It's not possible to overload keywords, so the syntax is slightly different than what you're used to, but the correlation is obvious. As a first example, we'll see how to create a simple if-then-else construct in a lambda expression. The form is *if_then_else(condition, then-statements, else-statements)*. There is also another syntactic form, which has the form *if_(condition)[then-statements].else_[else-statements]*.

```
#include <iostream>
#include <algorithm>
#include <vector>
```

```
#include <string>
#include "boost/lambda/lambda.hpp"
#include "boost/lambda/bind.hpp"
#include "boost/lambda/if.hpp"

int main() {
  using namespace boost::lambda;

  std::vector<std::string> vec;
  vec.push_back("Lambda");
  vec.push_back("expressions");
  vec.push_back("really");
  vec.push_back("rock");

  std::for_each(vec.begin(),vec.end(),if_then_else(
    bind(&std::string::size,_1)<=6u,
      std::cout << _1 << '\n',
      std::cout << constant("Skip.\n")));

  std::for_each(vec.begin(),vec.end(),
    if_(bind(&std::string::size,_1)<=6u)  [
      std::cout << _1 << '\n'
    ]
    .else_[
      std::cout << constant("Skip.\n")
    ] );
}
```

If you've read the whole chapter up to now, you probably find the preceding example quite readable; if you're jumping right in, this is probably a scary read. Control structures immediately add to the complexity of reading lambda expressions, so it does take a little longer to get used to. After you get the hang of it, it comes naturally (the same goes for writing them!). Deciding which syntactic form to use is merely a matter of taste; they do exactly the same thing.

In the preceding example, we have a vector of strings and, if their size is less than or equal to 6, they are printed to std::cout; otherwise, the string "Skip" is printed. There are a few things worth noting in the if_then_else expression.

```
if_then_else(
  bind(&std::string::size,_1)<=6u,
    std::cout << _1 << '\n',
    std::cout << constant("Skip.\n")));
```

First, the *condition* is a predicate, and it must be a lambda expression! Second, the *then*-statement must be a lambda expression! Third, the *else*-statement must be—get ready—a lambda expression! The first two come naturally in this case, but it's easy to forget the `constant` to make the string literal ("Skip\n") a lambda expression. The observant reader notices that the example uses `6u`, and not simply `6`, to make sure that the comparison is performed using two unsigned types. The reason for this is that we're dealing with deeply nested templates, which means that when a lambda expression like this happens to trigger a compiler warning, the output is really, really long-winded. Try removing the `u` in the example and see how your compiler likes it! You should see a warning about comparing signed and unsigned types because `std::string::size` returns an unsigned type.

The return type of the control structures is `void`, with the exception of `if_then_else_return`, which calls the conditional operator. Let's take a closer look at the whole range of control structures, starting with `if` and `switch`. Remember that to use `if`-constructs, `"boost/lambda/if.hpp"` must be included. For `switch`, `"boost/lambda/switch.hpp"` must be included. The following examples all assume that the declarations in the namespace `boost::lambda` have been brought to the current scope through using declarations or a using directive.

```
(if_then(_1<5,
 std::cout << constant("Less than 5")))(make_const(3));
```

The `if_then` function starts with a *condition*, followed by a *then*-part; in the preceding code, if the argument passed to the lambda function is less than 5 (`_1<5`), `"Less than 5"` is printed to `std::cout`. You'll note that when we invoke this lambda expression with the numeric value 3, we cannot pass it directly, like so.

```
(if_then(_1<5,std::cout << constant("Less than 5")))(3);
```

This would result in a compiler error, because 3 is an `int`, and an *rvalue* of type `int` (or any built-in type for that matter) cannot be `const` qualified. Thus, one has to use the utility `make_const` here, which does nothing more than return a reference to `const` of its argument. Another option is to wrap the whole lambda expression in a call to `const_parameters`, like so:

```
(const_parameters(
 if_then(_1<5,std::cout << constant("Less than 5"))))(3);
```

const_parameters is useful to avoid having to wrap each of several arguments with make_const. Note that when using this function, all of the parameters to the lambda expression are considered (references to) const.

Now look at how if_then looks using the alternative syntax.

```
(if_(_1<5)
  [std::cout << constant("Less than 5")])(make_const(3));
```

This notation has a greater resemblance to the C++ keyword, but it does exactly the same thing as if_then. The function if_ (note the trailing underscore) is followed by the parenthesized *condition*, which in turn is followed by the *then*-statement. Again, choosing between these syntax alternatives is simply a matter of taste.

Now, let's take a look at the *if-then-else* constructs; they're very similar to if_then.

```
(if_then_else(
  _1==0,
    std::cout << constant("Nothing"),
    std::cout << _1))(make_const(0));
(if_(_1==0)
  [std::cout << constant("Nothing")].
    else_[std::cout << _1])(make_const(0));
```

When adding the else-part using the alternative syntax, note that a period precedes the else_.

The return type of these lambda expressions is void, but there is also a version that returns a value, by using the conditional operator. There are some non-trivial rules for the types of such expressions (I won't go through them here, but see the online documentation for Boost.Lambda or the C++ Standard [§5.16] for the nitty-gritty details). Here's an example, where the return value is assigned to a variable, similar to how you would use the conditional operator for ordinary expressions.

```
int i;
int value=12;
var(i)=(if_then_else_return
  (_1>=10,constant(10),_1))(value);
```

There is no version of the alternative syntax for this construct. That's it for *if-then-else*, which brings us to the *switch*-statement, which differs somewhat from the standard C++ switch.

```
(switch_statement
  _1,
  case_statement<0>
    (var(std::cout) << "Nothing"),
  case_statement<1>
    (std::cout << constant("A little")),
  default_statement
    (std::cout << _1))
) (make_const(100));
```

The call to `switch_statement` starts with the condition variable, which in our case is `_1`, the first argument to the lambda expression. This is followed by (up to nine) case constants, which have labels of integer type; these must be constant integral expressions. We provide two such constants, for 0 and 1 (note that they could have any value acceptable for integral types). Finally, we add the optional `default_statement`, which is executed if the evaluation of `_1` doesn't match any of the other constants. Note that a `break`-statement is implicitly added to each case constant, so there's no need to explicitly exit from a switch (which is a Good Thing for those maintaining the code[6]).

Now let's examine the iteration statements, `for`, `while`, and `do`. To use any of these, you must include the header `"boost/lambda/loops.hpp"` first. Boost.Lambda's equivalent of C++'s `while` is `while_loop`.

```
int val1=1;
int val2=4;
(while_loop(_1<_2,
  (++_1,std::cout << constant("Inc...\n")))) (val1,val2);
```

A `while_loop` statement is executed until the condition becomes `false`; here the condition is `_1<_2`, which is followed by the body of the loop, the expression `++_1,std::cout << constant("Inc...\n")`. Of course, the condition and the loop body must, themselves, be valid lambda expressions. The alternative syntax is closer to the C++ syntax, just as was the case with `if_`.

---

6. Spokesmen of fall-through case-statements; please excuse this blasphemy.

```
int val1=1;
int val2=4;
(while_(_1<_2)
  [++_1,std::cout << constant("Inc...\n")])(val1,val2);
```

The form is `while_`(condition) [*substatement*], and it does save a couple of keystrokes...but personally I find the function call syntax easier to read for `while`, although I (irrationally) find `if_` easier to parse than `if_then(...)`. Go figure. `do_while_loop` is naturally very similar to `while_loop`, but the substatement is always executed at least once (unlike `while`, the condition is evaluated after each execution).

```
(do_while_loop(_1!=12,std::cout <<
constant("I'll run once")))(make_const(12));
```

The corresponding alternative syntax is

```
(do_[std::cout <<
constant("I'll run once")].while_(_1!=12))(make_const(12));
```

Finally, there's the `for` loop equivalent, `for_loop`. In the following example, a named, delayed variable is used to make the lambda expression more readable. We've come across delayed variables before through the use of `constant` and `var`. Delayed variables with names is a way of avoiding having to type `constant` or `var` for constants and variables, respectively. Instead, they're given a name of your choice with which they can later be referred. The general form for the loop is `for_loop`(*init-statement, condition, expression, statement*)—that is, it's like a regular for statement but the *statement* is part of the function (arguments).

```
int val1=0;
var_type<int>::type counter(var(val1));
(for_loop(counter=0,counter<_1,++counter,var(std::cout)
  << "counter is " << counter << "\n"))(make_const(4));
```

With the alternative syntax, *statement* is separated from initialization, *condition*, and *expression*.

```
(for_(counter=0,counter<_1,++counter)[var(std::cout)
  << "counter is " << counter << "\n"])(make_const(4));
```

The example initializes the delayed variable `counter` to 0, the *condition* is `counter<_1`, and the *expression* is `++counter`.

This concludes the section on control structures. For most problems that I've encountered and solved with lambda expressions, I can actually do without them, but sometimes, they are real lifesavers. Regarding the choice of syntactic version, the best way to figure out which to use is probably to experiment using both, and get a feel for which version suits your needs the best. It should be noted that when using `switch` and the loop constructs, the lambda expressions quickly become large enough to make them hard to follow if you're not fairly accustomed to using the library. Some care should thus be taken, and if an expression seems too hard to parse for your fellow programmers, consider a separate function object instead. (Or have them practice using Boost.Lambda more!)

Casting in Lambda Expressions

There are four special "cast operators"[7] that allow casting of types in lambda expressions: `ll_dynamic_cast`, `ll_static_cast`, `ll_reinterpret_cast`, and `ll_const_cast`. The names are different from the corresponding C++ keywords because these cannot be overloaded. To use these casts, include the header `"boost/lambda/casts.hpp"`. These functions work like their C++ cast operator equivalents; they take an explicit template argument, which is the type to cast to, and an implicit template argument, which is the source type. In our first example, we will use two classes, imaginatively named `base` and `derived`. We'll create two pointers to `base`, one of them will point to an instance of `base`, and the other to an instance of `derived`. Using `ll_dynamic_cast`, we will try to extract a `derived*` from both of these pointers.

```
#include <iostream>
#include "boost/lambda/lambda.hpp"
#include "boost/lambda/casts.hpp"
#include "boost/lambda/if.hpp"
#include "boost/lambda/bind.hpp"

class base {
public:
  virtual ~base() {}
```

---

7. Technically, they are template functions returning function objects.

```
    void do_stuff() const {
      std::cout << "void base::do_stuff() const\n";
    }
};

class derived : public base {
public:
    void do_more_stuff() const {
      std::cout << "void derived::do_more_stuff() const\n";
    }
};

int main() {
  using namespace boost::lambda;

  base* p1=new base;
  base* p2=new derived;

  derived* pd=0;

  (if_(var(pd)=ll_dynamic_cast<derived*>(_1))
    [bind(&derived::do_more_stuff,var(pd))].
      else_[bind(&base::do_stuff,*_1)])(p1);

  (if_(var(pd)=ll_dynamic_cast<derived*>(_1))
    [bind(&derived::do_more_stuff,var(pd))].
      else_[bind(&base::do_stuff,*_1)])(p2);
}
```

In `main`, the first thing we do is create `p1` and `p2`; `p1` points to a `base`, whereas `p2` points to an instance of `derived`. In the first lambda expression, the assigned `pd` becomes the condition; it is implicitly converted to `bool`, and if it yields `true`, *then*-part is evaluated. Here, we `bind` to the member function `do_more_stuff`. If the `ll_dynamic_cast` fails, the delayed variable representing `pd` will be 0, and the *else*-part is executed. So, in our example, the first invocation of the lambda expression should call `do_stuff` on `base`, and the second should call `do_more_stuff` in `derived`, which is confirmed when running this program.

```
void base::do_stuff() const
void derived::do_more_stuff() const
```

Note that in the example, the argument `_1` is dereferenced, but this is not really necessary; this is done implicitly if needed. If an argument to a `bind` expression must always be a pointer type, you can enforce that by dereferencing it yourself. Otherwise, leave that chore to Boost.Lambda.

ll_static_cast is really useful to avoid warnings. Don't use it to suppress important information, but to reduce noise. In a previous example, we created a bind expression that evaluated the length of a std::string (using std::string::size) and compared the length to another integral value. The return type of std::string::size is an unsigned type, and passing a signed integer type to the comparison (most likely) produces a warning from the compiler that signed and unsigned comparisons are risky business. However, because this happens in a lambda expression, the compiler dutifully traces the root of the problem by telling you which part of a nested template invocation is responsible for this horrible crime. The result is a very long warning message, which probably hides any other issues because of the low signal-to-noise ratio. In generic code, this can sometimes be an issue, because the types that are used are not within our control. Thus, after evaluating the potential problem, you often find it beneficial to suppress unwanted warnings using ll_static_cast. The following example includes code that exhibits this behavior.

```cpp
#include <iostream>
#include <string>
#include <algorithm>
#include "boost/lambda/lambda.hpp"
#include "boost/lambda/casts.hpp"
#include "boost/lambda/if.hpp"
#include "boost/lambda/bind.hpp"

template <typename String,typename Integral>
  void is_it_long(const String& s,const Integral& i) {
    using namespace boost::lambda;
    (if_then_else(bind(&String::size,_1)<_2,
      var(std::cout) << "Quite short...\n",
      std::cout << constant("Quite long...\n")))(s,i);
  }

int main() {
  std::string s="Is this string long?";
  is_it_long(s,4u);
  is_it_long(s,4);
}
```

The parameterized function is_it_long (and please try to ignore that this is a slightly more contrived example than usual) invokes a lambda expression using a reference to const variable of type `Integral`. Now, whether this type is signed or not is beyond our control, so chances are good that a user will inadvertently trigger a very verbose warning, which is exactly what the example illustrates, because one call to `is_it_long` uses a signed integer.

```
is_it_long(s,4);
```

The only way to make sure that the user doesn't accidentally cause this to happen (besides requiring only unsigned types) is to make the argument an unsigned integer type, regardless of what it originally is. This is a job for `ll_static_cast`, so we change the function `is_it_long` like so:

```
template <typename String,typename Integral>
  void is_it_long(const String& s,const Integral& i) {
    using namespace boost::lambda;
    (if_then_else(bind(&String::size,_1)<
      ll_static_cast<typename String::size_type>(_2),
        var(std::cout) << "Quite short...\n",
        std::cout << constant("Quite long...\n")))(s,i);
}
```

This situation does not arise often (at least I haven't seen it many times), but it does happen, and this solution works. Using `ll_const_cast` and `ll_reinterpret_cast` is similar to what we've seen here, so this example ends the cast functions. Use them wisely, and don't use `ll_reinterpret_cast` at all, without extremely compelling reasons (I can't think of any). It's mainly there for symmetry; if you need it, chances are good that you've done something that you shouldn't have.

Constructing and Destructing

When the need to create or destroy objects arises in lambda expressions, some special handling and syntax is required. To begin with, it's not possible to take the address of constructors or destructors, and it's thus not possible to use a standard `bind` expression for them. Moreover, operators `new` and `delete` have fixed return types, so they cannot return lambda expressions for arbitrary types. If you need to create or destroy objects in lambda expressions, make sure to include the header `"boost/lambda/construct.hpp"`, which contains the templates `constructor`, `destructor`, `new_ptr`, `new_array`, `delete_ptr`, and `delete_array`. We'll take a look at how to use them, and focus on `constructor` and `new_ptr`, which are the most commonly used of these constructs.

For our first example, consider a container that holds smart pointers as its elements, and we'll want to reset the contents of smart pointers in our lambda expression. This typically involves a call to operator new; the exception to that rule would be if some custom allocation scheme were used, or a factory method of some kind. We will need to use new_ptr to do that, and if you want or need to, it's often possible to also use constructor in an assignment expression. Let's do both. We'll set the table by defining two classes, base and derived, and a std::map of boost::shared_ptr<base>s indexed by std::strings. Take a deep breath before reading the lambda expressions in this example; they are two of the most complex lambda expressions you'll see in this chapter. Although complex, understanding what they do should be reasonably straightforward. Just take your time.

```cpp
#include <iostream>
#include <map>
#include <string>
#include <algorithm>
#include "boost/lambda/lambda.hpp"
#include "boost/lambda/construct.hpp"
#include "boost/lambda/bind.hpp"
#include "boost/lambda/if.hpp"
#include "boost/lambda/casts.hpp"
#include "boost/shared_ptr.hpp"

class base {
public:
  virtual ~base() {}
};

class derived : public base {
};

int main() {
  using namespace boost::lambda;

  typedef boost::shared_ptr<base> ptr_type;
  typedef std::map<std::string,ptr_type> map_type;

  map_type m;
  m["An object"]=ptr_type(new base);
  m["Another object"]=ptr_type();
  m["Yet another object"]=ptr_type(new base);
```

```
        std::for_each(m.begin(),m.end(),
          if_then_else(!bind(&ptr_type::get,
             bind(&map_type::value_type::second,_1)),
                (bind(&map_type::value_type::second,_1)=
                  bind(constructor<ptr_type>(),bind(new_ptr<derived>())),
                    var(std::cout) << "Created a new derived for \""
                       bind(&map_type::value_type::first,_1) << "\".\n"),
                        var(std::cout) << "\"" <<
                           bind(&map_type::value_type::first,_1)
                              << "\" already has a valid pointer.\n"));

    m["Beware, this is slightly tricky"]=ptr_type();
    std::cout << "\nHere we go again...\n";

        std::for_each(m.begin(),m.end(),
          if_then_else(!bind(&map_type::value_type::second,_1),
             ((bind(static_cast<void (ptr_type::*)(base*)>
               (&ptr_type::reset<base>),
              bind(&map_type::value_type::second,_1),
                bind(new_ptr<base>()))),
                   var(std::cout) << "Created a new derived for \""
                      << bind(&map_type::value_type::first,_1)
                         << "\".\n"),
                            var(std::cout) << "\"" <<
                               bind(&map_type::value_type::first,_1)
                                  << "\" already has a valid pointer.\n"));
}
```

You got all of that, right? Just in case there was any confusion, I'll explain what's happening in this example. First, note that the two lambda expressions do essentially the same thing. They set a valid pointer for any element in the `std::map` that is currently null. Here's the output when running the program:

```
"An object" already has a valid pointer.
Created a new derived for "Another object".
"Yet another object" already has a valid pointer.
"An object" already has a valid pointer.
"Another object" already has a valid pointer.
"Yet another object" already has a valid pointer.

Here we go again...
"An object" already has a valid pointer.
"Another object" already has a valid pointer.
Created a new derived for "Beware, this is slightly tricky".
"Yet another object" already has a valid pointer.
```

The output shows that we managed to put valid objects into each element of the map, but how?

The expressions do a similar task, but each takes a different tack. Starting with the first one, let's dissect the lambda expression to see how it works. The first part is the condition, of course, which is quite trivial:[8]

```
!bind(&ptr_type::get,bind(&map_type::value_type::second,_1))
```

Seeing it like this makes it a bit easier, right? Reading the expression starting with the innermost `bind` tells us that we're binding to the member `map_type::value_type::second` (which is a `ptr_type`), and to that we bind the member function `ptr_type::get` (which returns the `shared_ptr`'s pointee), and to the whole expression, we apply the `operator!`. Because a pointer is implicitly convertible to `bool`, that's a valid Boolean expression. That takes care of the *condition*, so we move on to the *then*-part.

```
bind(&map_type::value_type::second,_1)=
    bind(constructor<ptr_type>(),
        bind(new_ptr<derived>())),
```

There are three `bind` expressions here, the first one (we start reading from the left here, because the expression involves an assignment) extracts the member `map_type::value_type::second`, which is the smart pointer. This is the value that we assign a new `derived` to. The second and third expressions are nested, so we read them from the inside out. The innermost `bind` takes care of the default construction of an instance of `derived` on the heap, and to the result we `bind` a `constructor` call to `ptr_type` (the smart pointer type), which is then assigned (using the usual notation for assignment) to the very first `bind` expression. Then, we add another expression to this *then*-part, which simply prints out a short message and the element's key.

```
var(std::cout) << "Created a new derived for \"" <<
        bind(&map_type::value_type::first,_1) << "\".\n")
```

Finally, we add the *else*-part of the statement, which prints out the key of the element and some text.

---

8. It can be made even more trivial, as we shall soon see.

```
var(std::cout) << "\"" <<
  bind(&map_type::value_type::first,_1)
<< "\" already has a valid pointer.\n"));
```

When decomposing the expressions, it's clear that they're not really that complex, although looking at the whole thing can be quite intimidating. It's important to indent and separate the code so that reading becomes intuitive. We can write a similar expression for accomplishing our task, in a version that's quite different from this one but is much harder to read, although it is slightly more efficient. The thing to note here is that there are often several ways of attacking the problem of writing lambda expressions, just as is the case with other programming problems. It makes sense to apply some extra thought before writing, because the choices substantially affect the readability of the end result. For comparison, here's the other version I mentioned:

```
std::for_each(m.begin(),m.end(),
  if_then_else(!bind(&map_type::value_type::second,_1),
    ((bind(static_cast<void (ptr_type::*)(base*)>
      (&ptr_type::reset<base>),
    bind(&map_type::value_type::second,_1),
      bind(new_ptr<derived>()))),
        var(std::cout) << "Created a new derived for \"" <<
          bind(&map_type::value_type::first,_1) << "\".\n"),
            var(std::cout) << "\"" <<
              bind(&map_type::value_type::first,_1)
                << "\" already has a valid pointer.\n"));
```

This is not as nice, because the code is cluttered with casts and complicated nested binds, and we move away from the actual logic more than the previous version did. To understand it, let's again decompose the expressions to their constituent parts. First, we have the *condition*, which is actually simplified (nothing else is in this expression!); we utilize our knowledge of shared_ptr, which tells us that there is an implicit conversion to bool available. We can thus eliminate the bind to the member function get that we used in the previous expression.

```
!bind(&map_type::value_type::second,_1)
```

That *condition* works with the original expression, too. The next part is this:

```
bind(static_cast<void (ptr_type::*)(base*)>
  (&ptr_type::reset<base>),
bind(&map_type::value_type::second,_1),
    bind(new_ptr<derived>()))
```

This is arguably too hard to parse, so we should have avoided it in the first place. Rather than using assignment, we go directly for the member function `reset`, which is not only parameterized but also overloaded. We thus need to perform a `static_cast` to tell the compiler which version of `reset` we are interested in. In this case, it is mainly the `static_cast` that complicates the reading of the expression, but again starting from the innermost expression, we can work through it. We bind a call to `operator new`, creating an instance of `derived`, and to the result we bind the smart pointer (through the member `map_type::value_type::second`), to which we bind the `shared_ptr` member function `reset`. This results in a call to `reset` for the smart pointer in the element, with the argument being a newly constructed instance of `derived`. Although we've done basically the same thing as in the previous example, this version is much harder to understand.

Just remember that there can often be alternatives that lead to lambda expressions that are easier or harder to read and understand, so consider the alternatives and choose the easier forms when possible. It is imperative to treat the power that this library offers, and the effect it can have on your fellow programmers, with respect.

Throwing and Catching Exceptions

We have reached the final section of this chapter, which discusses exception handling in lambda expressions. If your reaction to this topic is to wonder exactly what justifies exception handling code in a lambda expression, that matches my first thoughts fairly well. However, it's not as far fetched as you might think. Surely you have written code that performs local exception handling when processing data in a loop? Well, handwritten loops can be avoided through usage of the Boost.Lambda library, so moving that exception handling into lambda expressions is quite natural.

To use the exception handling facilities of Boost.Lambda, include `"boost/lambda/exceptions.hpp"`. Let's reuse the classes `base` and `derived` that we saw earlier, and perform `dynamic_casts` almost like we did before—but this time we will perform casts to references rather than pointers, which means that upon failure, `dynamic_cast` will throw an exception. This makes the example more straightforward than what we did before, because we don't need to use an `if` statement.

```
#include <iostream>
#include "boost/lambda/lambda.hpp"
#include "boost/lambda/casts.hpp"
#include "boost/lambda/bind.hpp"
#include "boost/lambda/exceptions.hpp"

int main() {
  using namespace boost::lambda;

  base* p1=new base;
  base* p2=new derived;

  (try_catch(
    bind(&derived::do_more_stuff,ll_dynamic_cast<derived&>(*_1)),
      catch_exception<std::bad_cast>(bind(&base::do_stuff,_1))))(p1);
  (try_catch(
    bind(&derived::do_more_stuff,
      ll_dynamic_cast<derived&>(*_1)),
        catch_exception<std::bad_cast>(
          bind(&base::do_stuff,_1))))(p2);
}
```

These expressions reveal that you wrap an expression in a call to `try_catch`. The general form of `try_catch` is

```
try_catch(expression,
  catch_exception<T1>(expression),
  catch_exception<T2>(expression,
  catch_all(expression))
```

In the example code, the expressions use `dynamic_casts` to `derived&`. The first cast fails because `p1` points to an instance of `base`; the second cast succeeds, because `p2` points to an instance of `derived`. Note the dereferencing of the placeholders (`*_1`). This is required because we are passing pointers as arguments to the expressions, but the `dynamic_casts` we're interested in expect objects or references. If you need the `try_catch` to handle several types of exceptions, be sure to put the most specialized types first, just as with regular exception handling code.[9]

---

9. Otherwise, a more general type will match an exception and not find the handler for the more specific type. Consult your favorite C++ book for more details on this.

If we want to access the actual exception that was caught, we can do so using a special placeholder, _e. Of course, one cannot do that in catch_all, just as there is no exception object in a catch (...). Continuing the preceding example, we can print the reason for the failed dynamic_cast like so:

```
try_catch(
  bind(&derived::do_more_stuff,ll_dynamic_cast<derived&>(*_1)),
  catch_exception<std::bad_cast>
    (std::cout << bind(&std::exception::what,_e))))(p1);
```

When dealing with an exception type derived from std::exception—a common case—you can bind to the virtual member function what, as shown here.

Sometimes, however, you don't want to catch an exception, but rather throw one. This is done via the function throw_exception. Because you need to create an exception object to throw, you'll typically use constructor to throw an exception from inside a lambda expression. The following example defines an exception class, some_exception, which inherits publicly from std::exception, and creates and throws one in a lambda expression if the argument to the expression is true.

```
#include <iostream>
#include <exception>
#include "boost/lambda/lambda.hpp"
#include "boost/lambda/exceptions.hpp"
#include "boost/lambda/if.hpp"
#include "boost/lambda/construct.hpp"
#include "boost/lambda/bind.hpp"

class some_exception : public std::exception {
  std::string what_;
public:
  some_exception(const char* what) : what_(what) {}

  virtual const char* what() const throw() {
    return what_.c_str();
  }
  virtual ~some_exception() throw() {}
};
```

```
int main() {
  using namespace boost::lambda;

  try {
    std::cout << "Throw an exception here.\n";

    (if_then(_1==true,throw_exception(
      bind(constructor<some_exception>(),
        constant("Somewhere, something went \
        terribly wrong."))))))(make_const(true));

    std::cout << "We'll never get here!\n";
  }
  catch(some_exception& e) {
    std::cout << "Caught exception, \"" << e.what() << "\"\n";
  }
}
```

Running this program yields the following output:

```
Throw an exception here.
Caught exception, "Somewhere, something went terribly wrong."
```

The most interesting part is where the exception is thrown.

```
throw_exception(
  bind(constructor<some_exception>(),
    constant("Somewhere, something went \
      terribly wrong.")))
```

The argument to `throw_exception` is a lambda expression. In this case, it is created by binding a call to the `some_exception` constructor, to which we pass the `what` argument, a string literal.

That's all there is to exception handling in Boost.Lambda. As always, remember to treat these tools with care and respect, as they can make life easier or harder depending on how well and judiciously you utilize them.[10] Throwing and handling exceptions should not be common in your lambda expressions, but it's necessary and reasonable from time to time.

---

10. Beware the tendency to fulfill the old adage, "When all you have is a hammer, everything looks like a nail."

Lambda Summary

Use Lambda when

- You would otherwise create a simple function object

- You need to tweak argument order or arity for function calls

- You want to create standard-conforming function objects on-the-fly

- You need flexible and readable predicates

The preceding reasons are just some of the cases where using this library makes perfect sense. Although the most common uses arise together with Standard Library algorithms, that's at least in part due to the fact that such designs still aren't very common in other libraries (the Boost libraries notwithstanding). Although the notion of algorithmic configuration through function objects needs no further proof of its usefulness, there is a long way to go before we reach conclusive insights into what domains clearly can benefit from such designs. Just by thinking about potential uses of this library is a sure way to improve your current designs.

Boost.Lambda is one of my favorite libraries, mainly because it offers so much accessible functionality that isn't otherwise provided by the language. As the STL made its way into the hearts of programmers all over the world, there was still something missing. To work efficiently with the algorithms, something more than function objects was required. Such was the impetus for Boost.Lambda, with its plethora of features that enable a truly concise programming style. There are many areas where lambda expressions are usable, but there is still much to be explored. This is to some degree functional programming in C++, which is a paradigm yet to be explored in full. This introduction to the Lambda library can empower you to continue that exploration. It's only fair to state that the syntax sometimes can be a bit clumsy compared to "real" functional programming languages, and that it does take some time for new users to get accustomed to it. But, likewise, it's fair to say that there is great value for any C++ programmer in this library! I hope it becomes one of your favorite libraries, too.

Many thanks to Jaakko Järvi and Gary Powell, the authors of this library and true pioneers of functional programming in C++!

Library 11
Function

How Does the Function Library Improve Your Programs?

- Stores function pointers and function objects for subsequent invocation

The need to store functions and function objects is common in designs with callbacks, and where functions or classes are configured with custom functionality through either function pointers or function objects. Traditionally, function pointers have been used to accommodate the need for both callbacks and delayed functions. However, using only function pointers is too limiting, and what would be better is a generalized mechanism that defines the signature of the function to be stored, and leaves it up to the caller to decide which type of function-like entity (function pointer or function object) should be provided. It would then be possible to use anything that *behaves* like a function—for example, the result of using Boost.Bind and Boost.Lambda. This, in turn, means that it is possible to add state to such stored functions (because function objects are classes). This generalization is what Boost.Function offers. The library is used to store, and subsequently invoke, functions or function objects.

How Does Function Fit with the Standard Library?

The library provides functionality that does not currently exist in the Standard Library. Generalized callbacks are a natural part of virtually all frameworks decoupling the presentation layer from the business logic, and the uses are plentiful. As there is no support in the C++ Standard Library for storing function pointers and function objects for later invocation, this is an important addition to the tools offered by the Standard Library. Also, the library is compatible with the binders from the Standard Library (`bind1st` and `bind2nd`), as well as other binder libraries that extend the aforementioned binders, such as Boost.Bind and Boost.Lambda.

Function

Header: `"boost/function.hpp"`

The header `"function.hpp"` includes prototypes for functions with 0 to 10 arguments. (This is implementation defined, but 10 is the default limit for the current implementation.[1]) It is also possible to include only the header that corresponds to the number of arguments you need to use—the files are named `"function/functionN.hpp"`, where N is in the range 0 to 10. There are two different interfaces for Boost.Function, one that is most appealing because it is syntactically close to a function declaration (and doesn't require the signature to include the number of arguments), and the other is appealing because it works with more compilers. Which to choose depends, at least in part, on the compiler that you are using. If you can, use what we refer to as the *preferred syntax*. Throughout this chapter, both forms will be used.

Declarations Using the Preferred Syntax

A declaration of a `function` includes the signature and return type of the function or function object that the `function` is to be compatible with. The type of the result and the arguments are all supplied as a single argument to the template. For example, the declaration of a `function` that returns `bool` and accepts an argument of type `int` looks like this:

```
boost::function<bool (int)> f;
```

---

1. Boost.Function can be configured to support up to 127 arguments.

The argument list is supplied inside the parentheses, separated by commas, just like a function declaration. Thus, declaring a function that returns nothing (`void`) and takes two arguments, of type `int` and `double`, looks like this:

```
boost::function<void (int,double)> f;
```

Declarations Using the Compatible Syntax

The second way of declaring `functions` is to supply separate template type arguments for the return type and the argument types for the function call. Also, there's a suffix for the name of the `function` class, which is an integer that corresponds to the number of arguments the `function` will accept. For example, the declaration of a function that returns `bool` and accepts an argument of type `int` looks like this:

```
boost::function1<bool,int> f;
```

The numbering is based on the number of arguments that the function accepts—in the preceding example, there is one argument (`int`) and therefore `function1` is needed. More arguments simply means supplying more template type parameters to the template and changing the numeric suffix. A `function` that returns `void` and accepts two arguments of type `int` and `double` looks like this:

```
boost::function2<void,int,double> f;
```

The library actually consists of a family of classes, each taking a different number of arguments. There is no need to take this into account when including the header `"function.hpp"`, but if including the numbered versions, you must include the correct numbered header.

The preferred syntax is easier to read and is analogous to declaring a function, so you should use it when you can. Unfortunately, although the preferred syntax is perfectly legal C++ and easier to read, not all compilers support it as yet. If your compiler is among those that cannot handle the preferred syntax, you need to use the alternative form. If you need to write your code with maximum portability, you might also choose to use the alternative form. Let's take a look at the most important parts of a `function`'s interface.

Members

```
function();
```

> The default constructor creates an empty function object. If an empty function is invoked, it throws an exception of type bad_function_call.

```
template <typename F> function(F g);
```

> This parameterized constructor accepts a compatible function object—that is, a function or a function object that has a signature with a return type that is the same as, or implicitly convertible to, that of the function being constructed, and arguments the same as, or implicitly convertible to, that of the function being constructed. Note that another instance of function can also be used for construction. If that is the case, and the function f is empty, the constructed function will also be empty. This also applies to null function pointers and null pointers to members—the resulting function is empty.

```
template <typename F> function(reference_wrapper<F> g);
```

> This constructor is similar to the previous version, but takes its function object wrapped in a reference_wrapper, which is used to avoid passing by value, and thus creating a copy of the function or function object. The requirements on the function objects are that they be compatible with the signature of the function.

```
function& operator=(const function& g);
```

> The copy assignment operator stores a copy of g's stored function or function object; if g is empty, the function being assigned to will also be empty.

```
template<typename F> function& operator=(F g);
```

> The parameterized assignment operator accepts a compatible function pointer or function object. Note that another instance of function (with a different but compatible signature) can also be used for assignment. This also means that the function can be empty after assignment, which is the case if g is another instance of function and is empty. Assigning a null function pointer or a null pointer to member effectively empties the function.

```
bool empty() const;
```

This member returns a Boolean value that tells whether the function contains a function/function object or if it's empty. It returns `false` if there is a targeted function or function object that can be invoked. Because a function can already be tested in a Boolean context, or compared to 0, this member function may be deprecated in future versions of this library, so you might want to avoid it.

```
void clear();
```

This member function clears the `function`, which means that it is no longer targeting a function or function object. If the function is already empty, the call has no effect. After the call, the function is always empty. The preferred way to make a function empty is to assign 0 to it; `clear` may be deprecated in a future release of this library.

```
operator safe_bool() const
```

This conversion function returns an unspecified type (represented by `safe_bool`) that can be used in Boolean contexts. If the `function` is empty, the returned value is `false`. If the function is storing a function pointer or function object, the returned value is `true`. Note that using a type that is different from `bool` enables this conversion operator to be completely safe and not interfere with overloading, while still providing the idiomatic use of testing an instance of `function` directly in a Boolean context. It is also equivalent to the expression `!!f`, where `f` is an instance of `function`.

```
result_type operator()(Arg1 a1, Arg2 a2, ..., ArgN aN) const;
```

The function call operator is how a `function` is invoked. You cannot invoke an empty `function` or it will throw a `bad_function_call` exception—that is, `!f.empty()`, if `(f)`, or if `(!!f)` yields `true`. The invocation results in calling the function or function object in the `function`, and returns its result.

Usage

To start using Boost.Function, include `"boost/function.hpp"`, or any of the numbered versions, ranging from `"boost/function/function0.hpp"` to `"boost/function/function10.hpp"`. If you know the arity of the functions you want to store in `functions`, it taxes the compiler less to include the exact headers that are needed. When including `"boost/function.hpp"`, the other headers are all included, too.

The best way to think of a stored function is a normal function object that is responsible for wrapping another function (or function object). It then makes perfect sense that this stored function can be invoked several times, and not necessarily at the time when the `function` is created. When declaring `functions`, the most important part of the declaration is the function signature. This is where you tell the `function` about the signature and return type of the functions and/or function objects it will store. As we've seen, there are two ways to perform such declarations. Here's a complete program that declares a `boost::function` that is capable of storing function-like entities that return `bool` (or a type that is implicitly convertible to `bool`) and accept two arguments, the first convertible to `int`, and the second convertible to `double`.

```
#include <iostream>
#include "boost/function.hpp"

bool some_func(int i,double d) {
   return i>d;
}

int main() {
   boost::function<bool (int,double)> f;
   f=&some_func;
   f(10,1.1);
}
```

When the `function` f is first created, it doesn't store any function. It is empty, which can be tested in a Boolean context or with 0. If you try to invoke a `function` that doesn't store a function or function object, it throws an exception of the type `bad_function_call`. To avoid that problem, we assign a pointer to `some_func` to f using normal assignment syntax. That causes f to store the pointer to `some_func`. Finally, we invoke f (using the function call operator) with the arguments 10 (an `int`) and 1.1 (a `double`). When invoking a `function`, one must supply exactly the number of arguments the stored function or function object expects.

The Basics of Callbacks

Let's look at how we would have implemented a simple callback before we knew about Boost.Function, and then convert the code to make use of function, and examine which advantages that brings forth. We will start with a class that supports a simple form of callback—it can report changes to a value by calling whoever is interested in the new value. The callback will be a traditional C-style callback—that is, a free function. This callback could be used, for example, for a GUI control that needs to inform observers that the user changed its value, without having any special knowledge about the clients listening for that information.

```cpp
#include <iostream>
#include <vector>
#include <algorithm>
#include "boost/function.hpp"

void print_new_value(int i) {
  std::cout <<
    "The value has been updated and is now " << i << '\n';
}

void interested_in_the_change(int i) {
  std::cout << "Ah, the value has changed.\n";
}

class notifier {
  typedef void (*function_type)(int);
  std::vector<function_type> vec_;
  int value_;
public:
  void add_observer(function_type t) {
    vec_.push_back(t);
  }

  void change_value(int i) {
    value_=i;
    for (std::size_t i=0;i<vec_.size();++i) {
      (*vec_[i])(value_);
    }
  }
};

int main() {
  notifier n;
```

```
  n.add_observer(&print_new_value);
  n.add_observer(&interested_in_the_change);

  n.change_value(42);
}
```

Two functions, `print_new_value` and `interested_in_the_change`, have a signature that is compatible with what the `notifier` class supports. The function pointers are stored in a `vector`, and then invoked in a loop whenever the value changes. One syntax for invoking the functions is

```
(*vec_[i])(value_);
```

The dereferenced function pointer (which is what is returned from `vec_[i]`) is passed the value (`value_`). It's also valid to write the code differently, like this:

```
vec_[i](value_);
```

This may seem a bit nicer to the eye, but more importantly, it also allows you to replace the function pointer with Boost.Function without syntactic changes for invocation. Now, this works fine, but alas, function objects don't work at all with this `notifier` class. Actually, nothing but function pointers work, which is a serious limitation. It would work, however, if we were using Boost.Function. Rewriting the `notifier` class is fairly straightforward.

```
class notifier {
  typedef boost::function<void(int)> function_type;
  std::vector<function_type> vec_;
  int value_;
public:
  template <typename T> void add_observer(T t) {
    vec_.push_back(function_type(t));
  }

  void change_value(int i) {
    value_=i;
    for (std::size_t i=0;i<vec_.size();++i) {
      vec_[i](value_);
    }
  }
};
```

The first thing to do is to change the `typedef` to refer to `boost::function` rather than a function pointer. Before, we defined a function pointer; now we are using the generalization, which will soon prove its usefulness. Next, we change the signature of the member function `add_observer` to be parameterized on the argument type. We could have changed it to accept `boost::function` instead, but that means that users of our class would need to understand how `function` works[2] too, rather than just knowing about the requirements for the observer type. It should be duly noted that this change of `add_observer` is not a result of switching to `function`; the code would continue to work anyway. We make the change for generality; now, both function pointers, function objects, and instances of `boost::function` can be passed to `add_observer`, without any changes to existing user code. The code for adding elements to the `vector` is slightly altered, and now creates instances of `boost::function<void(int)>`. Finally, we change the code that invokes the functions to the syntax that can be used for functions, function objects, and instances of `boost::function`.[3] This extended support for different types of function-like "things" can immediately be put to use with a stateful function object, which represents something that could not be easily done using functions.

```
class knows_the_previous_value {
  int last_value_;
public:
  void operator()(int i) {
    static bool first_time=true;
    if (first_time) {
      last_value_=i;
      std::cout <<
        "This is the first change of value, \
        so I don't know the previous one.\n";
      first_time=false;
      return;
    }
    std::cout << "Previous value was " << last_value_ << '\n';
    last_value_=i;
  }
};
```

2. They *should* know about Boost.Function, but what if they don't? Everything that we add to an interface will need to be explained to users at some point in time.

3. Now we know that we should actually have been invoking like this from the beginning.

This function object stores the previous value and prints it to `std::cout` whenever the value changes again. Note that the first time it is invoked, it doesn't know about the previous value. The function object detects this using a static `bool` variable in the function, which is initially set to `true`. Because static variables in functions are initialized when the function is first invoked, it is only set to `true` during the first invocation. Although static variables can be used like this to provide state for free functions too, we must understand that it does not scale well, and is hard to do safely in a multithreaded environment. So, function objects with state are always to be preferred over free functions with static variables. The `notifier` class doesn't mind this function object at all—it complies with the requirements and is therefore accepted. This updated sample program demonstrates how this works.

```
int main() {
  notifier n;
  n.add_observer(&print_new_value);
  n.add_observer(&interested_in_the_change);
  n.add_observer(knows_the_previous_value());

  n.change_value(42);
  std::cout << '\n';
  n.change_value(30);
}
```

The important line to examine is where we add an observer that isn't a function pointer, but an instance of the function object `knows_the_previous_value`. Running the program gives the following output:

```
The value has been updated and is now 42
Ah, the value has changed.
This is the first change of value,
so I don't know the previous one.
The value has been updated and is now 30
Ah, the value has changed.
Previous value was 42
```

The great advantage here, more than relaxing the requirements on the functions (or rather, the additional support for function objects), is that we can introduce objects with state, which is a very common need. The changes that we made to the `notifier` class were trivial, and user code wasn't affected at all. As shown here, introducing Boost.Function into an existing design is typically straightforward.

Functions That Are Class Members

Boost.Function does not support argument binding, which would be needed to make each invocation of a `function` invoke a member function on the same class instance. Fortunately, it is possible to directly call member functions if the class instance is passed to the `function`. The signature of the `function` needs to include the type of the class, as well as the signature of the member function. In other words, the class instance is passed explicitly as what would normally be the implicit first parameter, `this`. The result is a function object that invokes a member function on the supplied object. Consider the following class:

```
class some_class {
public:
  void do_stuff(int i) const {
    std::cout << "OK. Stuff is done. " << i << '\n';
  }
};
```

The member function `do_stuff` is to be called from within an instance of `boost::function`. To do this, we need the function to accept an instance of `some_class`, and have the rest of the signature be a `void` return and an `int` argument. We have three choices when it comes to deciding how the instance of `some_class` should be passed to the function: by value, by reference, or by address. To pass by value, here's how the code would look.[4]

```
boost::function<void(some_class,int)> f;
```

Note that the return type still comes first, followed by the class where the member function is a member, and finally the arguments to the member function. Think of it as passing `this` to the function, which is implicitly the case when calling non-static member functions on an instance of a class. To configure the function `f` with the member function `do_stuff`, and then invoke the function, we do this:

```
f=&some_class::do_stuff;
f(some_class(),2);
```

---

4. There are seldom good reasons for passing the object parameter by value.

When passing by reference, we change the signature of the function, and pass an instance of some_class.

```
boost::function<void(some_class&,int)> f;
f=&some_class::do_stuff;
some_class s;
f(s,1);
```

Finally, to pass a pointer[5] to some_class, this is how we'd write the code:

```
boost::function<void(some_class*,int)> f;
f=&some_class::do_stuff;
some_class s;
f(&s,3);
```

So, all the likely variants for passing instances of the "virtual this" are provided by the library. Of course, there is a limitation to this technique: You have to pass the class instance explicitly; and ideally, you'd want the instance to be bound in the function object instead. At first glance, that seems to be a disadvantage of Boost.Function, but there are other libraries that support binding arguments, such as Boost.Bind and Boost.Lambda. We will examine the added value that a collaboration with such libraries brings to Boost.Function later in this chapter.

Stateful Function Objects

We have already seen that it is possible to add state to callback functions, because of the support for function objects. Consider a class, keeping_state, which is a function object with state. Instances of keeping_state remember a total, which is increased each time the function call operator is invoked. Now, when using an instance of this class with two instances of boost::function, the results may be somewhat surprising.

```
#include <iostream>
#include "boost/function.hpp"

class keeping_state {
  int total_;
```

---

5. Both raw pointers and smart pointers will do.

```
public:
  keeping_state():total_(0) {}

  int operator()(int i) {
    total_+=i;
    return total_;
  }

  int total() const {
    return total_;
  }
};

int main() {
  keeping_state ks;
  boost::function<int(int)> f1;
  f1=ks;

  boost::function<int(int)> f2;
  f2=ks;

  std::cout << "The current total is " << f1(10) << '\n';
  std::cout << "The current total is " << f2(10) << '\n';
  std::cout << "After adding 10 two times, the total is "
    << ks.total() << '\n';
}
```

When writing, and subsequently running, this program, the programmer probably expects that the total stored in ks is 20, but it's not; in fact, it's 0. This is the
output when running the program.

```
The current total is 10
The current total is 10
After adding 10 two times, the total is 0
```

The reason is that each instance of function (f1 and f2) contains a copy of
ks, and each of those instances winds up with a total value of 10, but ks is
unchanged. This may or may not be what is intended, but it is important to
remember that the default behavior of boost::function is to copy the function
object that it is to invoke. If that produces incorrect semantics, or if the copying
of some function objects is too expensive, you must wrap the function objects in
boost::reference_wrapper so that boost::function's copy will be a copy
of a boost::reference_wrapper, which just holds a reference to the original

function object. You rarely use `boost::reference_wrapper` directly, but rather you use two helper functions, `ref` and `cref`. Those functions return a `reference_wrapper` that holds a reference or `const` reference to the parameterizing type. To get the semantics that we want in this case, using the same instance of `keeping_state`, we need to change the code, like this:

```
int main() {
  keeping_state ks;
  boost::function<int(int)> f1;
  f1=boost::ref(ks);

  boost::function<int(int)> f2;
  f2=boost::ref(ks);

  std::cout << "The current total is " << f1(10) << '\n';
  std::cout << "The current total is " << f2(10) << '\n';
  std::cout << "After adding 10 two times, the total is "
    << ks.total() << '\n';
}
```

This usage of `boost::ref` informs `boost::function` that we want to store a reference to the function object, not a copy. Running this program produces the following output:

```
The current total is 10
The current total is 20
After adding 10 two times, the total is 20
```

This is exactly the behavior that we needed in this case. The difference between using `boost::ref` and `boost::cref` is exactly the same as the difference between references and references to `const`—you can only call constant member functions for the latter. The following example uses a function object called `something_else`, which has a function call operator that is `const`.

```
class something_else {
public:
  void operator()() const {
    std::cout << "This works with boost::cref\n";
  }
};
```

With this function object, we could use either `boost::ref` or `boost::cref`.

```
something_else s;
boost::function0<void> f1;
f1=boost::ref(s);
f1();
boost::function0<void> f2;
f2=boost::cref(s);
f2();
```

If we change the implementation of `something_else` and make the function non-const, only `boost::ref` will work, whereas `boost::cref` would produce an error at compile time.

```
class something_else {
public:
  void operator()() {
    std::cout <<
      "This works only with boost::ref, or copies\n";
  }
};

something_else s;
boost::function0<void> f1;
f1=boost::ref(s); // This still works
f1();
boost::function0<void> f2;
f2=boost::cref(s); // This doesn't work;
                   // the function call operator is not const
f2();
```

When a `function` contains a function object wrapped by `boost::reference_wrapper`, copy construction and assignment replicates the reference—that is, the copy of the `function` references the original function object.

```
int main() {
  keeping_state ks;
  boost::function<int,int> f1;
  f1=boost::ref(ks);

  boost::function<int,int> f2(f1);
  boost::function<short,short> f3;
  f3=f1;
```

```
std::cout << "The current total is " << f1(10) << '\n';
std::cout << "The current total is " << f2(10) << '\n';
std::cout << "The current total is " << f3(10) << '\n';
std::cout << "After adding 10 three times, the total is "
          << ks.total() << '\n';
}
```

This is equivalent to using `boost::ref` and assigning the function object `ks` to each instance of function.

The power that is wielded with the addition of state to callbacks is tremendous, and is one of the great advantages to using Boost.Function rather than function pointers.

Using Boost.Bind with Boost.Function

Things become even more interesting when we combine Boost.Function with a library that supports argument binding. Boost.Bind provides argument binding for free functions, class member functions, and class variables. This is a perfect fit for Boost.Function, where we often need this type of binding because the classes that we are working with are not themselves function objects. So, we transform them into function objects using Boost.Bind, and then we can store them for later invocation with Boost.Function. When separating graphical user interfaces (GUIs) from details on how to handle actions (events) from the user, callbacks of some sort are almost always used. If this callback mechanism is based on function pointers, it is hard to avoid severe limitations of the types that can be used with the callback, which in turn increases the risk of adding coupling between the presentation and the business logic. We can avoid this altogether by using Boost.Function, and when combined with a library that supports argument binding, we can supply the context to invocations of functions with ease. This is one of the most common uses of this library—to separate knowledge of the business logic from the presentation layer.

This example includes a state-of-the-art tape recorder, which is defined thusly.

```
class tape_recorder {
public:
  void play() {
    std::cout << "Since my baby left me...\n";
  }
```

```
    void stop() {
        std::cout << "OK, taking a break\n";
    }

    void forward() {
        std::cout << "whizzz\n";
    }

    void rewind() {
        std::cout << "zzzihw\n";
    }

    void record(const std::string& sound) {
        std::cout << "Recorded: " << sound << '\n';
    }
};
```

This tape recorder could be controlled from a GUI, or perhaps from a scripting client, or from any other source, which means that we don't want to couple the invocation of the functions to their implementation. A common way to create that separation is through special objects that are only responsible for executing a command, allowing the client to remain ignorant of how the command is executed. This is known as the *Command* pattern, and is very useful in its own right. One of the problems with the typical implementation of this pattern is the need to create separate classes to execute each command. The following snippet demonstrates how this might look:

```
class command_base {
public:
    virtual bool enabled() const=0;
    virtual void execute()=0;

    virtual ~command_base() {}
};

class play_command : public command_base {
    tape_recorder* p_;
public:
    play_command(tape_recorder* p):p_(p) {}

    bool enabled() const {
        return true;
    }
```

```
  void execute() {
    p_->play();
  }
};

class stop_command : public command_base {
  tape_recorder* p_;
public:
  stop_command(tape_recorder* p):p_(p) {}

  bool enabled() const {
    return true;
  }

  void execute() {
    p_->stop();
  }
};
```

This is not a very attractive solution, because it leads to code bloat in the form of numerous simple command classes, all with the sole responsibility of invoking a single member function on an object. Sometimes, this can prove necessary, because the commands may need to implement business logic as well as execute a function, but it is often just a result of limitations in the tools that we are using. These command classes can be used like this:

```
int main() {
  tape_recorder tr;

  // Using the command pattern
  command_base* pPlay=new play_command(&tr);
  command_base* pStop=new stop_command(&tr);

    // Invoked when pressing a button
  pPlay->execute();
  pStop->execute();

  delete pPlay;
  delete pStop;
}
```

Now, rather than creating an additional number of concrete command classes, we could generalize a bit if we take advantage of the fact that the commands we are implementing are all calling a member function with a `void` return, taking no argument (ignoring for the moment the function record, which does take an argument). Rather than creating a family of concrete commands, we could store a pointer to the correct member function in the class. This is a huge step in the right direction,[6] and it works like this:

```cpp
class tape_recorder_command : public command_base {
  void (tape_recorder::*func_)();
  tape_recorder* p_;
public:

  tape_recorder_command(
    tape_recorder* p,
    void (tape_recorder::*func)()) : p_(p),func_(func) {}

  bool enabled() const {
    return true;
  }

  void execute() {
    (p_->*func_)();
  }
};
```

This implementation of the commands is much nicer, because it relieves us from having to create separate classes that do basically the same thing. The difference here is that we are storing a pointer to a `tape_recorder` member function in `func_`, which is provided in the constructor. The execution of the command is not something you should show all your friends, because the pointer-to-member operators do have a habit of confusing people. However, this can be considered a low-level implementation detail, so that's fine. With this class, we have performed a generalization that proves useful in that we don't have to implement separate command classes anymore.

```cpp
int main() {
  tape_recorder tr;

  // Using the improved command
  command_base* pPlay=
    new tape_recorder_command(&tr,&tape_recorder::play);
```

---

6. Albeit slightly less efficient.

```
command_base* pStop=
  new tape_recorder_command(&tr,&tape_recorder::stop);

// Invoked from a GUI, or a scripting client
pPlay->execute();
pStop->execute();

delete pPlay;
delete pStop;
}
```

You may not realize it, but we're actually starting to implement a simplified version of `boost::function`, which already does what we want. Rather than reinvent the wheel, let's focus on the task at hand: separating the invocation and the implementation. Here is a new implementation of the command class, which is a lot easier to write, maintain, and understand.

```
class command {
  boost::function<void()> f_;
public:
  command() {}
  command(boost::function<void()> f):f_(f) {}

  void execute() {
    if (f_) {
      f_();
    }
  }

  template <typename Func> void set_function(Func f) {
    f_=f;
  }

  bool enabled() const {
    return f_;
  }
};
```

By using Boost.Function in the implementation, we can immediately benefit from the flexibility of being compatible both with functions and function objects—including function objects produced by binders. The command class stores the function in a `boost::function` that returns void and doesn't take any arguments. To make the class more flexible, we provide a way to change the

function object at runtime, using a parameterized member function, set_
function.

```
template <typename Func> void set_function(Func f) {
  f_=f;
}
```

By using parameterization, any function, function object, or binder is compatible with our command class. We could also have opted to have a boost::
function as argument, and achieve the same effect using the converting constructor of function. This command class is very general, and we can use it with our tape_recorder class or just about anything else. An additional advantage over the previous approach when using a base class and concrete derived classes (which in turn makes us use pointers for polymorphic behavior) is that it becomes easier to manage lifetime issues—we don't have to delete the command objects anymore, as they can be passed and saved by value. We test whether the command is enabled or not by using the function f_ in a Boolean context. If the function doesn't contain a target, a function or function object, this yields false, which means that we cannot invoke it. This is tested in the implementation of execute. Here's a sample program that uses our new class:

```
int main() {
  tape_recorder tr;

  command play(boost::bind(&tape_recorder::play,&tr));
  command stop(boost::bind(&tape_recorder::stop,&tr));
  command forward(boost::bind(&tape_recorder::stop,&tr));
  command rewind(boost::bind(&tape_recorder::rewind,&tr));
  command record;

  // Invoked from some GUI control...
  if (play.enabled()) {
    play.execute();
  }

  // Invoked from some scripting client...
  stop.execute();

  // Some inspired songwriter has passed some lyrics
  std::string s="What a beautiful morning...";
  record.set_function(
```

```
  boost::bind(&tape_recorder::record,&tr,s));
record.execute();
```

```
}
```

To create the concrete commands, we use Boost.Bind to create function objects that, when invoked through the function call operator, calls the correct member function of `tape_recorder`. These function objects are self-contained; they are nullary function objects, meaning that they can be directly invoked without passing any arguments, which is what a `boost::function<void()>` expects. In other words, the following code snippet creates a function object that invokes the member function play on the instance of `tape_recorder` that it is configured with.

```
boost::bind(&tape_recorder::play,&tr)
```

Normally, we wouldn't be able to store the returned function object from the call to `bind`, but because Boost.Function is compatible with any function object, this is possible.

```
boost::function<void()> f(boost::bind(&tape_recorder::play,&tr));
```

Notice that the class also supports calling `record`, which takes an argument of type `const std::string&`, because of the member function `set_function`. Because the function object must be nullary, we need to bind the context so that `record` still gets its argument. That, of course, is a job for binders. Thus, before calling `record`, we create a function object that contains the string to be recorded.

```
std::string s="What a beautiful morning...";
record.set_function(
  boost::bind(&tape_recorder::record,&tr,s));
```

Executing the function object stored in `record` passes the string to `tape_recorder::record`, invoked on the `tape_recorder` instance `tr`. With Boost.Function and Boost.Bind, it is possible to achieve the decoupling that makes it possible for the invoking code to know nothing about the code being invoked. It's immensely useful to combine these two libraries in this way. Having shown you the `command` class, it's time for me to come clean. All you really need, because of the power of Boost.Function, is the following:

```
typedef boost::function<void()> command;
```

Using Boost.Lambda with Boost.Function

Just as Boost.Function is compatible with the function objects that are created by Boost.Bind, it also supports Boost.Lambda, which also creates function objects. Any function object that you create with the Lambda library is compatible with the corresponding `boost::function`. We have covered some ground on binding in the previous section, and the main difference is that it is possible to do even more with Boost.Lambda. We can create these small, unnamed functions at ease, and store them in instances of `boost::function` for subsequent invocation. We have covered lambda expressions in the previous chapter—any of the examples that were provided there produced function objects that could be stored in an instance of `function`. The combination of `function` and libraries that create function objects is extremely powerful.

Thinking About the Cost

There's no such thing as a free lunch, as the saying goes, and this certainly applies to Boost.Function, too. There are some disadvantages of using Boost.Function compared to using function pointers, most notably the increase in size. A function pointer obviously occupies the space of one function pointer (duh!), whereas an instance of `boost::function` is three times as large. This can be an issue when there is a very large number of callbacks. Function pointers are also slightly more efficient when invoked, because where a function pointer is invoked directly, Boost.Function may require two calls through function pointers. Finally, there may be cases where the backward compatibility with C libraries makes function pointers the only choice.

Although these are potential disadvantages of Boost.Function, it is not very often that these are real-world issues. The extra size is still very small, and the overheard of the (potential) extra call through a function pointer usually comes at a very small cost indeed compared to the time it takes to actually perform the computations of the target function. It should be the rare situation that mandates using function instead of Boost.Function. The great advantages and the flexibility that is gained through using the library easily outweigh these costs.

Under the Hood

As always, it is valuable to understand at least the basics of how a library works. We shall consider the three cases of storing and invoking a function pointer, a pointer to member function, and a function object. These three are all different. To see exactly how Boost.Function works, just look at the source code—we are going to do things a bit differently, in an attempt to clearly show how different versions of such beasts demand slightly different approaches. We will also have a class with different requirements, namely that when calling a member function, a pointer to an instance of the class must be passed to the constructor of function1 (which is the name of our class). function1 supports functions taking exactly one argument. A relaxation of the requirements compared to Boost.Function is that even for member functions, only the type of the result and the argument need to be supplied. This is a direct consequence of the requirement that the constructor must be passed a pointer to an instance of the class for which the member is to be called (the type is automatically deduced).

The approach we shall take is to create a parameterized base class that declares a virtual function for the function call operator; then, three classes are derived from this base class for the different forms of function invocations that we are to support. These classes take care of all the work, while another, function1, decides which of these concrete classes to instantiate depending on the arguments to the constructor. Here is the base class for the invokers, invoker_base.

```
template <typename R, typename Arg> class invoker_base {
public:
  virtual R operator()(Arg arg)=0;
};
```

Next, we begin with the definition of function_ptr_invoker, which is a concrete invoker that derives publicly from invoker_base. Its purpose is to invoke free functions. The class also accepts two types, the return type and the argument type, and these are used for the constructor, which takes a function pointer as argument.

```
template <typename R, typename Arg> class function_ptr_invoker
  : public invoker_base<R,Arg> {
  R (*func_)(Arg);
public:
  function_ptr_invoker(R (*func)(Arg)):func_(func) {}

  R operator()(Arg arg) {
    return (func_)(arg);
  }
};
```

This class template can be used to call any free function that accepts one argument. The function call operator simply invokes the function stored in `func_` with the parameter it is given. Note the (admittedly strange) line that declares a variable to store the function pointer.

```
R (*func_) (Arg);
```

You can make that a little plainer using a `typedef`.

```
typedef R (*FunctionT) (Arg);
FunctionT func_;
```

Next, we need a class template that can handle member function calls. Remember that it should also require a pointer to an instance of the class type when constructed, which is different from the way that Boost.Function works. It does save us some typing, because the compiler, not the programmer, deduces the type of the class.

```
template <typename R, typename Arg, typename T>
  class member_ptr_invoker :
    public invoker_base<R,Arg> {
  R (T::*func_) (Arg);
  T* t_;
public:
  member_ptr_invoker(R (T::*func) (Arg),T* t)
    :func_(func),t_(t) {}

  R operator() (Arg arg) {
    return (t_->*func_) (arg);
  }
};
```

This class template is very similar to the version for free function pointers. It differs from the previous one in that the constructor stores a member function pointer and a pointer to an object and the function call operator invokes the member function (`func_`) on that object (`t_`).

Finally, we need a version that is compatible with function objects. This is actually the easiest implementation of all, at least when defining it our way. By using a single template parameter, we just state that the type T must indeed be a function object, because we intend to invoke it as such. Enough said.

```
template <typename R, typename Arg, typename T>
  class function_object_invoker :
    public invoker_base<R,Arg> {
  T t_;
public:
  function_object_invoker(T t):t_(t) {}

  R operator()(Arg arg) {
    return t_(arg);
  }
};
```

Now that we have these building blocks in place, all that remains is to put the pieces together in our version of boost::function, the function1 class. We want a way to detect which kind of invoker to instantiate. We can then save it in a pointer to invoker_base. The trick here is to provide constructors that are capable of detecting which type of invoker is correct for the supplied arguments. It's just overloading, with a little twist involving parameterizing two of the constructors.

```
template <typename R, typename Arg> class function1 {
  invoker_base<R,Arg>* invoker_;
public:
  function1(R (*func)(Arg)) :
    invoker_(new function_ptr_invoker<R,Arg>(func)) {}

  template <typename T> function1(R (T::*func)(Arg),T* p) :
    invoker_(new member_ptr_invoker<R,Arg,T>(func,p)) {}

  template <typename T> function1(T t) :
    invoker_(new function_object_invoker<R,Arg,T>(t)) {}

  R operator()(Arg arg) {
    return (*invoker_)(arg);
  }

  ~function1() {
    delete invoker_;
  }
};
```

As you can see, the hard part here is to correctly define the deduction system that is needed in order to support function pointers, class member functions, and function objects. This is true regardless of the actual design that is used to implement a library with this kind of functionality. To conclude, here is some sample code that we can use to test the solution.

```cpp
bool some_function(const std::string& s) {
  std::cout << s << " This is really neat\n";
  return true;
}

class some_class {
public:
  bool some_function(const std::string& s) {
    std::cout << s << " This is also quite nice\n";
    return true;
  }
};

class some_function_object {
public:
  bool operator()(const std::string& s) {
    std::cout << s <<
      " This should work, too, in a flexible solution\n";
    return true;
  }
};
```

All of these are acceptable for our function1 class:

```cpp
int main() {
  function1<bool,const std::string&> f1(&some_function);
  f1(std::string("Hello"));

  some_class s;
  function1<bool,const std::string&>
    f2(&some_class::some_function,&s);

  f2(std::string("Hello"));

  function1<bool,const std::string&>
    f3(boost::bind(&some_class::some_function,&s,_1));

  f3(std::string("Hello"));

  some_function_object fso;
  function1<bool,const std::string&>
    f4(fso);
  f4(std::string("Hello"));
}
```

It also works with function objects returned from binder libraries, such as Boost.Bind and Boost.Lambda. Our class is a lot more simplistic than the ones found in Boost.Function, but it should be sufficiently detailed to see the problems and the solutions involved when creating and using such a library. To know a little something about how a library is implemented is helpful for using it as effectively as possible.

Function Summary

Use Function when

- You need to store a callback function, or function object

- You want to decouple function calls from the implementation, for example between the GUI and the implementation

- You want to store function objects created by binder libraries to be invoked at a later time, or multiple times

Boost.Function is an important addition to the offerings from the Standard Library. The well-known technique of using function pointers as a callback mechanism is extended to include anything that behaves like a function, including function objects created by binder libraries. Through the use of Boost.Function, it is easy to add state to the callbacks, and to adapt existing classes and member functions to be used as callback functions.

There are several advantages to using Boost.Function rather than function pointers: relaxed requirements on the signature through compatible function objects rather than exact signatures; the possibility to use binders, such as Boost.Bind and Boost.Lambda; the ability to test whether functions are empty—that is, that there is no target—before attempting to invoke them; and the notion of stateful objects rather than just stateless functions. Each of these advantages favor using Boost.Function over the C-style callbacks that have been prevalent in solving this type of problem. Only when the small additional cost of using Boost.Function compared to function pointers is prohibitive should the function pointer technique be considered.

Boost.Function was created by Douglas Gregor. It is a library with many powerful features, and is expertly designed and implemented to provide exceptional user value.

Library 12
Signals

How Does the Signals Library Improve Your Programs?

- Flexible multicast callbacks for functions and function objects

- A robust mechanism for triggering and handling events

- Compatibility with function object factories, such as Boost.Bind and Boost.Lambda

The Boost.Signals library reifies signals and slots, where a signal is something that can be "emitted," and slots are connections that receive such signals. This is a well-known design pattern that goes under a few different names—*Observer*, *signals/slots*, *publisher/subscriber*, *events* (and event targets)—but these names all refer to the same thing, which is a one-to-many relation between some source of information and instances that are interested in knowing when that information changes. There are many cases where this design pattern is used; one of the most obvious is in GUI code, where certain actions (for example, the user clicks a button) are loosely connected to some kind of action (the button changes its appearance, and some business logic is performed). There are many more cases where signals and slots are useful to decouple the trigger of an action (signal) from the code that handles it (one or more slots). This can be used to dynamically alter the behavior of the handling code, to allow multiple handlers of the same signal, or to reduce type dependencies through an abstract connection between types via signals and slots. With Boost.Signals, it is possible to create signals that accept slots with any given function signature—that is, slots that accept arguments of arbitrary types. This approach makes the library very flexible; it accommodates the signaling needs of virtually any domain. By decoupling the source of the signal and the handlers thereof, systems become more robust in terms of both physical and logical dependencies. It's possible to let the signaling types be totally ignorant of the slot types, and vice versa. This is imperative to achieve a higher level of reusability, and it can help break cyclic dependencies. So, a signals and slots library isn't only about object-oriented callbacks, it's also about the robustness of the whole system to which it is applied.

How Does Signals Fit with the Standard Library?

There is nothing in the C++ Standard Library that addresses callbacks, yet there is an obvious need for such facilities. Boost.Signals is designed in the same spirit as the Standard Library, and it is a great addition to the Standard Library toolbox.

Signals

Header: `"boost/signals.hpp"`

This includes all of the library through a single header.

`"boost/signals/signal.hpp"`

contains the definition of `signals`.

`"boost/signals/slot.hpp"`

contains the definition of the `slot` class.

`"boost/signals/connection.hpp"`

contains definitions of the classes `connection` and `scoped_connection`.

To use this library, either include the header `"boost/signals.hpp"`, which ensures that the entire library is available, or include the separate headers containing the functionality that you need. The core of the Boost.Signals library exists in namespace `boost`, and advanced features reside in `boost::signals`.

The following is a partial synopsis for `signal`, followed by a brief discussion of the most important members. For a full reference, see the online documentation for Signals.

```
namespace boost {

  template<typename Signature,
  // Function type R(T1, T2, ..., TN)
    typename Combiner = last_value<R>,
    typename Group = int,
    typename GroupCompare = std::less<Group>,
    typename SlotFunction = function<Signature> >
  class signal : public signals::trackable,
                 private noncopyable {
  public:
    signal(const Combiner&=Combiner(),
           const GroupCompare&=GroupCompare());

    ~signal();

    signals::connection connect(const slot_type&);
    signals::connection connect(
      const Group&,
      const slot_type&);

    void disconnect(const Group&);

    std::size_t num_slots() const;

    result_type operator()
      (T1, T2, ..., TN);
  };
}
```

Types

Let's have a look first at the template parameters for `signal`. There are reasonable defaults for all but the first argument, but it helps to understand the basic meaning of these parameters. The first template parameter is the actual signature of the function to be invoked. In the case of `signals`, the `signal` itself is the entity to be invoked. When declaring this signature, use the same syntax as for ordinary function signatures.[1] For example, the signature for a function returning `double` and accepting one argument of type `int` looks like this:

```
signal<double(int)>
```

---

1. The alert reader might notice that this is how `boost::function` works, too.

The `Combiner` parameter denotes a function object responsible for iterating through and calling all of the connected slots for the `signal`. It also determines how to combine the results of invoking the handlers. The default type, `last_value`, simply returns the result of invoking the last slot.

The `Groups` parameter is the type to be used for grouping the slots that are connected to the `signal`. By connecting to different slot groups, it's possible to predict the order of slot invocation, and to disconnect groups of slots simultaneously.

The `GroupCompare` parameter decides how the `Groups` are ordered, and the default is `std::less<Group>`, which is almost always correct. If a custom type is used for `Groups`, some other ordering sometimes makes sense.

Finally, the `SlotFunction` parameter denotes the type of the slot functions, and the default is a `boost::function`. I am not familiar with any scenarios where changing this default would be wise. This template parameter is used to define the slot type, available through the public `typedef slot<SlotFunction> slot_type`.

Members

```
signal(const Combiner&=Combiner(),
   const GroupCompare&=GroupCompare());
```

When constructing a `signal`, it's possible to pass a `Combiner`, which is an object responsible for invoking the slots and handling the logic for the values returned when signaling to the slots.

```
~signal();
```

The destructor disconnects all of the slots that are connected at the time of destruction.

```
signals::connection connect(const slot_type& s);
```

The `connect` function connects the slot `s` to the `signal`. A function pointer, function object, a `bind` expression, or a lambda expression can be used as slots. `connect` returns a `signals::connection`, which is a handle to the created connection. Using that handle, the slot can be disconnected from the `signal`, or you can test whether the slot is still connected.

```
signals::connection connect(const Group& g, const slot_type& s);
```

This overloaded version of `connect` works like the previous one, and in addition, it connects the slot `s` to the group `g`. Connecting a slot to a group means that when a `signal` is signaling, slots that belong to groups that precede other groups are called before those (as described by the ordering for the groups, the `GroupCompare` parameter to the `signal` template), and all slots that belong to a group are called before those that aren't (it's possible to have only some of the slots in groups).

```
void disconnect(const Group& g);
```

Disconnects all of the connected slots that belong to the group `g`.

```
std::size_t num_slots() const;
```

Returns the number of slots that are currently connected to the `signal`. It is preferred to call the function `empty` rather than test the return value from `num_slots` against 0, because `empty` can be more efficient.

```
result_type operator()(T1, T2, ..., TN);
```

`signals` are invoked using the function call operator. When signaling, the appropriate arguments must be passed to the function call operator, as described by the signature of the `signal` (the first template parameter when declaring the `signal` type). The types of arguments must be implicitly convertible to the types required by the signal for the invocation to succeed.

There are other types available in Boost.Signals, but rather than distract you with a synopsis and discussion of each here, we'll discuss them in detail throughout the rest of this chapter. We will also discuss useful `typedefs` in the `signal` class.

Usage

When faced with needing more than one piece of code in a program to handle a given event, typical solutions involve callbacks through function pointers, or directly coded dependencies between the subsystem that fires the event and the subsystems that need to handle it. Circular dependencies are a common result of such designs. Using Boost.Signals, you gain flexibility and decoupling. To start using the library, include the header `"boost/signals.hpp"`.[2]

The following example demonstrates the basic properties of `signals` and slots, including how to connect them and how to emit the `signal`. Note that a *slot* is something that you provide, either a function or a function object that is compatible with the function signature of the `signal`. In the following code, we create both a free function, `my_first_slot`, and a function object, `my_second_slot`; both are then connected to the `signal` that we create.

```cpp
#include <iostream>
#include "boost/signals.hpp"

void my_first_slot() {
  std::cout << "void my_first_slot()\n";
}

class my_second_slot {
public:
  void operator()() const {
    std::cout <<
      "void my_second_slot::operator()() const\n";
  }
};

int main() {
  boost::signal<void ()> sig;

  sig.connect(&my_first_slot);
  sig.connect(my_second_slot());

  std::cout << "Emitting a signal...\n";
  sig();
}
```

We start by declaring a `signal`, which expects slots that return `void` and take no arguments. We then connect two compatible slot types to that `signal`. For one, we call `connect` with the address of the free function, `my_first_slot`. For the other, we default-construct an instance of the function object

2. The Boost.Signals library and the Boost.Regex library are the only libraries covered in this book that actually require compiling and linking for use. The process is simple, and it's described in great detail in the online documentation, so I won't cover it here.

my_second_slot and pass it to connect. These connections mean that when we emit a signal (by invoking sig), the two slots will be called immediately.

```
sig();
```

When running the program, the output will look something like this:

```
Emitting a signal...
void my_first_slot()
void my_second_slot::operator()() const
```

However, the order of the last two lines is unspecified because slots belonging to the same group are invoked in an unspecified order. There is no way of telling which of our slots will be called first. Whenever the calling order of slots matters, you must put them into groups.

Grouping Slots

It is sometimes important to know that some slots are called before others, such as when the slots have side effects that other slots might depend upon. *Groups* is the name of the concept that supports such requirements. It is a signal template argument named Group that is, by default, int. The ordering of *Groups* is std::less<Group>, which translates to operator< for int. In other words, a slot belonging to *group 0* is called before a slot in *group 1*, and so on. Note, however, that slots in the same group are called in an unspecified order. The only way to exactly control the order by which all slots are called is to put every slot into its own group.

A slot is assigned to a group by passing a Group to signal::connect. The group to which a connected slot belongs cannot be changed; to change the group for a slot, it must be disconnected and then reconnected to the signal in the new group.

As an example, consider two slots taking one argument of type int&; the first doubles the argument, and the second increases the current value by 3. Let's say that the correct semantics are that the value first be doubled, and then increased by 3. Without a specified order, we have no way of ensuring these semantics. Here's an approach that works on some systems, some of the time (typically when the moon is full and it's Monday or Wednesday).

```
#include <iostream>
#include "boost/signals.hpp"

class double_slot {
  public:
  void operator()(int& i) const {
    i*=2;
  }
};

class plus_slot {
public:
  void operator()(int& i) const {
    i+=3;
  }
};

int main() {
  boost::signal<void (int&)> sig;
  sig.connect(double_slot());
  sig.connect(plus_slot());

  int result=12;
  sig(result);
  std::cout << "The result is: " << result << '\n';
}
```

When running this program, it might produce this output:

```
The result is: 30
```

Or, it might produce this:

```
The result is: 27
```

There's simply no way of guaranteeing the correct behavior without using groups. We need to ensure that double_slot is always called before plus_slot. That requires that we specify that double_slot belongs to a group that is ordered before plus_slot's group, like so:

```
sig.connect(0,double_slot());
sig.connect(1,plus_slot());
```

This ensures that we'll get what we want (in this case, 27). Again, note that for slots belonging to the same group, the order with which they are called is unspecified. As soon as a specific ordering of slot invocation is required, make sure to express that using different groups.

Note that the type of Groups is a template parameter to the class signal, which makes it possible to use, for example, std::string as the type.

```cpp
#include <iostream>
#include <string>
#include "boost/signals.hpp"

class some_slot {
  std::string s_;
public:
  some_slot(const std::string& s) : s_(s) {}
  void operator()() const {
    std::cout << s_ << '\n';
  }
};

int main() {
  boost::signal<void (),
    boost::last_value<void>,std::string> sig;

  some_slot s1("I must be called first, you see!");
  some_slot s2("I don't care when you call me, not at all. \
    It'll be after those belonging to groups, anyway.");
  some_slot s3("I'd like to be called second, please.");

  sig.connect(s2);
  sig.connect("Last group",s3);
  sig.connect("First group",s1);

  sig();
}
```

First we define a slot type that prints a std::string to std::cout when it is invoked. Then, we get to the declaration of the signal. Because the Groups parameter comes after the Combiner type, we must specify that also (we'll just declare the default). We then set the Groups type to std::string.

```cpp
boost::signal<void (),boost::last_value<void>,std::string> sig;
```

We accept the defaults for the rest of the template parameters. When connecting the slots `s1`, `s2`, and `s3`, the groups that we create are lexicographically ordered (because that's what `std::less<std::string>` does), so `"First group"` precedes `"Last group"`. Note that because these string literals are implicitly convertible to `std::string`, we are allowed to pass them directly to the `connect` function of `signal`. Running the program tells us that we got it right.

```
I must be called first, you see!
I'd like to be called second, please.
I don't care when you call me, not at all.
It'll be after those belonging to groups, anyway.
```

We could have opted for another ordering when declaring the `signal` type—for example, using `std::greater`.

```
boost::signal<void (),boost::last_value<void>,
   std::string,std::greater<std::string> > sig;
```

Had we used that in the example, the output would be

```
I'd like to be called second, please.
I must be called first, you see!
I don't care when you call me.
```

Of course, for this example, `std::greater` produces an ordering that leads to the wrong output, but that's another story. Groups are useful, even indispensable, but it's not always trivial to assign the correct group values, because connecting slots isn't necessarily performed from the same location in the code. It can thus be a problem to know which value should be used for a particular slot. Sometimes, this problem can be solved with discipline—that is, commenting the code and making sure that everyone reads the comments—but this only works when there aren't many places in the code where the values are assigned and when there are no lazy programmers. In other words, this approach doesn't work. Instead, you need a central source of group values that can be generated based upon some supplied value that is unique to each slot or, if the dependent slots know about each other, the slots could provide their own group value.

Now that you know how to deal with issues of slot call ordering, let's take a look at different signatures for your `signals`. You often need to pass additional information along about important events in your systems.

Signals with Arguments

Often, there is additional data to be passed to a signal. For example, consider a temperature guard that reports drastic changes in the temperature. Just knowing that the guard detected a problem can be insufficient; a slot may need to know the current temperature. Although both the guard (the signal) and the slot could access the temperature from a common sensor, it may be simplest to have the guard pass the current temperature to the slot when invoking it. As another example, consider when slots are connected to several signals: The slots will most likely need to know which signal invoked it. There are myriad use cases that require passing some information from signal to slot. The arguments that slots expect are part of a signal's declaration. The first argument to the signal class template is the signature for invoking the signal, and this signature is also used for the connected slots when the signal calls them. If we want the argument to be modifiable, we make sure that it is passed by non-const reference or pass a pointer, else we can pass it by value or reference to const. Note that besides the obvious difference that the original argument is either modifiable or not, this also has implications for the types of acceptable arguments to the signal itself and to the slot types—when the signal expects an argument by value or as reference to const, types that are implicitly convertible to the argument's type can be used to emit a signal. Likewise for slots—if the slot accepts its arguments by value or reference to const, this means that implicit conversion to that type from the actual argument type of the signal is allowed. We'll see more of this soon, as we consider how to properly pass arguments when signaling.

Consider an automatic parking lot guard, which receives notifications as soon as a car enters or leaves the parking lot. It needs to know something unique about the car—for example, the car's registration number, so it can track the coming and going of each. (That would also permit the system to know just how ridiculous a sum to charge the owner according to the elapsed time.) The guard should also have a signal of its own, to be able to trigger an alarm when someone is trying to cheat. There needs to be a few security guards to listen to that signal, which we'll model using a class called security_guard. Finally, let's also add a gate class, which contains a signal that is signaled whenever a car enters or leaves the parking lot. (The parking_lot_guard will definitely be interested in knowing about this.) Let's look first at the declaration for the parking_lot_guard.

```
class parking_lot_guard {
  typedef
    boost::signal<void (const std::string&)> alarm_type;
  typedef alarm_type::slot_type slot_type;

  boost::shared_ptr<alarm_type> alarm_;

  typedef std::vector<std::string> cars;
  typedef cars::iterator iterator;

  boost::shared_ptr<cars> cars_;
public:

  parking_lot_guard();
  boost::signals::connection
    connect_to_alarm(const slot_type& a);
  void operator()(bool is_entering,const std::string& car_id);

private:
  void enter(const std::string& car_id);
  void leave(const std::string& car_id);
};
```

There are three especially important parts to look at closely here; first of these is the alarm, which is a `boost::signal` that returns `void` and takes a `std::string` (which will be the identifier of the car). The declaration of such a `signal` is worth looking at again.

```
boost::signal<void (const std::string&)>
```

It's just like a function declaration, only without a function name. When in doubt, try to remember that there's really nothing more to it than that! It is possible to connect to this `signal` from outside using the member function `connect_to_alarm`. (We'll address how and why we would want to sound this alarm when implementing this class.) The next thing to note is that both the alarm and the container of car identifiers (a `std::vector` containing `std::strings`) are stored in `boost::shared_ptrs`. The reason for this is that although we only intend to declare one instance of `parking_lot_guard`, there are going to be multiple copies of it; because this guard class will also be connected to other `signals` later on, which will create copies (Boost.Signals copies the slots, which is required for managing lifetime correctly); but we still want all of the data to be available, so we share it. We could have avoided copying altogether—for example, by using pointers or externalizing the slot behavior from this class—but doing it this way nicely illuminates a trap that's easy to fall into. Finally, note that we have declared a function call operator, and the reason for this is that we are going to connect the `parking_lot_guard` to a `signal` in the `gate` class (that we have yet to declare).

Let's turn our attention to the `security_guard` class.

```cpp
class security_guard {
  std::string name_;
public:
  security_guard (const char* name);

  void do_whatever_it_takes_to_stop_that_car() const;
  void nah_dont_bother() const;

  void operator()(const std::string& car_id) const;
};
```

The `security_guards` don't really do much. The class has a function call operator, which is used as a slot for alarms from the `parking_lot_guard`, and just two other functions: One is for trying to stop cars for which the alarm goes off, and the other is used to do nothing. This brings us to the `gate` class, which detects when cars arrive at the parking lot, and when they leave it.

```cpp
class gate {
  typedef
    boost::signal<void (bool,const std::string&)> signal_type;
  typedef signal_type::slot_type slot_type;

  signal_type enter_or_leave_;
public:
  boost::signals::connection
    connect_to_gate(const slot_type& s);
  void enter(const std::string& car_id);
  void leave(const std::string& car_id);
};
```

You'll note that the `gate` class contains a `signal` that is to be emitted when a car either enters or leaves the parking lot. There is a public member function (`connect_to_gate`) for connecting to this `signal`, and two more functions (`enter` and `leave`) that are to be called as cars come and go.

Now that we know the players, it's time to take a stab at implementing them. Let's start with the gate class.

```cpp
class gate {
  typedef
    boost::signal<void (bool,const std::string&)> signal_type;
  typedef signal_type::slot_type slot_type;

  signal_type enter_or_leave_;
public:
  boost::signals::connection
    connect_to_gate(const slot_type& s) {
    return enter_or_leave_.connect(s);
  }

  void enter(const std::string& car_id) {
    enter_or_leave_(true,car_id);
  }

  void leave(const std::string& car_id) {
    enter_or_leave_(false,car_id);
  }
};
```

The implementation is trivial. Most of the work is forwarded to other objects. The function connect_to_gate simply forwards a call to connect for the signal enter_or_leave_. The function enter signals the signal, passing true (this means that the car is entering) and the identifier of the car. leave does the same thing, but passes false, indicating that the car is leaving. A simple class for a simple chore. The security_guard class isn't much more complicated.

```cpp
class security_guard {
  std::string name_;
public:
  security_guard (const char* name) : name_(name) {}

  void do_whatever_it_takes_to_stop_that_car() const {
    std::cout <<
      "Stop in the name of...eh..." << name_ << '\n';
  }

  void nah_dont_bother() const {
    std::cout << name_ <<
      " says: Man, that coffee tastes f i n e fine!\n";
```

```
      }

    void operator()(const std::string& car_id) const {
      if (car_id.size() && car_id[0]=='N')
        do_whatever_it_takes_to_stop_that_car();
      else
        nah_dont_bother();
    }
};
```

security_guards know their names, and they can decide whether to do something when the alarm goes off (if the car_id starts with the letter *N*, they spring into action). The function call operator is the slot function that is called—security_guard objects are function objects, and adhere to the requirements for parking_lot_guard's alarm_type signal. Things get a little more complicated with parking_lot_guard, but not too much.

```
class parking_lot_guard {
  typedef
    boost::signal<void (const std::string&)> alarm_type;
  typedef alarm_type::slot_type slot_type;

  boost::shared_ptr<alarm_type> alarm_;

  typedef std::vector<std::string> cars;
  typedef cars::iterator iterator;

  boost::shared_ptr<cars> cars_;
public:

  parking_lot_guard()
    : alarm_(new alarm_type), cars_(new cars) {}

  boost::signals::connection
    connect_to_alarm(const slot_type& a) {
    return alarm_->connect(a);
  }

  void operator()
    (bool is_entering,const std::string& car_id) {
    if (is_entering)
      enter(car_id);
    else
      leave(car_id);
  }
```

```
private:
  void enter(const std::string& car_id) {
    std::cout <<
      "parking_lot_guard::enter(" << car_id << ")\n";

    // If the car already exists here, sound the alarm
    if (std::binary_search(cars_->begin(),cars_->end(),car_id))
      (*alarm_)(car_id);
    else // Insert the car_id
      cars_->insert(
        std::lower_bound(
          cars_->begin(),
          cars_->end(),car_id),car_id);
  }

  void leave(const std::string& car_id) {
    std::cout <<
      "parking_lot_guard::leave(" << car_id << ")\n";

    // If there are no registered cars,
    // or if the car isn't registered, sound the alarm
    std::pair<iterator,iterator> p=
      std::equal_range(cars_->begin(),cars_->end(),car_id);
    if (p.first==cars_->end() || *(p.first)!=car_id)
      (*alarm_)(car_id);
    else
      cars_->erase(p.first);
  }
};
```

That's it! (Of course, as we haven't connected any slots to any `signals` yet, there's a bit more to do. Still, these classes are remarkably simple for what they're about to do.) To make the `shared_ptrs` for the alarm and the car identifiers behave correctly, we implement the default constructor, where the `signal` and the `vector` are properly allocated. The implicitly created copy constructor, the destructor, and the assignment operator will all do the right thing (thanks to these fine smart pointers). The function `connect_to_alarm` forwards to call to the contained `signal`'s `connect`. The function call operator tests the Boolean argument to see whether the car is entering or leaving, and makes a call to the corresponding function `enter/leave`. In the function `enter`, the first thing that's done is to search through the `vector` for the identifier of the car. Finding it would mean that something has gone wrong; perhaps someone has stolen a license plate. The search is performed using the algorithm `binary_search`,[3] which expects a sorted sequence (we make sure that it always is sorted). If we do find the identifier, we immediately sound the alarm, which involves invoking the `signal`.

```
(*alarm_) (car_id) ;
```

We need to dereference `alarm_` first, because `alarm_` is a `boost::shared_ptr`, and when invoking it, we pass to it the argument that is the car identifier. If we don't find the identifier, all is well, and we insert the car identifier into `cars_` at the correct place. Remember that we need the sequence to be sorted at all times, and the best way to ensure that is by inserting elements in a location such that the ordering isn't compromised. Using the algorithm `lower_bound` gives us this location in the sequence (this algorithm also expects a sorted sequence). Last but not least is the function `leave`, which is called when cars are leaving through the gates of our parking lot. `leave` starts with making sure that the car has been registered in our container for car identifiers. This is done using a call to the algorithm `equal_range`, which returns a pair of iterators that denote the range where an element could be inserted without violating the ordering. This means that we must dereference the returned iterator and make sure that its value is equal to the one we're looking for. If we didn't find it, we trigger the alarm again, and if we did find it, we simply remove it from the `vector`. You'll note that we didn't call any code for charging the people who park here; such evil logic is well beyond the scope of this book.

With all of the participants in our parking lot defined, we must connect the `signals` and slots or nothing will happen! The `gate` class knows nothing about the `parking_lot_guard` class, which in turn knows nothing about the `security_guard` class. This is a feature of this library: Types signaling events need not have any knowledge of the types receiving the events. Getting back to the example, let's see if we can get this parking lot up and running.

```
int main() {
  // Create some guards
  std::vector<security_guard> security_guards;
  security_guards.push_back("Bill");
  security_guards.push_back("Bob");
  security_guards.push_back("Bull");
```

---

3. `binary_search` has the attractive complexity $O(logN)$.

```
// Create two gates
gate gate1;
gate gate2;

// Create the automatic guard
parking_lot_guard plg;

// Connect the automatic guard to the gates
gate1.connect_to_gate(plg);
gate2.connect_to_gate(plg);

// Connect the human guards to the automatic guard
for (unsigned int i=0;i<security_guards.size();++i) {
  plg.connect_to_alarm(security_guards[i]);
}


std::cout << "A couple of cars enter...\n";
gate1.enter("SLN 123");
gate2.enter("RFD 444");
gate2.enter("IUY 897");

std::cout << "\nA couple of cars leave...\n";
gate1.leave("IUY 897");
gate1.leave("SLN 123");

std::cout << "\nSomeone is entering twice - \
   or is it a stolen license plate?\n";
gate1.enter("RFD 444");
}
```

There you have it—a fully functional parking lot. We did it by creating three security_guards, two gates, and a parking_lot_guard. These know nothing about each other, but we still needed to hook them up with the correct infrastructure for communicating important events that take place in the lot. That means connecting the parking_lot_guard to the two gates.

```
gate1.connect_to_gate(plg);
gate2.connect_to_gate(plg);
```

This makes sure that whenever the signal enter_or_leave_ in the instances of gate is signaled, parking_lot_guard is informed of this event.

Next, we have the `security_guards` connect to the `signal` for the alarm in `parking_lot_guard`.

```
plg.connect_to_alarm(security_guards[i]);
```

We have managed to decouple these types from each other, yet they have exactly the right amount of information to perform their duties. In the preceding code, we put the parking lot to the test by letting a few cars enter and leave. This real-world simulation reveals that we have managed to get all of the pieces to talk to each other as required.

```
A couple of cars enter...
parking_lot_guard::enter(SLN 123)
parking_lot_guard::enter(RFD 444)
parking_lot_guard::enter(IUY 897)

A couple of cars leave...
parking_lot_guard::leave(IUY 897)
parking_lot_guard::leave(SLN 123)

Someone is entering twice - or is it a stolen license plate?
parking_lot_guard::enter(RFD 444)
Bill says: Man, that coffee tastes f.i.n.e fine!
Bob says: Man, that coffee tastes f.i.n.e fine!
Bull says: Man, that coffee tastes f.i.n.e fine!
```

It's a sad fact that the fraudulent people with license plate RFD 444 got away, but you can only do so much.

This has been a rather lengthy discussion about arguments to `signals`—in fact, we have covered much more than that when examining the very essence of Signals' usefulness, the decoupling of types emitting `signals` and types with slots listening to them. Remember that any types of arguments can be passed, and the signature is determined by the declaration of the `signal` type—this declaration looks just like a function declaration without the actual function name. We haven't talked at all about the return type, although that is certainly part of the signature, too. The reason for this omission is that the return types can be treated in different ways, and next we'll look at why and how.

Combining the Results

When the signature of a `signal` and its slots have non-`void` return type, it is apparent that something happens to the return values of the slots, and indeed, that invoking the `signal` yields a result of some kind. But what is that result? The `signal` class template has a parameterizing type named *Combiner*, which is a type responsible for combining and returning values. The default *Combiner* is `boost::last_value`, which is a class that simply returns the value for the last slot it calls. Now, which slot is that? We typically don't know, because the ordering of slot calls is undefined within the groups.[4] Let's start with a small example that demonstrates the default *Combiner*.

```
#include <iostream>
#include "boost/signals.hpp"

  bool always_return_true() {
    return true;
  }

  bool always_return_false() {
    return false;
  }

int main() {
  boost::signal<bool ()> sig;

  sig.connect(&always_return_true);
  sig.connect(&always_return_false);

  std::cout << std::boolalpha << "True or false? " << sig();
}
```

Two slots, `always_return_true` and `always_return_false`, are connected to the signal `sig`, which returns a `bool` and takes no argument. The result of invoking `sig` is printed to `cout`. Will it be `true` or `false`? We cannot know for sure without testing (when I tried it, the result was `false`). In practice, you either don't care about the return value from invoking the `signal` or you need to create your own *Combiner* in order to get more meaningful, customized behavior. For example, it may be that the results from all of the slots accrue into the net result

---

4. So, assuming that the last group has only one slot, we do know.

desired from invoking the `signal`. In another case, it may be appropriate to avoid calling any more slots if one of the slots returns `false`. A custom *Combiner* can make those things, and more, possible. This is because the *Combiner* iterates through the slots, calls them, and decides what to do with the return values from them.

Consider an initialization sequence, in which any failure should terminate the entire sequence. The slots could be assigned to groups according to the order with which they should be invoked. Without a custom *Combiner*, here's how it would look:

```cpp
#include <iostream>
#include "boost/signals.hpp"

bool step0() {
  std::cout << "step0 is ok\n";
  return true;
}

bool step1() {
  std::cout << "step1 is not ok. This won't do at all!\n";
  return false;
}

bool step2() {
  std::cout << "step2 is ok\n";
  return true;
}

int main() {
  boost::signal<bool ()> sig;
  sig.connect(0,&step0);
  sig.connect(1,&step1);
  sig.connect(2,&step2);

  bool ok=sig();

  if (ok)
    std::cout << "All system tests clear\n";
  else
    std::cout << "At least one test failed. Aborting.\n";
}
```

With the preceding code, there is no way that the code will ever know that one of the tests has failed. As you recall, the default combiner is `boost::last_value`, and it simply returns the value of the last slot call, which is the call to `step2`. Running the example as-is gives us this disappointing output:

```
step0 is ok
step1 is not ok. This won't do at all!
step2 is ok
All system tests clear
```

This is clearly not the right result. We need a *Combiner* that stops processing when a slot returns `false`, and propagates that value back to the `signal`. A *Combiner* is nothing more than a function object with a couple of additional requirements. It must have a `typedef` called `result_type`, which is the return type of its function call operator. Furthermore, the function call operator must be parameterized on the iterator type with which it will be invoked. The *Combiner* that we need right now is quite simple, so it serves as a good example.

```cpp
class stop_on_failure {
public:
  typedef bool result_type;

  template <typename InputIterator>
  bool operator()(InputIterator begin,InputIterator end) const
  {
    while (begin!=end) {
      if (!*begin)
        return false;
      ++begin;
    }
    return true;
  }
};
```

Note the public `typedef` `result_type`, which is `bool`. The type of `result_type` doesn't necessarily relate to the return type of the slots. (When declaring the `signal`, you specify the signature of the slots and the arguments of the `signal`'s function call operator. However, the return type of the *Combiner* determines the return type of the `signal`'s function call operator. By default, this is the same as the return type of the slots, but it doesn't have to be the same.) `stop_on_failure`'s function call operator, which is parameterized on a slot iterator type, iterates over the range of slots and calls each one; unless we encounter an error. For `stop_on_failure`, we don't want to continue calling the slots on an error return, so we test the return value for each call. If it is `false`, the function returns immediately, else it continues invoking the slots. To use `stop_on_failure`, we simply say so when declaring the `signal` type:

```
boost::signal<bool (),stop_on_failure> sig;
```

If we had used this in the bootstrap sequence from the previous example, the output would have been exactly as we had intended.

```
step0 is ok
step1 is not ok. This won't do at all!
At least one test failed. Aborting.
```

Another useful type of *Combiner* is one that returns the maximum or the minimum, of all of the values returned by the invoked slots. Many other interesting *Combiners* are possible, including one to save all results in a container. The (excellent) online documentation for this library has an example of just such a *Combiner*—be sure to read it! It's not every day you'll need to write your own *Combiner* class, but now and then doing so creates an especially elegant solution to an otherwise complicated problem.

Signals Can Never Be Copied

I have already mentioned that `signals` cannot be copied, but it's worth mentioning what one should do about classes that contain a `signal`. Must these classes be non-copyable too? No they don't have to be, but the copy constructor and the assignment operator needs to be implemented by hand. Because the `signal` class declares the copy constructor and the assignment operator private, a class aggregating `signals` has to implement the semantics that apply for it. One way to handle copies correctly is to use shared `signals` between instances of a class, which is what we did in the parking lot example. There, every instance of `parking_lot_guard` referred to the same `signal` by means of `boost::shared_ptr`. For other classes, it makes sense to simply default-construct the `signal` in the copy, because the copy semantics don't include the connection of the slots. There are also scenarios where copying of classes containing a `signal` doesn't make sense, in which one can rely on the non-copyable semantics of the

contained `signal` to ensure that copying and assignment is verboten. To give a
better view of what's going on here, consider the class `some_class`, defined here:

```
class some_class {
  boost::signal<void (int)> some_signal;
};
```

Given this class, the copy constructor and the assignment operator that the
compiler generates isn't usable. If code is written that tries to use these, the compiler complains. For example, the following example tries to copy construct the
`some_class sc2` from `sc1`:

```
int main() {
  some_class sc1;
  some_class sc2(sc1);
}
```

When compiling this program, the compiler-generated copy constructor tries to
perform a member-by-member copy of the members of `some_class`. Because of
the private copy constructor of `signal`, the compiler says something like this:

```
c:/boost_cvs/boost/boost/noncopyable.hpp: In copy constructor  `
  boost::signals::detail::signal_base::signal_base(const
  boost::signals::detail::signal_base&)':
c:/boost_cvs/boost/boost/noncopyable.hpp:27: error:  `
  boost::noncopyable::noncopyable(
    const boost::noncopyable&)' is private
noncopyable_example.cpp:10: error: within this context
```

So whatever your copying and assignment of classes containing `signals` need
to do, make sure that need doesn't include copying of the `signals`!

Managing Connections

We have covered how to connect slots to `signals`, but we haven't yet seen how
to disconnect them. There are many reasons to not leave a slot connected permanently to a `signal`. Until now, we've ignored it, but `boost::signal::connect`
returns an instance of `boost::signals::connection`. Using this `connection`
object, it is possible to disconnect a slot from the `signal`, as well as test whether
the slot is currently connected to the `signal`. `connections` are a sort of handle to

the actual link between the `signal` and the slot. Because the knowledge of the connection between a `signal` and a slot is tracked separately from both, a slot doesn't know if or when it is connected. If a slot won't be disconnected from a `signal`, it's typically fine to just ignore the `connection` returned by `signal::` `connect`. Also, a call to `disconnect` for the group to which a slot belongs, or a call to `disconnect_all_slots` will disconnect a slot without the need for the slot's `connection`. If it's important to be able to test whether a slot is still connected to a `signal`, there is no other way than by saving the `connection` and using it to query the `signal`.

The `connection` class provides `operator<`, which makes it possible to store connections in the Standard Library containers. It also provides `operator==` for completeness. Finally, the class provides a `swap` member function that swaps the signal/slot connection knowledge of one `connection` with that of another. The following example demonstrates how to use the `signals::connection` class:

```cpp
#include <iostream>
#include <string>
#include "boost/signals.hpp"

class some_slot_type {
  std::string s_;
public:
  some_slot_type(const char* s) : s_(s) {}

  void operator()(const std::string& s) const {
    std::cout << s_ << ": " << s << '\n';
  }
};

int main() {
  boost::signal<void (const std::string&)> sig;

  some_slot_type sc1("sc1");
  some_slot_type sc2("sc2");

  boost::signals::connection c1=sig.connect(sc1);
  boost::signals::connection c2=sig.connect(sc2);

  // Comparison
  std::cout << "c1==c2: " << (c1==c2) << '\n';
  std::cout << "c1<c2:  " << (c1<c2) << '\n';
```

```
// Testing the connection
  if (c1.connected())
    std::cout << "c1 is connected to a signal\n";

// Swapping and disconnecting
  sig("Hello there");
  c1.swap(c2);
  sig("We've swapped the connections");
  c1.disconnect();
  sig("Disconnected c1, which referred to sc2 after the swap");
}
```

There are two `connection` objects in the example, and we saw that they can be compared using `operator<` and `operator==`. The ordering relation that `operator<` implements is unspecified; it exists to support storing `connections` in the Standard Library containers. Equality through `operator==` is well defined, however. If two `connections` reference the exact same physical connection, they are equal. If two `connections` do not reference any connection, they are equal. No other pairs of `connections` are equal. In the example, we also disconnected a `connection`.

```
c1.disconnect();
```

Although `c1` originally refers to the `connection` for `sc1`, at the time of disconnecting it refers to `sc2`, because we swap the contents of the two connections using the member function `swap`. Disconnecting means that the slot no longer is notified when the `signal` is signaled. Here is the output from running the program:

```
c1==c2:  0
c1<c2:   1
c1 is connected to a signal
sc1: Hello there
sc2: Hello there
sc1: We've swapped the connections
sc2: We've swapped the connections
sc1: Disconnected c1, which referred to sc2 after the swap
```

As you can see, the last invocation of the `signal` `sig` only invokes the slot `sc1`.

Sometimes, the lifetime of the `connection` for a slot relates to a certain scope in the code. This is similar to any other resource that is required for a given scope, something that is handled using smart pointers or other mechanisms for scoping. Boost.Signals provides a scoped version for `connections` called `scoped_connection`. A `scoped_connection` makes sure that the `connection` is disconnected as the `scoped_connection` is destroyed. The constructor of `scoped_connection` takes a `connection` object as argument, which it assumes ownership of in a way.

```cpp
#include <iostream>
#include "boost/signals.hpp"

class slot {
public:
  void operator()() const {
    std::cout << "Something important just happened!\n";
  }
};

int main() {
  boost::signal<void ()> sig;
  {
    boost::signals::scoped_connection s=sig.connect(slot());
  }
  sig();
}
```

The `boost::signals::scoped_connection s` is given a small scope inside of `main`, and after leaving that scope the `signal sig` is invoked. There is no output from that, because the `scoped_connection` has already terminated the connection between the slot and the `signal`. Using scoped resources like this simplifies the code and maintenance thereof.

Creating Slots Using Bind and Lambda

You've seen how useful and flexible Signals is. However, you'll find even more power when you combine Boost.Signals with Boost.Bind and Boost.Lambda. Those two libraries, covered in detail in "Library 9: Bind" and "Library 10: Lambda," help to create function objects on-the-fly. That means it is possible to create slots (and slot types) right at the point where they are connected to a `signal`, rather than having to write a special, single-purpose class for a slot, create an instance, and then connect it. It also puts the slot logic right where it's used rather than in a separate part of the source code. Finally, these libraries even make it possible to adapt existing classes that don't provide a function call operator but have other, suitable means for handling signals.

In the first example to follow, we'll have a look at how neatly lambda expressions can be used to create a few slot types. The slots will be created right in the call to connect. The first one simply prints a message to std::cout when the slot is invoked. The second checks the value of the string passed through the signal to the slot. If it equals "Signal", it prints one message; otherwise, it prints another message. (These examples are rather contrived, but the expressions could perform any kind of useful computation.) The last two slots created in the example will do exactly what double_slot and plus_slot did in an example earlier in the chapter. You'll find the lambda versions far more readable.

```cpp
#include <iostream>
#include <string>
#include <cassert>
#include "boost/signals.hpp"
#include "boost/lambda/lambda.hpp"
#include "boost/lambda/if.hpp"

int main() {
  using namespace boost::lambda;

  boost::signal<void (std::string)> sig;

  sig.connect(var(std::cout)
    << "Something happened: " << _1 << '\n');
  sig.connect(
    if_(_1=="Signal") [
      var(std::cout) << "Ok, I've got it\n"]
    .else_[
      std::cout << constant("Yeah, whatever\n")]);

  sig("Signal");
  sig("Another signal");

  boost::signal<void (int&)> sig2;
  sig2.connect(0,_1*=2); // Double it
  sig2.connect(1,_1+=3); // Add 3
  int i=12;
  sig2(i);
  assert(i==27);
}
```

If you aren't yet familiar with lambda expressions in C++ (or otherwise), don't worry if the preceding seems a bit confusing—you may want to read the chapters on Bind and Lambda first and return to these examples. If you already have, I am sure that you appreciate the terse code that results from using lambda expressions; and it avoids cluttering the code with small function objects, too.

Now let's take a look at using binders to create slot types. Slots must implement a function call operator, but not all classes that would otherwise be suitable as slots do so. In those cases, it's often possible to use existing member functions of classes, repackaged for use as slots using binders. Binders can also help readability by allowing the function (rather than function object) that handles an event to have a meaningful name. Finally, there are situations in which the same object must respond to different events, each with the same slot signature, but different reactions. Thus, such objects need different member functions to be called for different events. In each of these cases, there is no function call operator suitable for connecting to a `signal`. Thus, a configurable function object is needed, and Boost.Bind provides (as the `bind` facility in Boost.Lambda) the means to do that.

Consider a `signal` that expects a slot type that returns `bool` and accepts an argument of type `double`. Assuming a class `some_class` with a member function `some_function` that has the correct signature, how do you connect `some_class::some_function` to the `signal`? One way would be to add a function call operator to `some_class`, and have the function call operator forward the call to `some_function`. That means changing the class interface unnecessarily and it doesn't scale well. A binder works much better.

```cpp
#include <iostream>
#include "boost/signals.hpp"
#include "boost/bind.hpp"

class some_class {
public:
  bool some_function(double d) {
    return d>3.14;
  }

  bool another_function(double d) {
    return d<0.0;
  }
};
```

```
int main() {
  boost::signal<bool (double)> sig0;
  boost::signal<bool (double)> sig1;

  some_class sc;

  sig0.connect(
    boost::bind(&some_class::some_function,&sc,_1));
  sig1.connect(
    boost::bind(&some_class::another_function,&sc,_1));

  sig0(3.1);
  sig1(-12.78);
}
```

Binding this way has an interesting side effect: It avoids unnecessary copying of some_class instances. The binder holds a pointer to the some_class instance and it's the binder that the signal copies. Unfortunately, there's a potential lifetime management issue with this approach: If sc is destroyed and then one of the signals is invoked, undefined behavior results. That's because the binder will have a dangling pointer to sc. By avoiding the copies, we must also assume the responsibility of keeping the slots alive so long as a connection exists that (indirectly) references them. Of course, that's what reference-counting smart pointers are for, so the problem is easy to solve.

Using binders like this is common when using Boost.Signals. Whether you use lambda expressions to create your slots or binders to adapt existing classes for use as slot types, you'll soon value the synergy among Boost.Signals, Boost.Lambda, and Boost.Bind. It will save you time and make your code elegant and succinct.

Signals Summary

Use Signals when

- You need robust callbacks

- There can be multiple handlers of events

- The connection between the `signal` and the connected slots should be configurable at runtime

That Boost.Signals supersedes old-style callbacks should be blatantly clear by now, and this library is one of the best signals and slots implementations available. The design pattern that the library captures is well known and has been studied for a long time, so the domain is mature. Some programming languages already have such mechanisms available directly in the language—for example, delegates and events in .NET. In C++, the problem is elegantly solved with libraries. Signals and slots are used to separate the trigger mechanism of an event from the code that handles it. This separation decouples subsystems and makes them more comprehensible. It also solves the problem of updating multiple interested parties when important events take place. There are numerous places in a typical program or library where signals and slots are useful. Whether you are writing a GUI framework or an intrusion detection system for a power plant, Signals is ready to take care of all your signaling needs. It is easy to learn how to use, yet it also offers the advanced functionality that is required for complex tasks. For example, custom *Combiners* make it possible to write event mechanisms that are tailor-made for a certain domain.

Boost.Signals was written by Douglas Gregor (who incidentally also wrote Boost.Function). This is a great library; thank you Doug!

Bibliography

[1] *Advanced C++ Programming Styles and Idioms* (James O. Coplien)

This book has been around for some time, but it's still immensely valuable. It teaches important C++ idioms from the ground up, in a way that is sure to capture the reader's interest and stimulate further research. Professor Coplien invites you to a journey that might just last a lifetime.

[2] *C++ FAQs 2nd Edition* (Marshall Cline/Greg Lonow/Mike Girou)

This great book includes short (a page or so) questions and answers that are often asked by C++ programmers. Topics vary wildly, from why private inheritance is seldom a good idea to the intricacies of how to correctly use `typename`. If you've got a technical C++ question, chances are that the answer exists in this book.

[3] *C++ Template Metaprogramming: Concepts, Tools, and Techniques from Boost and Beyond* (David Abrahams/Aleksey Gurtovoy)

This is your definitive guide to template metaprogramming. C++ gurus David Abrahams and Aleksey Gurtovoy (who are also the authors of Boost.Mpl) teach readers template metaprogramming in general, and applied template metaprogramming using the fabulous Boost.Mpl library. Mpl is similar to the STL, but for compile time programming! You cannot afford to miss this fantastic book on a topic that's so hot you might burn your fingers.

[4] *C++ Templates—The Complete Guide* (David Vandevoorde/Nicolai Josuttis)

Don't you just love templates? Whether you do or not, this book is one of only two in existence (the other one is *C++ Template Metaprogramming* mentioned previously) that thoroughly discusses the ins and outs of templates; this is not a topic to be taken lightly, and the authors of the book don't. This is indeed the complete guide. Get it.

[5] *Design Patterns—Elements of Reusable Object-Oriented Software*
(Erich Gamma, Richard Helm, Ralph Johnson, John Vlissides)

This classic probably doesn't need an introduction. If you haven't yet read this book about one of the most important movements in the software industry, do so now. Almost every programmer in the known universe should know the design patterns in this book. These four gentlemen have, through this book, changed the world.

[6] *Effective C++: 50 Specific Ways to Improve Your Programs and Design* (Scott Meyers)

This series is well known to most professional C++ programmers. If you haven't read it, you should. If you have, read it again. Scott Meyers teaches best practices and never forgets to explain why they are indeed best practices.

[7] *Effective STL* (Scott Meyers)

Here, Scott Meyers takes on effective and correct usage of the STL. A must-read for all that are making extensive use of the Standard Library containers and algorithms.

[8] *Efficient C++: Performance Programming Techniques* (Dov Bulka/David Mayhem)

There are few books that cover optimization techniques for C++. In fact, I don't think there is any other than this one. There is good coverage of the traditional means of speeding up those inner loops. Complement this with a book on template metaprogramming techniques and you're all set for optimum performance programming.

[9] *Exceptional C++* (Herb Sutter)

This is a book that should be read by all intermediate to advanced C++ programmers. The approach is to challenge the reader with a puzzle, and then provide an answer that explains, in great detail, good and bad solutions. It's a very challenging and rewarding read.

[10] *Generative Programming: Methods, Tools and Applications* (Krzysztof Czarnecki/Ulrich Eisenecker)

This is another modern classic. Probably the first book to talk in detail about templates as a tool for metaprogramming. It describes methods and tools to use for generative programming—programs that generate programs. It's an extensive book, but reading it is well worth the time.

[11] *Generic Programming and the STL: Using and Extending the C++ Standard Template Library* (Matthew Austern)

Matt Austern is an unquestionable authority when it comes to the STL. In the first part of this book, he teaches the reader about the design decisions that influence the STL, and how to build on that design to properly extend the existing components of the STL. The other part of the book is a reference (for SGI STL). The first part is what makes this book so interesting; it's the most concise and correct introduction to "the STL way" I've ever read.

[12] *Imperfect C++* (Matthew Wilson)

Always with a glint in the eye, Matthew Wilson guides the reader through the trenches of real-world C++: language peculiarities, useful idioms, anti-idioms, and more. A book that teaches the inner workings of C++ and invites the reader to the occasional laugh is a rare treat. This book's definitely worth reading.

[13] *International Standard ISO/IEC 14882*

The C++ Standard is definitely not a textbook or tutorial, but having the actual definition of the language at hand is a must for serious programmers. If nothing else, you'll be able to quote the Standard at meetings and parties. People love that.

[14] *Modern C++ Design* (Andrei Alexandrescu)

The title says it best. This book covers modern techniques (in particular using templates in mysterious ways) of C++ programming (and design). This book definitely has the potential of making the reader feel daft (at least that's how I felt during my first read), but that's not really important (read it again). What's important is that it teaches techniques not seen elsewhere.

[15] *More Effective C++: 35 New Ways to Improve Your Programs and Designs* (Scott Meyers)

The second volume in the *Effective C++...* series picks up where *Effective C++* left off—more advice from Scott, and his advice is known to be good. This is an excellent companion to its predecessor.

[16] *More Exceptional C++* (Herb Sutter)

As if the challenges brought forth by Herb Sutter in *Exceptional C++* weren't enough to humble us, here's another set of intriguing puzzles. I think that this sequel is even better than the first book in the series, and if you're just buying one of them, choose this one. Better yet is to get both.

[17] *STL Tutorial and Reference Guide, Second Edition* (David Musser/Gillmer Derge/Atul Saini)

The first part of this book is a tutorial-style introduction to the STL. Written by STL experts, this book manages to convey to the reader how the different parts of the STL fit together. The second part is a reference section. For a good and solid introduction to using and understanding the STL, consider reading this book. You'll want to read this before Matthew Austern's book ([11]).

[18] *The Boost Graph Library User Guide and Reference Manual* (Jeremy Siek/Lie-Quan Lee/Andrew Lumsdaine)

This book covers the Boost.Graph library. It gives a nice introduction to mathematical graphs, and goes on to demonstrate how to use the library to build algorithms that operate on graphs. It demonstrates the large number of graph algorithms that are included in the library. If you find yourself in need of using graphs to solve your programming problems, look no further than Boost.Graph. When it comes to learning how to use the library, look no further than this book!

[19] *The C++ Programming Language 3rd Edition* (Bjarne Stroustrup)

Written by the Creator himself, this book discusses most parts of the C++ language, and the C++ Standard Library. You owe it to yourself to own a copy.

[20] *The C++ Standard Library* (Nicolai Josuttis)

This is my favorite book on the STL. Although the book covers more parts of the C++ Standard Library than the STL, it's the parts on containers, iterators, and algorithms that really make this book stand out from the rest. It keeps a steady pace and never leaves the reader behind.

[21] *Thinking in C++, Volume 2* (Bruce Eckel/Chuck Allison)

This is an 800-page tome that tries to teach most of the features in C++, and more importantly, how to use them correctly. The book's a magnificent achievement, because it actually works. Reading this book helps you to think in C++. Best of all, it's available both online[1] and in print, so you can check it out before buying it (it's much more comfortable to hold a book than a monitor when reading in bed).

---

1. Check out http://www.mindview.net.

Index

Also available from Addison-Wesley

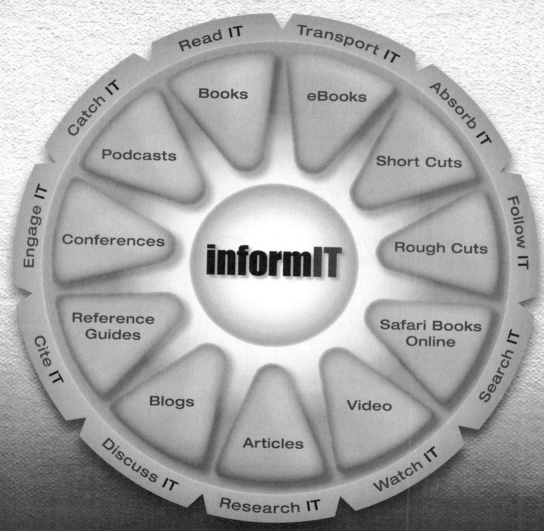

Safari Library
Subscribe Now!
http://safari.informit.com/library

Safari's entire technology collection is now available with no restrictions. Imagine the value of being able to search and access thousands of books, videos, and articles from leading technology authors whenever you wish.

EXPLORE TOPICS MORE FULLY

Gain a more robust understanding of related issues by using Safari as your research tool. With Safari Library you can leverage the knowledge of the world's technology gurus. For one flat, monthly fee, you'll have unrestricted access to a reference collection offered nowhere else in the world—all at your fingertips.

With a Safari Library subscription, you'll get the following premium services:

- **Immediate access to the newest, cutting-edge books**—Approximately eighty new titles are added per month in conjunction with, or in advance of, their print publication.

- **Chapter downloads**—Download five chapters per month so you can work offline when you need to.

- **Rough Cuts**—A service that provides online access to prepublication information on advanced technologies. Content is updated as the author writes the book. You can also download Rough Cuts for offline reference

- **Videos**—Premier design and development videos from training and e-learning expert lynda.com and other publishers you trust.

- **Cut and paste code**—Cut and paste code directly from Safari. Save time. Eliminate errors.

- **Save up to 35% on print books**—Safari Subscribers receive a discount of up to 35% on publishers' print books.

Addison Wesley
Cisco Press
Microsoft Press
Peachpit Press
Redbooks
Adobe Press
FT Press FINANCIAL TIMES
New Riders
PRENTICE HALL
Wharton School Publishing
SAMS
ALPHA
lynda.com
O'REILLY
que
IBM Press